The Ultimate Guide to

Commercial Vehicle

Fleet Management

The Ultimate Guide to Commercial Vehicle Fleet Management

First Edition Published 2021 by The DW Consultancy

www.thedwconsultancy.com

dwilson@thedwconsultancy.com

ISBN number 978-1-7398273-0-4

Production - Mark Gedye InterPro Solutions

The Ultimate Guide to Commercial Vehicle Fleet Management

Foreword

David Wilson has built on his substantial business experience and detailed knowledge developed in commercial fleet management and consultancy to produce this comprehensive guide, which covers all aspect of commercial vehicle specification, acquisition, and management through to redundancy and disposal.

The Guide is also very useful in setting the scene, by recording the history of commercial vehicle operations industry over the last 20 years, and the current legal and technical position. It identifies the complex technical, legal and operational challenges which the commercial vehicle operator, as well as vehicle designers and manufacturers, will have to face over the next decade as we address environmental challenges, moving towards the delivery of Net Zero and the requirements of ever increasingly complex supply chains, which commercial vehicles serve.

In my view, this book belongs on the desks of Chief Executives and Management of vehicle fleet operators across all sectors of British industry at all levels, not left on a bookshelf, but rather in easy reach as an authoritative reference.

It also will make a very useful tool for vehicle designers, manufacturers, automotive engineers and repairers alike, to ensure that all involved in the commercial vehicle industry sector are aligned to deliver safe, legal, economical and environmentally sound operations.

Chris Sturman FCILT FRSA

Director of Craymere Consulting Ltd. and Former CEO of the FSDF (The Food Storage & Distribution Federation)

August 2021

The Ultimate Guide to Commercial Vehicle Fleet Management

About the Author

Most books provide you with a brief overview of the author's experience and background, simply to demonstrate to the reader the credibility of the advice and information contained in the pages that follow: this book is no different, so here it is:

The author, David Wilson, has been the principal consultant for the DW Consultancy for over 30 years. In that time, it has helped a wide variety of transport and logistics clients to improve their fleet management, from Blue Chip private sector companies to public sector organisations such as the London Boroughs, the Police and the Fire Services. In the private sector, the larger customers included well-known organisations such as Hovis, Serco and the RAC, saving them many millions of pounds in annual fleet costs.

After obtaining a degree in Mechanical Engineering, David's initial manufacturing experience was in Ford's Special Vehicle division, offering operators a very wide range of bespoke vehicle specifications. This was followed by a move into logistics for the next 15 years, managing vehicle fleets for United Biscuits, Tate & Lyle and Philips Electronics, before moving into consultancy.

As well as initially undertaking specialist consultancy for some of the larger consultancies such as Coopers & Lybrand and KPMG, the DW consultancy assisted many clients in reducing costs and improving efficiency in a wide and interesting range of transport sectors, including: oil exploration, vehicle rescue services, the waste and recycling industry, gas, the food industry & FMCG, wet & dry tanker operations, pharmaceutical and for added excitement, considerable experience in emergency blue light fleets.

Later government clients included more specialist work for the Knowledge Transfer Networks (KTN's) and the Energy Savings Trust (EST). As well as consultancy, David also undertook interesting spells as an interim manager, helping to keep management skills up to date. Of course, over this time, David has also been involved in industry education, presenting for universities, institutes and trade bodies on varying aspects of fleet management, also sitting on steering committees for these same organisations.

Just for completeness, a sister organisation, called Fleet Technology Ltd., (www.fleettechnology.co.uk) gains efficiency savings for clients through improved utilisation of their vehicle telematics, resulting in considerable cost savings through improved driver behaviour. That telematics experience has been exceedingly useful in compiling this book, as the feedback demonstrates precisely how vehicles are driven in real life and how most commercial vehicles and drivers will respond, both physically and mentally, when out on the road.

The Ultimate Guide to Commercial Vehicle Fleet Management

Brief explanation of the Terms & Units used throughout the book

In times gone past, books of this type may have included conversion tables, or similar, to explain and convert any units used throughout the text. In 2021, I have taken the view that there are now so many other ways to convert units of measurement, not least using the internet (in just a couple of seconds), so it would be a waste of and space to include them in this volume.

However, I should just explain to potential readers that they will find a mix of units in the script – I have therefore used whatever is in common usage in the industry and in particular, by most of my clients, to make the book easier to read. So for example, although fuel is now almost universally sold in litres, I have used miles per gallon, or mpg, as the prime measure of vehicle fuel efficiency, simply because most other people still do. In fact, for some reason, I think it makes more logical sense to have a fixed unit of fuel and then describe how far you can get with it, rather than the other way around. Litres per 100 Km has never had the same significance to me, however, if you still want to convert, please feel free; there are lots of ways of doing so.

Perversely then, when talking about tyres, you will find I use p.p.k. or pence per kilometre as a measure of cost efficiency. For some reason, for almost as long as I have been in the industry, that has been the norm, so that is what is referred to in this book. To be honest, I don't much care which units you use, as long as you do compare like-with-like, by measuring the distance travelled per £ (or $ or Euro or whatever) spent.

You will also find that I refer to heavy vehicles as HGV's not LGV's or any other acronym as almost everyone, whether in transport or not, still understands the term HGV as a Heavy Goods Vehicle and knows what one looks like, so any attempts to change the term, I think, are misguided and perhaps misleading. In O licence terms, HGV is anything over 3.5T, in reality, it's probably anything over 7.5T and I still use GVW for gross vehicle weight, rather than any other term.

I would also like to apologise in advance for the number of acronyms used in this book. There are many industries around today that delight in trying to confuse the layman by utilising far too many acronyms; unfortunately transport is just one more of them. I try to explain each acronym the first time it is used in the text and sometimes include the explanation again later, just to assist the reader. If you get stuck and can't think what an acronym means (even though you may know you know it really), I have included a full listing in the appendix.

I really hope that by taking the above approach, you will find the text much easier to read and enjoy.

The Ultimate Guide to Commercial Vehicle Fleet Management

Contents

Page No.

Chapter 8 – Telematics 141

Deciding on the right type of Telematics for you to fit and selecting from the large number of suppliers; the pros and cons of the various systems. Potential results that would be realistic for your operation and getting the best out of the system with the minimum effort.

Chapter 9 – Fleet Management Systems 165

The differing types of systems now all called 'fleet management'; selecting from the wide variety available, catering for both internal and external workshops. Using the system to maximum advantage and utilising true whole life costs for comparisons; when to integrate the system with other IT platforms.

Chapter 10 – Vehicle Repair & Maintenance 187

The basics of maintaining both heavy and light commercial vehicles. The pros and cons of running your own workshops against externalising maintenance operations and how to best manage both routes. Managing vehicle records along with the important daily vehicle checks. Ensuring the quality of parts supply and managing breakdowns.

Chapter 11 – Fuel, Oil & AdBlue Management 227

The key factors in managing one of your biggest operating costs, fuel; choosing internal bulk supplies or contracting out to external suppliers; how to keep control of your expenditure through fuel cards. The interventions that work best to reduce the amount of fuel your drivers use and how to manage your Oil and AdBlue supplies.

Chapter 12 – Tyres & Wheels 257

Deciding on the most appropriate tyre policy for your fleet, how to handle replacement, decide on manufacturers and tyre types. Minimising tyre expenditure, also the monitoring, management and maintenance of all your vehicle tyres, including the care of vehicle wheels.

Summary 283

Summarised Key Advice, chapter by chapter.

Acknowledgements 293

Explanation of Acronyms used throughout the book 295

INDEX 301

The Ultimate Guide to Commercial Vehicle Fleet Management

Chapter 1 – introduction

In essence, this book has been designed specifically for new fleet managers, transport managers, finance directors, fleet engineers, managing directors, operational managers or directors; in short, anyone who has the responsibility for managing a fleet of commercial vehicles, large or small, and feels they would like to do more to improve the organisation's efficiency and reduce costs.

The book is chock full of the best available advice and guidance on how to run your fleet of commercial vehicles. All the ideas contained within these pages have come from a lifetime spent in either managing vehicles directly, or advising organisations of all sizes on how to manage their fleets effectively.

The contents are intended to help you understand which issues you need to focus on and gives guidance on how to make the right strategic fleet policy decisions. It will be greatly beneficial to someone recently taking up a post as well as being a very useful resource to seasoned fleet professionals.

By fleet, this means more than just one vehicle. By commercial vehicle, that means anything from a small van up to a maximum weight vehicle, in the UK, normally an articulated vehicle up to 44 tonnes. Commercial obviously means the driver is generally driving for a living, whether delivering goods, or carrying equipment to enable them to operate a service.

It should be clearly said at the outset that the guidance given in the following pages steers away from pure compliance, but focuses very much on the largely forgotten art of fleet management and looking after vehicles. I say forgotten, because the emphasis within the industry for the last three to five years has been almost exclusively compliance and regulatory advice. In fact so much has been written on this subject in recent years, especially with the advent of operator recognition schemes, I feel it has been more than adequately covered elsewhere.

Although compliance is obviously a key component of keeping your fleet and drivers safe on the road, for some time there has been a distinct lack of focus on the operational and financial aspects of the vehicles themselves. Many of the detailed fleet decisions that need to be made have largely been offloaded to manufacturers and suppliers in general, as they are now seen by many operators as the 'experts'.

Such advice from suppliers is usually up-to-date and often is representative of a wider industry picture, however, it can never take into account the full and detailed range of an organisation's longer-term strategies such as potential site changes or closures, company acquisitions and changes to operating principles, leading to possible sub-optimal decisions being taken over time. This book will assist fleet and transport managers in redressing the balance and will enable decision makers to meet the fleet business needs of their organisation.

Let us also be very clear on what this book is NOT about, so as not to waste your time. This book is not a pure reference book; if you want to find chapter and verse on vehicle legislation, the document that I would recommend is the Logistics UK (formally the FTA or Freight Transport Association) yearbook. Full of detail, it will answer all your questions on weights, dimensions, driver's hours, compliance and all things technical, legal and regulatory. Of course, as ever, other similar publications are available.

Nor is this book a manual to help you undertake a Transport Manager's CPC (Certificate of Professional Competence). In essence, that would be full of tutorial content to help you pass an examination. Having said what the book is not about, I should just mention that you will find mention of driver psychology within these pages, as this has a big effect on getting the best out of your drivers and hence your fleet.

In order to give the whole subject some structure, and help you get the best from the contents, this handbook has been logically divided into 12 chapters, separated into four groups.

- **How to acquire your fleet**

Firstly, to establish the background, we look at how things have changed in fleet management in the last 20 years, along with what is likely to change in the next 10, to provide you with some direction to your forward fleet procurement plans.

We then look at the best ways to arrive at the right fleet in the right way to assist your organisation, by examining how to plan your fleet and fleet strategy, followed by how best to acquire your vehicles. This is coupled with the issue of how to finance your choice, completed by a look at how to calculate the right time and the best way to dispose of them.

- **Using new technology**

Here, we examine the effect of changing the way vehicles will be fuelled in the near future and all that decarbonising entails. We also look at the implications of recent exciting vehicle technology developments employed by manufacturers, coupled with the more peripheral technology that you may either want, or be required to employ by legislation. We also examine the whole subject of telematics, which has truly revolutionised vehicle and staff operations in recent years and will feature highly in the future of all fleet operations.

- **Vehicle Repair & Maintenance**

Thirdly, we review the complex and important issue of how to keep vehicles fully and economically maintained. We look briefly at whether to operate internal workshops or sub-contract maintenance, along with the management implications of both choices and what performance indicators to use in either case to ensure an efficient and safe operation.

- **Using Fleet Management Systems, Fuel & Tyres**

Lastly, we look at the importance of what fleet management systems can do for you and the risks of not fully utilising a good system. We also examine the importance of knowing whole life costs for your vehicles, and how to really maximise a fleet management system's effectiveness for the minimum outlay and minimum clerical input. There is also an examination of the opportunities for efficiency in one of the biggest cost areas of all, namely fuel, along with the oft overlooked, but important subject of managing tyres.

In order to get the best out of this book, I strongly suggest that you familiarise yourself with the entire contents and then dip into the sections and chapters that interest you most, or are relevant to issues you may be dealing with at the time. However, each chapter is written in such a way that, of course, it be read as a discrete subject in its own right. Each section within each chapter provides the answer to the ten or so questions posed at the start, so if you are looking for the answer to a specific issue, check out the chapter questions at the start of each chapter for the subject you desire.

To assist you, throughout the book, there are many 'Top Tips' highlighted at the end of each chapter, along with some classic mistakes to avoid, which can often happen simply due to human nature and time pressures. The text is also sprinkled with a few 'handy hints' which generally better explain some of the more important points. All of these are a reflection of hard-won management experience, or what I have uncovered in my many years consulting.

And for those of you who are short on time or you just want to get to the end result very quickly, the final summary at the end of the book brings together the most important tips and advice contained within these pages.

It is probable that after reading this book you will come away with a list of ideas and actions that will help you improve the management of the fleet in your organisation. Do not despair with the length of any list. It is strongly suggested that you highlight and pick out one or two of your priority areas - it obviously helps if these are also relatively easy to complete. Then implement just a few potential improvements, achieving some positive results, before moving on to make progress in other areas. This is obviously what is generally described as "picking the low hanging fruit".

The Ultimate Guide to Commercial Vehicle Fleet Management

Chapter 2 – The Commercial Vehicle Industry Yesterday, Today & Tomorrow

1) *What was the Commercial Vehicle industry like 20 years ago, what sort of challenges did it face?*
2) *What other improvements happened 10 to 20 years ago?*
3) *What has happened to the Commercial Vehicle industry in the last 10 years?*
4) *What other improvements have happened in the last 10 years?*
5) *What effect did the introduction of emission controls have in the two decades?*
6) *How have emissions measurement changed and what has been the effect of "Dieselgate"?*
7) *How did changes in society effect the commercial vehicle industry?*
8) *What other changes happened in the last decade?*
9) *What will the future bring for Commercial Vehicle operations?*

In order to understand the current state of play of the commercial vehicle industry, I believe it is important to have a brief look at where we have come from in the last 10 to 20 years; in other words, how did we get to here, what progress have we made, where have things improved and conversely, what is now more difficult? Then I think it is equally important to get a realistic picture as to where the industry is likely to go over the next 10 years, as this will obviously affect every fleet's planning and acquisitions. There is plenty of hot air and predictions about what may be the 'next big thing' in terms of how vehicles will be powered and what technology will they use; looking back at the last 10 to 20 years should help to provide a sensible backdrop about how quickly new technology was introduced, what got abandoned along the way and what ultimately survived or was improved and refined over time.

1) *What was the Commercial Vehicle industry like 20 years ago, what sort of challenges did it face?*

So, what has led to the current legislation and operating practices we have in operation today? 20 years ago, the commercial vehicle industry was similar to today in many respects, but also very different in others. Vehicles may have looked a little more basic and less refined, but the building blocks for modern commercial vehicles were all there. Weights were slightly lower, but the same type of power trains and vehicle bodies were in operation then as now. Obviously, technology has advanced in leaps and bounds in that time, just think of the changes to our personal lives that have happened in the last decade or so. As an example, take the iPhone, established in (believe it or not), 2007, so it has been with us for only 14 years. Look at how its computing power and all the accompanying apps have revolutionised modern life and have advanced in that short period. That increase in technical development is also reflected in the transport world.

Fleet engineers and fleet managers 20 years ago were more concerned about the physical aspects, or the nuts and bolts, of running vehicles. That meant they were debating items such as the introduction of synthetic and semi-synthetic oils. Looking back, it is easy to see the benefits of longer drain and service periods, however, at the time many operators were concerned about a relatively large increase in cost and they felt more comfortable with regular, traditional oil changes. The thinking at the time was that this kept engines cleaner and regularly removed any wear particles and products of combustion. Largely because of those misgivings, that technology change is still in progress today and some of those concerns still stand. The rate of change is now perhaps being forced by vehicle manufacturers who emphasise that due to technology changes, their vehicles must now use a more modern specification oil. This change is aided by the obvious advantages of much increased drain intervals. However, that reluctance to move away from tried and tested methods is a fairly common theme throughout the transport arena.

In a similar vein, another topic still under discussion in some areas now, but very important at that time was that of brakes on heavier commercial vehicles, the issue here being one of whether newly introduced disc brakes were as good as the tried and tested drum variety. Years of trials generated measurements, cost comparisons and wear rates, to help fuel the debate. In addition, disc brakes better suited electronic braking systems which were still fairly much in their infancy at the time and perhaps not fully understood by all operators. In the intervening period, most HGVs have adopted discs, whilst there are still many trailers relying on drums. But the advantages of disc brake technology over drum brakes became apparent to early adopters; shorter stopping distances coupled to lower maintenance times and hence reduced repair costs, providing their more exacting service requirements were being met. Weight was also reduced and there was less or no brake fade, which could still be experienced with drum brakes.

There were disadvantages though, initial cost again being the big one, although prices have since evened somewhat. There is still sometimes a problem of incompatibility, primarily on articulated vehicles and trailers, where the latter were, and still are, more likely to retain drums, especially on rental trailers, a significant part of the market. It is also true that a well set up drum braked trailer will probably withstand more abuse than a disc braked trailer, providing they are compatible. The expansion of EBS (Electronic Braking systems) may lead to increased imbalance issues and perhaps increased trailer brake wear. It is important to understand the inertia of the transport industry, who on the whole, are often reluctant to accept a change of historical practices. We can view this as an important indicator for the future, again a reason why to some extent, that these changes in braking setups are still not fully complete today, 20 years later.

2)   What other improvements happened 10 to 20 years ago?

Well, the introduction of regulations on manual handling of loads became a big issue for operators at the time and resulted in changes to loading practices along with lots of ingenious mechanical devices being introduced in order to reduce the physical efforts of delivery. This included a rise in the use of lorry mounted cranes, a much-increased use of caged loads and other mechanical aids, all designed to minimise the physical effort required. You can see the effect of these developments in today's vehicle specifications, where manual handling continues to be reduced wherever possible.

Predictive maintenance for vehicles had been talked about for many years, but was very much in its infancy and there were a number of methodologies in use, all trying to improve preventive maintenance and reduce vehicle downtimes. Around the year 2000 we saw the start of a significant rise in more sophisticated electronics around the vehicle, including a big increase in sensors, which were becoming both smaller and more robust, providing real data about important vehicle components. Back then, almost everything was changed on a mileage or time interval basis. Sensors now started flagged up health indicators allowing technicians and managers to make better decisions about when best to replace items to help avoid later problems in service.

Increasing the number and efficacy of these sensors over time allowed greater accuracy and availability of the data returned and hence a more intelligent view of mechanicals. Now, in the last decade, (especially the last half), this has been supplemented by predictive algorithms and machine learning to increasingly automate the process of making better maintenance decisions. What all this means in practice is that maintenance teams can optimise the use of workshop repair times, attempting to service vehicles such that a predicted event never becomes a problem on the road and able to spot recurring issues across groups of vehicles of a certain type. In practice, the last few years have seen the emergence of a service routine that was envisaged up to two decades earlier.

General safety standards were also gradually increasing over this time, such as the introduction of LOLER regulations and inspections for lifting equipment. Systems like ABS braking moved from being optional to becoming a standard feature on virtually all vehicles during the course of this decade.

It is quite sobering to think that at the beginning of just the last decade, around 11 road users per week were still being killed or seriously injured in collisions involving a rear impact with an HGV. One of the results of this carnage was the introduction of vehicle conspicuity marking tape on the sides and rear of HGVs. This is one example of the many safety benefits EU legislation had on UK transport; this one alone was estimated to save 76 lives per year. The benefits of this innovation were largely self-explanatory and were introduced in quite a short time, helped by the fact that markings (especially if fitted when new) were relatively inexpensive, but vehicle incidents, generally, were not.

3) What has happened to the Commercial Vehicle industry in the last 10 years?

Moving forward 10 years to 2010, what had changed as far as vehicles were concerned? Quite a lot as it happens. The industry as a whole was still recovering from the 2008 financial crash, so vehicle numbers and general business were on the increase from their low point. For example, the van sector was coming back from a 50% drop in sales from their highs in 2007. Fuel prices and fuel duty were also on the increase, so fuel saving was high on the agenda until the last few years of the decade, where low oil prices and no duty increases for some years meant it was no longer flavour of the month. Alternative fuels started to become a mainstream subject rather than just being promoted by enthusiasts and public knowledge on the effect that transport had on the environment increased greatly during the last 10 years.

Carbon reduction was important throughout the decade and it is hard to remember that for environmental reasons, refrigerant gas and fluid use was still being legislated heavily at the beginning of this period. Unfortunately, in recent years, politicians and industry commentators alike have confused the issue of decarbonisation with that of emissions control, which are really two separate areas. For example, politicians and commentators are forever saying that the way to decarbonise transport is to have everybody driving electric vehicles. They also have a habit of referring to them as 'zero emission' vehicles. Whilst battery electric vehicles result in zero emissions at the tailpipe, good for local air quality, currently, electricity in the UK is around 50% produced by fossil-fuelled sources, thus not fully cutting out transport carbon production for the country or, the planet. In addition, their production leaves a larger footprint on the planet, as well as leaving some difficult materials to clean up or recycle at the end of their lives.

4) What other improvements have happened in the last 10 years?

Possibly the biggest single factor in improving vehicle operations in this decade was the widespread introduction of telematics, either manufacturer fitted, or more probably from one of the many telematics suppliers available at that time. It is impossible to underestimate the benefit of not having to constantly telephone a driver to find out where the vehicle was (always an optimistic exercise) or what it was doing. Telematics not only gave precise vehicle location information but a whole raft of other information and was also a major enabler behind the big increase in just-in-time (JIT) delivery, effectively resulting in overall lower stock levels across the UK. Telematics benefited not only the operator, but the customer as well, who could also utilise the wealth of data provided. Think of how you can now track your parcel delivery driver to your door, something that would just not have been thinkable before the introduction of telematics.

Many technological and more general innovations added up to gradual, but ever-increasing, improvements in vehicle safety & operation. European Whole Type Vehicle Approval (EWTVA) was introduced in 2010 allowing vehicles to be registered across all European Union (EU) states. Tyre labelling was introduced identifying fuel economy, wet grip and noise performance, along with the introduction of Tyre Pressure Monitoring Systems (TPMS), first on cars then later on commercial vehicles. Commercial vehicles massively increased the use of LED (Light-Emitting Diode) lighting, thus reducing energy consumption and the constant need to keep replacing traditional incandescent bulbs, a notionally small, but really important environmental and safety advance.

There was huge increase in commercial vehicle product complexity and sophistication during this period resulting, for example, in the last decade to a fourfold increase in vehicle electronic control units and the associated lines of computer code. The reliability of vehicle electronics, thankfully, improved greatly in the period. These sorts of advances are not immediately visible to the layman as the vehicles look remarkably similar from the outside. There was also an accompanying increase in ADAS (Advanced Driver Assistance Systems). These included safety features such as lane departure warning systems, Advanced Emergency Braking Systems (AEBS) and Electronic Vehicle Stability Controls (ESC). All these safety systems were introduced in the early part of the decade and can clearly be seen as the precursor to fully autonomous vehicles, probably in the next decade.

5) What effect did the introduction of emissions controls have in the last two decades?

As far as emissions regulations were concerned, Euro 3 was introduced in 2001 followed by Euro 4 in 2006, both having a significant improvement in air quality, although somewhat later worsened by a longer-term general increase in traffic, numbers of vehicles and increased mileages. It is fair to say that, although the introduction of these regulations generated plenty of turmoil at the time, they did not have such a large impact as the introduction of Euro 5 and 6 in the following decade. Whenever a new emissions regulation was introduced, there was always an effect on the rate of vehicle purchase, generally operators buying more of the older specification to avoid any increases in costs associated with the new.

At the time, this situation temporarily worked to the benefit of the vehicle manufacturers who were able to sell increased numbers of vehicles, sometimes at discounted prices, that would be no longer be compliant with the new Euro emission legislation after a certain date. The unintended consequence of this was a surge in the purchase and thus the use of vehicles with higher emissions which somewhat undermined the original purpose of the regulations. It also, somewhat unfortunately, meant a natural fall in sales of the newer vehicles for quite a period after the legislation introduction date, once again meaning that 'cleaner' vehicles were delayed in being adopted.

The introduction of increased emission controls, however, did lead to considerable research at the time on improved combustion, especially for diesel vehicles. This was a time when a certain level of smoke and emissions from commercial vehicles were expected by both the transport industry and the public, as vehicles were generally thought of, and often described as, "dirty". Even 20 years ago there was considerable debate about the health hazards of diesel exhaust emissions, although you can be forgiven for thinking it is a more modern problem.

Without a doubt, the biggest single issue of discussion amongst vehicle buyers in the last decade was the introduction of Euro 5 emissions legislation in 2011 and Euro 6 emissions in 2015. It has been said that every time one of these Euro levels was announced, dating back to Euro 1 in 1992, the manufacturers continuously held their hands up claiming that these regulations could not be met technically, or at a sensible price, in the time available and that a calamity would occur with increased fuel consumption, heavier weights and non-viable vehicles. On every occasion, for all 6 emission regulations, they managed to meet both the challenges and the deadlines, generally reduce the fuel consumption and at sensible weights and just about sensible prices.

Having said how well manufacturers met the regulations, it is important to note that the final and current level Euro 6 became very complex, involving the use of Exhaust Gas Recirculation (EGR), Selective Catalytic Reduction (SCR), Diesel Oxidation Catalysts (DOC) and Diesel Particulate Filters (DPF) in a number of combinations, depending on engine design. This, quite naturally, involved a vehicle price increase as well as a weight increase.

Before we beat ourselves up for not moving faster towards decarbonised transport, let's just celebrate the impressive net result of these emission regulations which was a reduction in CO2 (Carbon Dioxide) emissions by 82%, hydrocarbons and NOx (Nitrogen Oxide) also by 82% and particulate matter, the villain of the piece, by 96% over their original Euro 1 figure in 1992. It did also generally result in a fuel consumption reduction, however not everywhere, with some operations finding it gave a slight fuel consumption increase. These reductions look particularly impressive when viewed in graphical format, as shown below:

Development of European Heavy-duty Legislated Emissions Limits

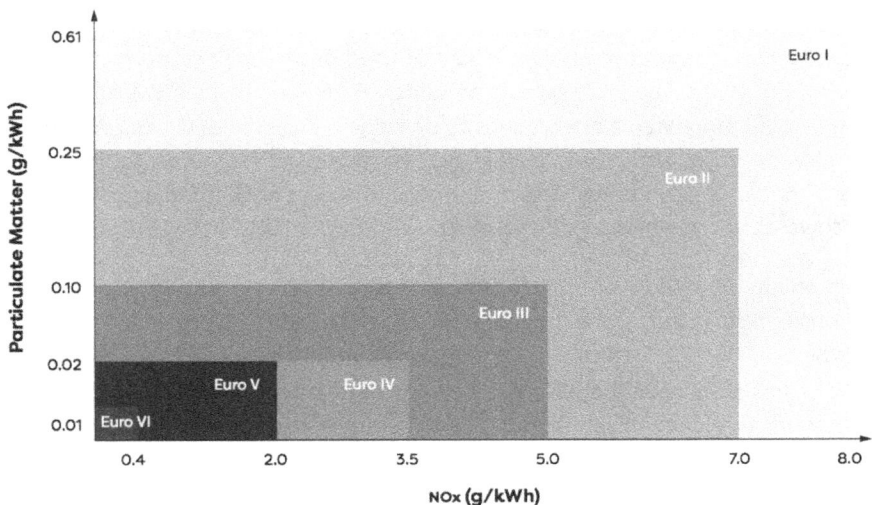

Source: The Association for Emissions Control by Catalyst (AECC), Brussels, Belgium: https://www.aecc.eu/legislation/heavy-duty-vehicles/

Perhaps the biggest problem with Euro 6 was finding places on the vehicle chassis that were still free to install all the various pieces of required kit, becoming quite a jigsaw puzzle in some instances. This presented an even more significant headache for bodybuilders, who managed an amazing conjuring trick in some cases, to accommodate their fittings in the very few spaces remaining on the vehicle.

6) How have emissions measurement changed and what has been the effect of "Dieselgate"?

At the beginning of the last decade there was a clear and definite objective of reducing carbon emissions from all modes of energy production, but especially transport. Largely this was due to an understanding that humans were contributing to global warming through production of CO_2, although this was still highly contested by some people, including politicians, at the beginning of the decade, less so at the end. This meant that early in the decade, the thrust of government advice for commercial vehicle operators, not least from organisations such as the Energy Saving Trust (EST), was to move all their fleet as fast as possible to become powered by diesel engines, in order to reduce CO_2 production.

For heavy commercials there was, and still is, no other real widely available current viable option other than diesel, due to the energy density of the fuel compared with other available alternatives. Not forgetting the fact, of course, that the diesel engine still remains probably the most efficient way to convert hydrocarbon into transport energy. At the time, many van operators still used petrol engines, so conversion to diesel would have saved considerable amounts of fuel and hence CO_2, although for vans there are more viable alternatives to petrol and diesel fuel, which some people were already using although they did not even begin to become comparable in terms of price, range and weights until nearer the end of the decade. Despite the drive towards decarbonisation, diesel still powers about 96% of the UK's vans.

We are still in the middle of introducing comparisons of how we may compare HGV fuel consumption figures and hence emission production before buying a vehicle using the EU's 'VECTO' Vehicle Energy Consumption Calculation Tool. There will be a review of this system by the end of 2022 – currently much of the data comes from the manufacturers themselves, but this is supported by independent testing conducted by external organisations. This system has a little way to go before being fully adopted by operators and indeed comparisons between the predicted figures and real-life are all important.

Official fuel consumption and emission figures for vans (in the UK) have only been available for slightly longer, since around 2017. It is probably fair to say that these figures also still need a little more work, again more experience of operators comparing real-life data with predictions is required. However, they are so much better than nothing at all and look reasonably representative for most types of vehicle. What can obviously dramatically affect van official fuel statistics will be the payload which can vary enormously even on one trip.

Official fuel and emission figures for cars have been available for many years however in recent years, the test result figures have been getting further and further away from real-life outcomes. Manufacturers and especially end users were becoming increasingly more dissatisfied with the picture they gave. Then came the VW 'Dieselgate' fiasco, the outcomes of which are still being understood even now. Just to put their situation into perspective, up until the start of 2021, VW claim the diesel cheating scandal has cost the organisation over 31 billion euros in fines and settlements, the equivalent to the Gross Domestic Product of a small country.

Possibly one major result of discovering that VW had deliberately falsified emission figures was the introduction in 2018 of a new EU test program programme known as Worldwide harmonised Light vehicle Test Procedure (WLTP). Again, these figures probably need a little more work but they represent much more realistic figures than their predecessors. There is also a harsher Real Driving Emissions (RDE) test which measures emissions figures on the road and the end result will be a reducing published ratio, over time, of the WLTP. This means manufacturers will have to reduce their emissions over time to continue meeting the targets.

7) How did changes in society effect the commercial vehicle industry?

I think you can safely say you would not normally read anything about politics and social change in a fleet management handbook. However, there is no doubt that the subject had a major effect on transport operations between 2010 and 2020 and will do for some time to come. The Internet, together with online buying habits, promoted a massive cultural change which accelerated towards the end of the decade, helped by the huge increase in social media and the rise in the use of personal devices, meaning IT and purchasing became far more mobile.

A huge rise in van numbers, both being made and registered on the road, occurred right the way through this decade, until 2017 when the Brexit effect dropped consumer confidence and demand, reversed when deliveries became so important in the Covid-19 crisis. Casual observers believed that the increase in vans was directly due to the rise of online shopping, although statistics say, it was far more to do with a large rise in self-employed and small independent trades business, all needing vans to ply their trade.

A coalition government at the start of the decade was replaced by a Brexit government towards the end of the decade. One result of these styles of leadership has been considerable uncertainty during the period for both business and transport. One immediate effect after the 2016 referendum was a sharp drop in the value of the pound, resulting in increased costs for imported goods into the UK, including trucks, vans and the cost of vehicle parts and services not produced in the UK. It presents considerable and as yet largely undetermined problems for vehicle manufacturers in the future, where parts for vehicle production criss-cross many international boundaries. Companies such as Jaguar Land Rover, Ford, Nissan, Honda and Vauxhall have all announced plant closures or decided to produce model lines in countries other than the UK since 2016.

Happily, a Trade and Cooperation Agreement (TCA) deal was signed at the last minute in December 2020 between the EU & the UK, just before the end of the transition period. However, this gave all parties, including vehicle manufacturers and logistics operations virtually no time to prepare for any new arrangements, including increased customs controls from mid-2021. Already, it would appear that new arrangements will add considerably to the bureaucracy involved in crossing borders, most importantly, causing time delays in transit. This will inevitably give rise to upward price pressures on both parts and vehicles. This has been a major factor in increasing vehicle build lead-times and reducing availability in 2021 along with shortages in parts availability.

Possibly the biggest change to the automotive industry after Brexit will be the introduction of new rules concerning the 'country of origin'. In order to export to the EU, it will be necessary for materials used in production to meet very specific criteria relating to where a part, or an assembly, was produced. This obviously becomes quite complex for assemblies of components, including whole vehicles, some of which are both produced and worked upon in many different countries. There is currently a period of grace in place meaning documentation to show origin will not be required until 2022.

However, there are plans for the UK or EU content of electric vehicles (EV's) to ramp up between now and 2027, such that the entire battery assembly should also be sourced from either the UK or EU by that date, in order to keep selling into Europe. These requirements mean that the UK industry are urgently considering ways to source more local parts production and especially battery production, where we currently lag behind the EU. This action will obviously be required to avoid additional tariffs which would make UK vehicles uncompetitive and also to meet the increasing EV demand. Recent news of investment in a so-called "Gigafactory" to supply batteries for Nissan's Sunderland plant is a welcome step in that direction.

Increased decentralisation of government during the decade also had a series of consequences on vehicle specifications. Led mostly by London, a whole series of local regulation such as Clean Air Zones (CAZ) and Ultralow Emission Zones (ULEZ) were introduced along with operator recognition schemes, ostensibly introduced to reduce accidents and save lives, an obviously admirable target. The latest extension to the ever-increasing mountain of local legislation is the introduction of a Direct

Vision Standard (DVS) for the cabs of vehicles over 12 tonnes in London, effectively from early in 2021.

This standard will have a considerable commercial impact on many operators and at least some version of it is likely to be specified in public sector contracts in many other locations in the UK, so could have far-reaching impacts on any UK organisation involved in transport. However, more cynical transport commentators may say these regulations have now become an overcomplicated revenue earning scheme, especially for commercial vehicles, as they have no choice but to enter a specified zone in order to deliver to, or service, their customers.

Perversely, this huge increase in local legislation means that for the first time, a vehicle that was perfectly legal say, in Sussex, could now be "illegal" when running in London, or at the very least, subject to penalty fines. This causes users a major headache as national operators have to decide which vehicles to operate in particular locations and also are forced to fit considerable amounts of additional equipment, not necessary in the national context, but simply to be compliant in specific areas or for certain customers. It has however, massively boosted sales of ancillary equipment manufacturers, such as cameras and proximity sensors. It has also had the beneficial effect of raising the overall level of understanding of vehicle related safety issues and changed operators' attitude to compliance forever.

These political and legislative changes have given rise to major problems for commercial vehicle manufacturers and operators alike. Manufacturers find it very difficult to predict what legislation is required in their various markets across Europe and further afield, and are therefore reluctant to commit huge sums of development money for vehicle programs that may not see the light of day for another two to four years. Similarly, operators are equally nervous about expending large sums of money on capital equipment that may cease to be compliant before the end of its natural economic life. The only answer is for all parties to be as flexible as possible. However, that is easier said than done.

8)   What other changes happened in the last decade?

One very strange phenomenon in operators buying behaviour occurred during the middle of this decade. Almost forever, manual gearboxes were the normal choice for HGV vehicles. This was mainly due to AMT's (Automated Manual Transmissions) being more expensive (at least £1000 extra, more for fully automatic) and slightly less efficient, therefore costing more to run in terms of fuel. Over time, manufacturers continued to improve the performance of automated gearboxes, mainly through increased electronics, until they were very close, or in some circumstances, better in performance to manual. Coupled to this has been an ever-increasing lack of numbers and quality of HGV drivers, so operators started to choose AMT and fully automatic boxes that would perform as well or better in terms of fuel consumption, even in the hands of a very poor driver.

So within a period of not much more than two years, HGV vehicles purchased effectively went from virtually all being equipped with a manual gearbox to virtually all being equipped with an automated version. It did strike me at the time that if government or the DfT had insisted all vehicles would now be automatic, the industry would be up in arms, saying it would take 10 years to plan and 10 years to put into effect. Instead, the entire process happened almost overnight, almost without anybody really noticing. Perversely, the same has not been the case for the van market, which still remains stubbornly in favour of a manual box, despite some of the apparent advantages which an auto box could bring. Because of this reluctance from buyers, auto boxes are usually available only on selected van models and most are automated versions of a manual box rather than a true automatic. They do have the advantage of retaining higher resale values, however, probably due to their scarcity.

What does the commercial vehicle marketplace look like today? According to the Society of Motor Manufacturers and Traders (SMMT) the current volume of vehicles (2021 figures for the previous year) on the UK roads is just over 40 million vehicles, made up of around 35 million cars, 4.6 million vans, just under 600 thousand trucks and nearly 75,000 buses and coaches. No wonder we find it difficult to move around!

The automotive industry in total occupies around one-tenth of the total manufacturing output in the UK. Many of the commercial vehicles we use are now made outside the UK, however, according to the SMMT, pre-pandemic UK production was as follows: around 63,000 vans were made by Vauxhall each year; 17,000 trucks were made by Leyland; 2,000 busses came from Alexander Dennis; nearly 1,000 vehicles from Dennis Eagle and LEVC steadily increased production to over 1,500 electric vehicles (mostly electric taxis, now vans are part of the mix). The 2021 figures for the equivalent 2020 covid year are Stellantis Group (including Vauxhall) nearly 50,000 units; Leyland Trucks nearly 13,000; LEVC still just over 1,500; Dennis Eagle still just over 1,000 and Alexander Dennis now 874. Not bad considering the upheavals we have just gone through. Considerable political & economic upheaval at the time of writing will mean these figures are likely to continue to vary one way or another.

Even if a vehicle is produced overseas, there is still a complex and sophisticated dealer network in the UK providing a sales function and all the required service, after sales support and back-up. Most manufacturers are now looking nervously at the outcome of the Brexit deal, especially as world demand increases as we exit the Covid-19 shutdown. There is no doubt trading conditions will remain tough for quite some time yet.

9) What will the future bring for Commercial Vehicle operations?

Where is the commercial vehicle industry likely to be in the year 2030? Well, I could say almost anything I like here and by the time these things happen, it would be too late to challenge them and irrelevant anyway. That, of course, is what most industry pundits bank on when they make their bold statements about the future. However, there are some definite trends appearing in the transport world, and with some intelligent interpretation it is possible to predict what is likely to happen in the next decade, with a view to assisting operators in their all-important future vehicle buying and strategic fleet decisions.

First and foremost is the blindingly obvious issue of the massive trend towards carbon free transport in any shape or form. This will have to increase in the coming decade not least because of international, national and local commitments and targets to move to a zero-carbon world. For vans, the future is highly likely to be electric using renewable battery power. At the moment, mass adoption would require even better, lighter batteries or other energy storage methods, a number of which are coming up on the outside rails, such as super capacitors. It will also require huge improvements in infrastructure supporting increased electric vehicle use. Currently, the high cost of electric vans is balanced by very low running costs, resulting in total life costs similar to petrol or diesel vehicles, depending on mileages and lifespan.

However, when revenue from hydrocarbon fuel starts to drop, some way of taxing electricity for vehicles, or a charge on road use will most likely be introduced. This change will be a huge paradigm shift away from the current transport model based on hydrocarbon fuel that has sustained and supported much of the transport industry for over 100 years. This change has probably not been fully appreciated by governments and operators; to some extent we are all working in the dark – the full picture of this "new world" will emerge gradually over time.

For those of you connected in any way with workshops and the repair side of the industry, one of the knock-on effects a move to electric vehicles will have, is a reduction in service time, although hybrid vehicles, perversely, actually slightly increase service requirements. So, your total fleet service requirement will depend very much on the mix of vehicles you have at any given time. In fact much of the servicing on electric vehicles revolves around software updates, rather than mechanical items, something that workshops will have to reflect in their staff profile, although items such as brakes and tyres will still need replacing as before.

For HGVs, the future is not so clear as there is no obvious alternative to diesel fuel. Oil prices are rising again and are likely to continue to rise over this period, not least because over the last few years they had sunk to a relative low. However, any price increase is not thought by industry experts to be significant enough on its own to act as a driver for alternative developments. Gas is often suggested by its proponents, but this is only viable at the margins and is still generally a fossil fuel. Biofuel again is only viable at the margins and could not be adopted on a global scale because of the increasing need for land to grow food. Many people suggest hydrogen is the way forward and it is the most likely option for HGVs, mainly due to its energy density when transporting heavy vehicles. However, the big drawback here is the huge energy required to make it, the difficulty of storing and transporting it, and the inefficiency of turning it back into electric power at the wheels. There are currently also interesting trials of electric trucks being held, generally powered by overhead cables, but which lack flexibility when off trunk roads. All these potential options are examined in more detail in chapter 6.

Electric Self-Driving Van – Vision of the not-too Distant Future?

Autonomous vehicles look to be a pretty safe bet and will probably come into being in five to ten years' time, so available towards the end of the decade, very much depending on their commercial viability. (See chapter 6 for a brief explanation and further examination of autonomous vehicles). Many people tend to forget that most of the technology is largely available now and the fact they are not in use is actually more about standards, systems, security and interoperability, which is effectively delaying the introduction of more of these vehicles right now. For example, around half of cars coming off the production line have autonomous emergency braking and/or adaptive cruise control.

Some commentators suggest that the introduction of autonomous vehicles may be helped by the introduction of improved alternative technology elsewhere, such as better storage capacity, or with the development of more effective solar panels covering a vehicle, meaning the vehicle becomes self-powered. This would eliminate the need for most "docking" manoeuvres in order to charge.

A little more futuristic perhaps, is the use of VTOL (Vertical Take-Off and Landing) craft, probably electric powered, which fly in a similar fashion to drones. The issue here is currently one of safety and the protocols that would have to be inbuilt as to where, when and how they can fly. Experts tend to agree we will not have "drone corridors" which can often be seen in many science-fiction films. Passenger carrying craft are probably some way off due to safety concerns and production in large numbers is not predicted by the end of the next decade.

However, the use of drones for deliveries, especially parcel deliveries, would be so beneficial to the efficiency of the so-called "last mile" delivery, that this will drive rapid research and development with a much more likely early commercial uptake. A 2016 report by consultants McKinsey, predicted autonomous robots and drones could be carrying out up to 80% of last-mile deliveries by 2030. Their calculations show robotic vehicles could achieve a 40% cost saving over current style manual last-mile deliveries, (depending on labour rates and transport costs) particularly in rural and areas of lower population. Find their report here: https://tinyurl.com/4evedkvh

Vehicle ownership is likely to have a tremendous shakeup in the next 10 years. The recent Covid lock down has shown just how many people can effectively work from home. On a normal travel day (pre-Covid) it is estimated that only 5 to 10% of the total vehicle parc is actually in use at any given time therefore 90 to 95% of all cars are sat stationary somewhere, not in use. It is unlikely that depreciation and maintenance costs will dramatically fall, therefore the demand for alternative transport options will increase and the amount of vehicle ownership will fall. Having access to a vehicle will become massively more important than actually owning one, a factor many people are waking up to even today, especially in congested urban areas with high parking charges and perhaps no access to charging facilities. Covid has delayed this "pay-by-use" concept marginally, due to owners wanting their own vehicle space for hygiene reasons, however, that is likely to reverse if and when the effects of the pandemic (hopefully) finally disappear.

This ownership model is unlikely to have a significant effect on the way commercial vehicles are owned, however, it should have a significant effect on one of the biggest problems of the last two decades, that of congestion. Therefore, overall road traffic should decrease in this period as there will be fewer other vehicles on the road, and those cars that are on the highways should have a much higher utilisation as they are likely to be rented temporarily by individual drivers.

Top Issues in the Commercial Vehicle Industry, Past & Future

- Vehicle progress over the last 10 to 20 years gives us some indication of where we are likely to go over the next 10 years.

- 20 years ago, fleet engineers and managers were more concerned about the mechanics of running vehicles.

- 10 years ago, advanced electronics systems started to improve significantly, giving improved control of vehicles and feedback data.

- EU emission controls have resulted in over 80% reduction in emissions and 96% reduction in particulates since Euro 1 was introduced in 1992.

- There were considerable welcome technical advances in transport in the last decade such as; telematics, tyre labelling, TPMS, LED lights, ADAS; mainly increasing road safety or reducing breakdowns.

- Societal changes, such as the uptake of broadband and personal devises plus an increase in small businesses, helped give rise to a large increase in van use.

- Decentralising government has given rise to increased traffic control schemes and operator recognition schemes, resulting in increased legislation and the fitting of expensive additional equipment.

- Emission classification and reporting is moving from laboratory testing towards real life testing, producing more realistic results.

- Brexit has given the industry massive challenges which are still in the process of being resolved at a time of global crisis.

- Battery Electric Vehicles are likely to be the vehicle of choice for most van users in the near to middle future, with reducing weight, increasing range and a wide extension to the charging infrastructure.

- HGVs will stay diesel powered for the foreseeable future, with continued technical advances and Euro 7 introduced around 2025; pundits don't all agree, but oil prices are likely to rise over the period.

- HGVs are likely to move to hydrogen in the medium to long term, supported by gas and biofuel in the shorter term and electric (including hybrid) in the medium or longer term.

- Changed vehicle ownership models in the next 10 years are likely to see a move towards 'pay-by-use' rather than ownership, the result being much increased utilisation of each vehicle and therefore less vehicles on the road, generally reducing congestion for commercial vehicles.

- There is highly likely to be an increase in robots or drones for last mile deliveries, further reducing urban congestion.

- Autonomous vehicles, in some format, are likely to appear towards the end of the decade, one result being it will start to resolve the issue of a shortage of HGV drivers.

David's Don'ts ✖

- Don't assume the cost of electricity for vehicles will stay low for ever; it is likely to be either taxed directly, if use can be measured, or some form of road user charge introduced when tax revenue from hydrocarbon fuel drops significantly.

The Ultimate Guide to Commercial Vehicle Fleet Management

Chapter 3 – Fleet Strategy & Planning

1) *Why is a fleet strategy so important to my organisation?*
2) *How do I align the fleet strategy to our corporate strategy?*
3) *How do I devise a fleet strategy; where do I start? What issues should a fleet strategy document cover?*
4) *How do I make sure users are happy with our fleet strategy?*
5) *How do I separate my fleet into sensible discrete groups?*
6) *How does replacement fit into the fleet strategy?*
7) *How does maintenance and administration fit into the fleet strategy?*
8) *How does disposal fit into the fleet strategy?*
9) *How do I make sure our fleet strategy is working? (Fleet KPI's)*

1) *Why is a fleet strategy so important to my organisation?*

There literally hundreds of dictionary definitions of the word "strategy". However, two definitions of 'business strategy' sum up the issue for me regarding fleet. One describes it as:

"A set of guiding principles that, when communicated and adopted in the organisation, generates a desired pattern of decision making".

The other shorter definition states:

"Strategy, in short, bridges the gap between 'where we are' and 'where we want to be' ".

There is no doubt that spending some time thinking through all the requirements of your fleet at an early stage and recording them clearly for others to see will result in far better decisions being taken at all levels in the business later down the track, a clear benefit to the organisation as a whole, also saving you precious management time. An effective fleet strategy defines your organisation's approach to fleet management in a clear and concise manner, so that everyone involved in fleet activities can understand and follow it. It should set out a vision for how you intend to manage the fleet effectively, both now and for the future, such that it will meet the needs of the organisation for some time to come.

The process of deciding on your fleet strategy is the probably most important part of managing the fleet, but sadly, it is often the part that most organisations either skimp on, or even miss entirely. Many more organisations than I would like, generally the smaller ones, often arrive at their fleet strategy mainly by accident. Luckily, no matter what the size of your fleet, the basic principles remain the same.

Organisations whose core function is transport or distribution tend to be more likely to have, by definition, a fleet strategy that is more closely aligned to the business. It is the organisations where fleet is merely a tool to support the real business where vehicle provision can end up almost as an adjunct to the business strategy, falling victim to the latest fleet trend or amazing supply deal. It is human nature to get excited about new vehicles; the smells, the latest gadgets, but without clearly setting out how you will meet business needs this excitement can become a distraction. Buying the latest trend or great deal results in poor management decisions and a sub-optimal fleet profile that seldom meets the real needs of the business.

I would strongly advise that a strategy should be written, for two reasons. Firstly, because putting anything down in writing clarifies issues wonderfully in the minds of those producing and reading the document. Secondly, so that it can be distributed to anyone in the organisation involved in fleet along with all the associated processes. It could be said that if you have not got a written strategy then you don't have a strategy at all. Some people fear that a written document will not be flexible enough to meet the changing needs of the business, but it should be regularly reviewed and updated (at least once a year), so should be a fluid document rather than one set in stone.

Although we talk about Fleet Strategy throughout this chapter, in truth, some of the advice strays into the area of Fleet Policy and occasionally into Fleet Procedures. From time to time, I am asked 'what's the difference between these three?', which is a very good question. In essence, Strategy is about your vision for the future and a high-level view of how you are going to get there. Policy is one level down and describes the actions you are going to take, whereas Procedure describes exactly what to do to achieve the objective. So, for example, your environmental fleet strategy might be to go carbon free by 2035. Your policy may state that every depot will possess 15% electric vehicles within the next three years and your procedure would state details such as which vehicles you will buy and how many chargers are required, of what type, where and by when.

Handy Hint   ☝

- Whenever you update your strategy document (or policy or procedures for that matter) make sure you distribute the revised version to all fleet personnel concerned. It really helps to include a short note of what has changed and if not self-explanatory, why. This may take a little more time, but it will save so much more time downstream when trying to sort out the problems that occur because some users did not notice the changes.

Ultimately, the strategy document should:

- help you achieve a fleet that is fit for purpose
- identify the business needs for each sector of the fleet
- set out goals for how your organisation intends to manage its fleet in the future
- allow for any potential future changes in the business
- be part of your organisation's overall approach to effective asset management
- must link to your environmental aims

To be fully effective, the Fleet Strategy should also look outside your organisation and consider the potential benefits of working with external organisations, such as trade bodies and specialised transport associations, to help provide your organisation with the most effective, efficient and compliant fleet.

Ideally, the management of the fleet should be an integral part of the organisation's overall business plan and reflect service objectives and more detailed targets linking to the organisation's corporate objectives. There should be a clear link from the fleet budgets to both corporate financial budgets and capital programmes, as well as staff development and training. To be honest, this was not always the case in years past, but almost all organisations now take the running of fleets more seriously and most do include managing its performance at a strategic level, not least due to the introduction of corporate responsibility legislation.

Most importantly of all, but often not fully recognised, it is not sufficient for your fleet strategy simply to be integrated into your organisation's business plans and objectives. There must be buy-in from the very top for all aspects of your fleet strategy. This factor has obviously become more important with the advent of increased corporate responsibility. The CEO or MD of the organisation and the senior management team must have read, agreed and fully signed up to all aspects of the strategy. This means that management decisions taken in other areas must also support the fleet strategy. If not, staff will notice these little anomalies and cease to believe that the organisation is serious about the aims of the fleet function. It also means your strategy will carry weight across the organisation for when challenges are made. Of course, it also means that fleet decisions can no longer be made "on the hoof" and more serious decisions need to be ratified with the senior management tiers before implementation, which has always been best practice.

Fleet Strategy is important whatever the size of your Fleet

2)   How do I align the fleet strategy to our corporate strategy?

Although to arrive at a genuinely effective vision for your fleet, the fleet management strategy must link up with your organisation's other strategic aims and priorities, I sometimes get called into fleets where, in places, the fleet processes can work against achieving operational aims, or at the very least, are not actively helping to achieve them. Although this sounds like a criticism, it is actually a function of how complex modern business is.

Fleet procedures and processes are often drawn up over time, usually for sound reasons, probably underpinned by legislation and it is human nature to stick to them, for no lesser reason than they have worked well for years and everyone (well, most people) understand them. It is useful if that is the case, and you probably do not want to be changing working practices every 5 minutes, otherwise staff will end up confused and possibly demotivated. However, if the business is changing, at sensible points in the story, support services may need to match those changes to keep in step.

So, all that sounds great in theory; of course, your fleet strategy should reflect or mirror your business strategy, but how does that look in practice? Let's look at an example of a fairly straightforward case of fleets involved in grocery distribution and parcels. Both these sectors suffer perennially from a lack of available vehicles in the run-up to Christmas. They usually have to pre-order hire and short-term vehicles immediately after the previous Christmas to stand any chance of having enough vehicles in this extremely busy period. In the next chapter we look at how to decide on lead times for ordering vehicles, but, if the vehicles for these sectors are ordered such that they arrive in September and October, but the vehicles they are replacing are not sold until January or February the following year, the increase in fleet almost exactly matches the need of the business. If, for example, these vehicles were on a five-year replacement cycle that means effectively a 20% increase in fleet availability for the crucial Christmas period.

This is not a perfect strategy by any means, as normally you would wish to sell the replaced vehicle immediately to help recoup a proportion of the cost of purchase. Also, January or February is not generally a good time of year for selling vehicles as the second hand and auction market is often flat. It also assumes you are not replacing many vehicles at other times of the year. However, if the alternative is that you just cannot get enough vehicles to run your business, it becomes a great way of getting over a known business issue.

For this method to work fully it needs to be documented such that all the appropriate people in the business understand the need for this strategy. Nowhere is that quite so important as for maintenance, where operators and technical staff alike, need to understand when vehicles are going to appear and disappear in order to manage maintenance budgets in the best possible fashion. In print, this looks so blindingly obvious, but I cannot tell you the number of organisations I have visited and asked the question "when is x going to be replaced?" to receive a reply along the lines of "no idea mate, your guess is as good as mine!".

Handy Hint 👍

- As well as all your internal staff, whenever updating strategy, policy or procedural documents, consider if organisations outside of your own (for example, a hire company) also need to know of the changes. Keeping them in the loop helps build your relationship with suppliers and helps them to help you. Far better for them to feel inclusive and hear directly from you, rather than from a driver or other suppliers.

One caveat here about aligning yourself to your organisations' environmental objectives. Be a little careful at this early stage in a cultural change about declaring objectives for alternatively fuelled vehicles. I have seen many organisations, probably more from the public sector, who boldly declare "X% of our fleet will be emissions free by Y". The problem here, especially for early electric vehicles, is one of suitability. Early electric vehicles suffered from increased prices, reduced range and increased weight.

So, one of two things can happen; either the vehicles are forced into the fleet, in which case you end up with disillusioned and upset operations and staff, because the vehicles are not as good as their predecessors at certain aspects of the operation. Or you just do not achieve the objectives of introducing enough vehicles, so end up with disillusioned stakeholders. Either way, you are on a hiding to nothing, so it is probably best to declare clear aims, but give yourself a range to operate within, to allow for variations in prices, infrastructure and technology advances.

3) How do I devise a fleet strategy; where do I start? What issues should a fleet strategy document cover?

Thankfully, there are no right or wrong answers here. Your fleet strategy should be specific to your organisation and your needs, however, there are some basics that should probably be included in any strategy document. These include:

- Firstly, an introduction on why your organisation has a fleet strategy in the first place, incorporating some of the reasons outlined in sections 1 & 2 above, emphasising the benefits of the strategy to the reader

- Then, what is the business use and business need for each group of vehicles in the fleet? This is perhaps a more important question than most people give credit for; without it you may well be carrying out some fleet operations that perhaps are more effectively sub-contracted to another supplier. Being as specific as possible at this stage often helps decision making down the line

- The method of purchase, lease or hire, with reasoning, needs to be clearly spelt out as the logic of these decisions can change with new legislation or changes in the business status and require adjustment

- Once the method of acquisition is decided, then you need to spell out how often this will happen, when, from whom and what the process of acquisition is – what information is required and what is the decision-making process, together with all the required administrative procedures

- Some indication of what the intended average age of the fleet will be, along with the maximum age and mileage for each vehicle group, so colleagues know when vehicles will always get replaced (all other things being equal). A regularly published replacement schedule for the whole fleet is possibly one of the most useful things you can do to avoid unnecessary expense on vehicles ready for disposal

- You probably (and unfortunately) will need to include a statement within your strategy that fleet vehicles will be selected on the basis of their projected whole life costs being the lowest available on the market – you may need to state this to counter inevitable comments from certain quarters of the organisation that an alternative vehicle to one you have selected is "cheaper" – i.e., its purchase price may be cheaper, but total life costs may not be.

- Your current vehicle numbers, by group of vehicles, relative to the current business activities need to be specified and any trends identified – for example, if mileages have been reducing due to changes in the business, average vehicle ages may be allowed to increase (providing total costs reduce, of course). It helps everyone involved in fleet if this ambition is shared, otherwise those managers not "in the know" become disillusioned, mainly because their vehicles are not being replaced so regularly

- If the demand on fleet is not fairly static, due to seasonal or changing business patterns, how the fleet will meet these demands needs to be explained and spelt out. This may be by flexible vehicle design or by hiring in to meet business peaks

- The types of vehicles and bodies for each vehicle group need to be broadly specified, along with their function, size and weight capacity, power and fuel figures, so operators know which vehicle to pick when replacing. As mentioned elsewhere, it is really important to reduce the number of types or groups of fleet vehicles to a minimum, so the logic of how you have arrived at these groups needs spelling out. If the specification of vehicles can be slightly modified, it may be that differing functions can be catered for using the same vehicle, thus increasing standardisation. The reasoning behind such planning needs explaining in the strategy to avoid misunderstandings

- Describe any specialist requirements within the fleet and how they will be catered for. Explain very briefly how you arrived at the specification criteria for each vehicle. It helps to try to answer the question "why" in the minds of some of your operational managers, who might not understand the reasons some specifications were arrived at; a little logic at this stage helps acceptance of the reasons why decisions were made

- Along with your fleet strategy, depending on the size of your organisation, a vehicle (and body) specification manual is really helpful, with one-page descriptions and dimensions, together with an outline sketch or picture of each type of vehicle. It takes a little effort, but will be so useful to operations, and you may be able to get suppliers to assist you assemble some of the details

- Maintenance operations need to be specified, when, where, how often and how vehicles will be maintained, internally or externally and how this fits in with your fleet profile and your acquisition and disposal regimes. Most important is to fully describe how the driver and daily inspection regime fits into the maintenance strategy and how important it is for the organisation to help keep fleet costs, safety and quality under control

- Disposal procedures need specifying carefully, so everyone knows exactly who does what when it is time to get rid of your vehicles. For example, if you are leasing, you may need a de-fleet activity which removes all ancillary equipment and logos, then evaluates what, if any, wear or damage requires repairing before returning, as that can really save money, depending on the contract conditions

- At some point, you will need to discover how well your fleet management strategy is working. In order to do that, you have to install Key Performance Indicators (KPI's) – see section 9 below. The strategy should explain which KPI's you have selected to measure your fleet's performance and in particular, why these have been selected and what it tells you about fleet performance for your organisation. You also need to state publicly what happens if the figures do not meet your published targets or guidelines; in broad terms, what actions are you going to take in order to get the figures to where they should be? This is required so there are no surprises for anyone involved, if and when the KPI's do not meet the required standards.

- The fleet strategy will intersect with other departments in the organisation, such as finance, operations and HR; these relationships need to be spelt out in clear terms of what communication needs to happen and when. There needs to be clear guidelines for interaction between departments, so responsibilities are clear and the best business decisions can be made with each department being given the data they require for the tasks at hand. This is especially true for your relationship with Transport or Operational managers. Under O licence obligations, they are accountable for the condition of the fleet, which means there could be ambiguity about responsibilities for fleet assets; these need carefully spelling out to avoid misunderstandings.

- A strategy document in today's climate probably will not be complete without some mention of your environmental targets; how will you be trying to reduce your organisation's fuel use, how are you attempting to reduce mileages, what mitigating activities will you employ, what is your future strategy on alternative fuels? If you are seeking to utilise significant numbers of alternative fuelled vehicles, how will any additional capital and hopefully reduced revenue costs (almost certainly these will change) be handled? They may well also have differing mileage and age replacement criteria to the existing fleet which needs clarifying

- Also necessary for today's fleet is a description of the supporting technology and IT that will almost certainly be fitted to vehicles in order to assist the operation, and how this fits into the organisation as a whole. For example, how cameras will be used and how the images will be stored and managed (important now under GDPR). If, for example, hand-held terminals, together with telematics, are used to capture Proof of Deliver, some explanation of who manages the technology, how it will be used and how the data will integrate with the organisation's other systems is essential. Without an overarching strategy here, these add-ons can be supplier led and become a bit of a muddle to manage, giving sub-optimal results.

- Your strategy should also recognise that for a whole variety of reasons, there is currently a shortage of skilled technicians to maintain vehicles in the UK. Even if all your maintenance is totally external, you need to have thought through and describe what standards you require from your maintenance provider and their team. If your maintenance is in-house, you should consider what standards you require from your staff, evidenced by such qualifications as irtec or from the IMI (Institute of the Motor Industry), also specifying the standards and accreditation you require both now and for the future for your workshops themselves.

Considering the phenomenal rate at which vehicle technology is currently changing, it has become increasingly important for the entire fleet function to incorporate a Continuous Professional Development (CPD) culture, which is hopefully reflected elsewhere in your organisation. In addition, as the use of electric vehicles increases, utilising potentially lethal high voltages, it becomes increasingly important to ensure that all members of staff associated with vehicles receive at least a basic awareness level of training so they are not fazed (no pun intended!) by the new technology. As electric vehicles become a greater proportion of your fleet, if you run your own workshops, there will fast come a time when all technicians will require training. Under duty of care, there is a limit to how long you can leave all EV repairs to just one or two technicians. In any case, this is not a very practical solution.

- One other issue that tends to get forgotten in a fleet strategy is staff succession planning. It is easy to see why, it is something that can be put off until further down the track. Unfortunately, that 'later' time often comes up all too quickly. The transport industry probably suffers from this problem as much, if not more than other sectors of the UK industry. In particular, the shortage of skilled drivers and technicians is not helped by the age demographic, meaning many staff are at, or approaching, retirement age. Spend some time, therefore, on formalising a plan for bringing staff through the business, receiving appropriate training at a time that maximises knowledge retention and is most beneficial to your staff performance.

And lastly, please do make full use of whatever grants and inducements are available for apprenticeships. Many operators do not think of utilising this method of employment on the basis that staff can leave after receiving considerable training. Sometimes I feel that could be more of a reflection on the organisation, in that conditions are not attractive enough to retain the talent. The benefits for both the employee and employer can be really attractive, by combining on-the-job training with classroom learning and attaining qualifications from GCSE equivalent to degree level. This makes it suitable for almost any operation within fleet, so the apprentice can end up with functional skills, NVQ's, technical certificates or even advanced academic qualifications. To me, the biggest asset is that after training, the apprentice is fully versed in your operating procedures and the culture of the organisation, so can 'hit the ground running' when fully employed.

4) How do I make sure users are happy with our fleet strategy?

Vehicle drivers, loading staff, vehicle technicians, passengers and other fleet users can often offer a broad perspective on the strategic direction of fleet management. If the organisation grows to any size at all, it is incredibly useful to devise a Service Level Agreement (SLA) to specify exactly what the fleet department will do for operations and vice-versa. Some SLAs I have seen are dreadful long-winded documents, full of details which look as though they are there solely to punish each side for non-compliance.

Instead, the SLA should simply state, in very clear and concise language, what the standards are for providing the fleet to operations and conversely, how operations can help in that process. The process of writing the SLA will again focus the minds of those involved on what is really important about fleet provision and what else is just nice to have. Items like lead times for defect reporting and the servicing process itself just help clarify issues for everyone concerned. The top-level Fleet KPI's (see examples below) should also be included in the SLA to indicate what performance is targeted, hopefully, improving gradually over time.

User groups for any fleet with more than a handful of vehicles are, in my view, absolutely essential. Many fleet managers see these groups as a bit of a chore, but regular meetings are a key method for operational staff to understand fleet provision and maintenance problems and just as importantly, for fleet providers to get to grips with operations and understand exactly how vehicles are being used. There is often a mismatch in understanding between these two views which can only really get resolved by regular consultation. These user groups can also contribute greatly to the creation and updating of a fleet strategy, making it adaptable, current and well informed.

Vehicle users must be consulted at regular intervals to ensure the fleet strategy stays well informed and captures all the key issues for devising a fleet that is fully fit for purpose. The user groups, by definition, will be the people using your vehicles, so their operational knowledge and experience is crucial in ensuring the strategy focuses on the right issues.

Conversely, if sufficient user consultation has not taken place, especially by seeking input on trial vehicles and during the process of drawing up operational specifications, it is unfortunately very likely that there may be some driver opposition to using the vehicles that you have procured on behalf of your organisation. User input is also vitally important when considering the needs of users in terms of fleet size, fleet groupings, vehicle type, legislative changes and training requirements.

However, it needs to be said that whilst consultation and participation with users is a must, there will almost certainly come a time when the views of the user have to be over-ridden by the fleet manager, backed by senior management. If so, this must be factually based and not just rely on "feelings". For example, when talking to operators at vehicle replacement time they will often declare that they "cannot do without" a particular replacement vehicle.

Chapter 8 on Telematics points out that very often, a detailed and factual examination of mileages and usage will almost certainly reveal a significant number of vehicles in your fleet that are just not being properly utilised. However, very often the manager concerned will still want a replacement, quite naturally, to give themselves some flexibility, although this will not be the declared reason. In this case, the replacement should probably go elsewhere and the underutilised vehicle withdrawn, being replaced by a shared vehicle, short-term hire or similar, if necessary. Most operational managers, in my experience, actually understand this issue and if properly handled, soon adapt to slightly reduced fleet numbers. In any event, their capital costs should reflect this reduction which will make their overall performance figures look better.

I usually get resistance from fleet managers when I suggest conducting a regular survey of users on the fleet. I think there is a belief amongst fleet management staff that users do not understand how difficult fleet management is and they feel a survey will just encourage negative comments. However, over time, I have found them to be a really useful tool in helping focus management time on areas causing particular problems. The feedback is yet another way of steering the decision making on the fleet strategy, based upon real user feedback.

Also, surveys are especially good to repeat at sensible intervals to measure trends; hopefully to show things are improving. In fact, I find fleet staff are sometimes too pessimistic and surveys often return some really good comments which need sharing with the appropriate staff. The wording needs to be carefully thought through of course; do not ask too many open questions unless you really want to encourage a wide variety of opinions, but similarly, don't close the questions too much so managers and staff do not get to say what they mean.

5) How do I separate my fleet into sensible discrete groups?

Most organisations that I work with have usually already split their fleet listing into fairly logical groups. Some, however, are not so logical, but because reorganising the listing and the groups may be quite a major task, and I am invariably brought in to investigate other issues, I work with whatever has been set up previously. The way these groups are setup can have a marked effect on the efficiency of managing the fleet. The prime objective for grouping vehicles in this way is to make comparisons of fleet management performance figures such as fuel use, maintenance and operating costs both logical and easy.

The first logical and easy split is to divide the vehicles by their gross weight and hence carrying capacity, depending on the number of vehicles within the fleet. Logical split points can be used to separate groups, so for example, a split for vans could be car derived vans, small and medium vans up to 3.5 tonnes and vans over 3.5 tonnes. Small fleets may not need this level of definition; larger fleets may split down even further, again by weight or type of operation. The next possible differentiator is the make and model of the vehicle, again more practical for larger fleets. For very mixed fleets, such as local authorities, this idea is probably not so useful, but can still usefully be carried out to some extent. For fleets who have truly practised standardisation and run perhaps a solus or dual make buying policy, this makes absolute sense.

Another possible prime differentiator is the basic job function, closely followed by a second differentiator such as wheelbase or engine power. So, for example, compaction vehicles, 6x2 or 6x4. Engine power is a good differentiator as operating costs can often, but not always, escalate in line with increased power. Further differentiators can also make logical sense, such as trailers with and without tail lifts or ancillary equipment, which will have an effect on operating efficiency and maintenance costs, making costs difficult to compare without the split.

It is virtually impossible on this page to describe exactly how to set up a fleet listing and how to split your fleet into all the possible group permutations. However, many fleet listings are arrived at over time, on largely a 'hit or miss basis, where vehicles are often added as they come into the fleet and groups just expanded to cater for the latest additions, with subtle variations.

What also often happens, because different admin personnel are used in this process, is that definitions on the fleet management system for the same vehicles are not always the same. A colleague of mine once found 60 separate names on a fleet system for the same model of vehicle! This makes comparisons very difficult, if not impossible, as computers do not discriminate over these things, so ensuring a standard format for input may seem a little trivial, but is so helpful when trying to produce meaningful fleet figures. Modern fleet management systems are really good at allowing you to select a raft of differentiators when running reports, but that, of course, means the initial listing data really must be accurate for the results to make sense.

My point here is that when beginning an initial listing of your fleet, or at certain points in the expansion of your vehicle fleet profile, some thought about, and reorganisation of, your vehicle groupings will be massively beneficial to the comparisons you are making further down the line. The aim, of course, is to always be comparing eggs with eggs. You will know this is not always achievable in practice, but it should be a constant target to keep managing your vehicle listings to aid your overall fleet management. When your managing director asks you for some simple fleet statistics, or indeed looks at them for themselves, it is really tedious, time wasting and inefficient to have to keep explaining or making adjustments for vehicles that should or should not be in the same vehicle grouping.

6) How does replacement fit into the fleet strategy?

One of the first aspects of the strategy to be decided is how to acquire your fleet. There are many aspects of this process, such as deciding on vehicle life cycles and what type of vehicle finance is needed that requires some quite detailed analysis and may well be determined by factors outside of fleet. Finance, for example, is often determined by an organisation's cash flow, level of profits or their tax and VAT position. Many of these issues are dealt with separately elsewhere in this book.

Thinking about the strategy document however, it will be useful to take a "helicopter" view, stepping back from the detail and look at the more basic and strategic issues. So, asking yourself questions such as:

- Why do we need vehicles in the first place?
- If we do not use vehicles, what are the alternatives, do they fit our business model?
- Can we subcontract aspects of transport or do we consider it a core part of the business?
- Do we really need people constantly travelling the countryside, or can we cope more on a virtual basis, an issue that became very relevant in the pandemic?

By thinking through these issues, analysing your particular approach and describing them clearly, you are laying the foundations for far better fleet decisions at all levels of the organisations at a later time.

When it comes to vehicle replacement policies, most fleets use fixed cycles driven by a variety of factors such as age, total mileage run, operating and maintenance costs or lease contract or financing terms. All these policies will vary, often due to differing operational requirements, however, in most cases relatively fixed replacement intervals are in place. These intervals have usually been in place for so long, they often go unquestioned and the logic behind them is probably forgotten.

Standardising your Fleet is core to Making Savings

I would recommend and suggest utilising more flexible vehicle replacement cycles, focusing on the best performing, but least costly makes and models for your operations. In order for your fleet vehicle replacement policy to become more flexible, consider mixing different strategies for different functions, maximising the benefits for each vehicle grouping. Although replacement cycles should keep to a stated nominal interval, do not be afraid of shortening or lengthening cycles for particular groups of vehicles if a definite business advantage can be shown, but as ever, base this on the statistics and make sure everyone involved in fleet knows why and when this is happening through good communications.

Deciding the most effective replacement cycles for your vehicles is not always simple, especially if mileages vary considerably across different parts of your operation. In chapter 4 we investigate briefly how to determine the optimum economic point to replace your vehicles. You probably will not have time to carry out this full calculation on a regular basis, but I would suggest at least once a year, probably at budget time, going through the figures to check that you are still replacing each group of vehicles at the optimum point. Your fleet data should be providing enough information to decide if a change within each group would give operational savings on a long-term basis.

Fleets often delay vehicle replacement during periods of economic uncertainty like the one we experienced due to a pandemic. This is, of course, a legitimate practice of managing risk and cash flow. However, as fleet manager, do ensure that all the decision-makers involved in delaying vehicle purchases understand the economic on-costs this will have on the business by providing them with your calculations of what the increases in running costs are likely to be. Provide the on-going evidence from fleet data and refer to it regularly in whatever senior management reports you are circulating. Most senior decision makers will have no problems in kicking this particular can down the road but then get quite heated when they see maintenance budgets rising steeply, so you need to have clearly forewarned them, and I would advise, in writing.

Do not be frightened to vary from your declared replacement strategy if the need arises. One possible alternative option to consider is obtaining vehicles on a short-term lease or similar, to provide vehicles for one or two years until the economy is in a more stable situation or the business need for a vehicle has been proven.

The fleet strategy should also be flexible enough to allow you to maximise the use of vehicles you already use. Most operators tend to think of the vehicle as "theirs", in other words it belongs to them or their depot or operation. Instead consider them all as assets of the business and your job is to maximise their use. As fleet manager you should constantly be scanning the mileages of the vehicles within the various groups and deciding if vehicles need reallocating because their use and mileages are either too high or too low. Operations tend to hate this practice, so they try to avoid it like the plague, which is why, in my humble opinion, most fleet managers are not very proactive in this area. Try to think strategically in this regard, in order to maximise the use of vehicles across the fleet and hence minimise total operating costs.

7) How does maintenance and administration fit into the fleet strategy?

Once you have decided how you are to acquire vehicles, for a commercial fleet, possibly the most important decision of all is how, when and where are you going to maintain them. For most of my career, heavy commercial vehicles have had their inspection regimes largely laid out for them by legislation. The service regime is separate from inspection and mainly determined by the manufacturers, something that is not always understood fully by operators, but obviously inextricably linked to the inspection regime.

With predictive maintenance and self-diagnosis getting more prevalent, this may change future maintenance practices, but for the time being, inspection and service schedules they are still largely time based. In fact, largely due to the advent of operator compliance demonstration schemes, the effect has been to push these more formal maintenance regimes down the weight range to vans. Van fleets are now generally expected to be carrying out daily inspections on basic safety items, exactly as HGVs' and keeping accurate maintenance records in a similar fashion. Vans are also moving toward service intervals being determined by their engine management system. Such service intervals are also being extended, not least by the increased use of synthetic oils. Depending on your operation, it may make a lot of sense for vans with long service intervals to have at least one interim inspection scheduled in between their service visits. This may look like an additional cost, but can often save money by picking up issues early, allowing for a minor repair rather than major expenditure.

The core of a good fleet maintenance strategy is a sound and robust administration system to ensure fleet maintenance takes place in a timely, professional and legal manner, whether or not these are 'O' licenced vehicles. The system can be electronic, paper, wallchart, wallets, cards; in short, anything you like as long as it works, anyone can follow it and it is fully auditable.

Any mechanical asset will need regular and routine maintenance, with discrete operations serviced at specific points in their life cycle and a record to show what has been carried out. Your system, whatever you choose to operate, should keep you and your organisation fully legal, cover your corporate responsibility and ensure the maximum cost-effective life for the asset. Everyone has their own way of doing things, the core requirement is that it demonstrably works. If, for example, you start missing MoT dates, for whatever reason, you obviously need to look at the system again. The fleet administration system needs to be clearly specified as part of the core Fleet strategy.

The strategy document needs to specify who will be doing what when it comes to fleet issues. The fleet administration function will vary from organisation to organisation depending on their size, internal structure and operation. Sometimes other departments may take on a particular function, such as HR holding driver records and checking driving licences. However, there are some core competencies that are generally dealt with by fleet administration and need to be specified in the fleet strategy, which are:

- the organisation and recording of vehicle maintenance & inspection.
- the organisation and recording of any vehicle related safety inspections.
- checking defect reports are actioned & completed.
- checking service documentation against schedules and invoices.
- managing tyre replacements and records
- ensuring VED Vehicle Excise Duty is paid and up to date for all vehicles
- ordering replacement vehicles (often assisted by finance and/or procurement).
- receiving new vehicles, inspection, delivery, managing paperwork & keys.
- updating driver records, initial checks, driver licence & medical checks such as driver eyesight.
- managing and ordering hire vehicles.
- ordering and managing fuel and/or fuel cards.
- monitoring fuel use, vehicle down time and utilisation.
- providing fleet statistical and financial information, reconciling invoices, recharging, warranty management.

You are obviously going to have to review at some stage whether maintenance provision should be provided using an in-house facility, or whether it would be better outsourced. If the service is provided in-house, the location and types of services should be regularly reviewed in line with any business changes to see if they still make strategic sense, or if some parts of the operation should be perhaps rationalised, extended or sub-contracted, whatever is financially and logistically appropriate.

In-house facilities will provide more control and flexibility, providing you employ the correct number of skilled staff in a flexible workshop, with workshop hours closely aligned to vehicle operating hours so as to maximise vehicle utilisation, which often means extending or staggering working times to enable vehicles to be repaired during their 'downtime'. Sadly, this latter benefit is not yet seen so often in public sector workshops, but hopefully will extend as budgets are reduced. A common occurrence is for an internal workshop to use outside contractors in order to supplement internal provision during peak periods, which helps to keep workshop overheads lower. In addition, contractors and main dealers may well have specialist equipment or skills which may not always be available in house.

In some circumstances, it may be easier to find the relevant skills outside the organisation as it is currently difficult to find the right level of skills when recruiting workshop staff and there is a cost to training internal staff. As technology moves on, the need to refit the workshop will become a significant overhead. This latter cost can be mitigated by carrying out third party work such as running an Authorised Test Facility (ATF), but the numbers must be investigated carefully before investing.

Normally, leased vehicles will specify that maintenance is usually carried out by a main dealer or authorised non-franchised service agent. That used to be a cast iron guarantee of quality, however, it has to be said that in recent years, the nationwide lack of skilled technicians has also affected main dealerships, so the quality of service and repair from these establishments has sometimes sadly dropped somewhat.

As far as skills for internal organisations are concerned, fleet managers should keep up to date with current maintenance and legislative requirements with CPD (Continuous Professional Development) training and staff should do likewise. In order to ensure internal work is of sufficient standard, it is becoming the norm that workshop staff benefit enormously from their staff being irtec accredited. Irtec is an independent accreditation, set up to validate the competence of technicians maintaining commercial vehicles, trailers and passenger carrying vehicles. It was developed and is managed by the IRTE (Institute of Road Transport Engineers, a professional sector of the SOE - Society of Operational Engineers) in order to raise standards and encourage industry self-regulation. The accreditation is delivered by the IMI (Institute of the Motor Industry). The quality control of the workshop itself can be demonstrated by becoming IRTE accredited.

Continuous Development of all staff involved in fleet, at whatever level, should be an integrated and important part of the fleet strategy, not least due to the current shortage of qualified staff, so developing your staff's capabilities from within makes very good business sense.

8)   How does disposal fit into the fleet strategy?

So, you have acquired the vehicles, run and maintained them for a significant period of time; now you have to get rid of them in the most cost-effective manner for the business.

One of the first things to say is that good communication between all the relevant departments involved with Fleet is essential to ensure the vehicle is in the best condition to be disposed and all relevant details about the vehicle prior to disposal are captured on the fleet management administration system; your procedures should also allow for updating records that may be held elsewhere, such as the asset register. It should also act as a prompt for items such as recovering VED and cancelling fuel cards. Good communication also helps ensure that the correct maintenance and repairs are undertaken during the last few months of the vehicle's life with you. Developing a robust disposal strategy, that is fully communicated to all staff, helps your organisation to take a consistent and cost-effective approach to disposing of vehicles.

The number one disposal method for owned fleet vehicles from most organisations is through auctions. This method has considerable advantages and provides the best opportunity to gain a fair price for the vehicle, whilst also saving time on advertising, storing vehicles, hosting open days and managing bids. If your organisation has a track record of providing nicely prepared and well-maintained vehicles at the end of their lives, you will find you attract a loyal following of dealers looking to buy your vehicles. Regular communication with the auction house remarketing manager of what vehicles are about to be disposed is an absolute must and will also help to provide the best possible attendees at any auction selling your vehicles.

It helps to prepare vehicles before disposal to a particular standard. Discussions with auction management and results from a number of auctions will soon educate you as to the most cost-effective standards to prepare vehicles and you will quickly know which items to repair, or alternatively leave alone, before sale. Any leased or finance owned vehicle will require returning to the leasing company or finance house at the end of its contractual life, unless you have an option to purchase. Similar to auction, there should be a preparation phase prior to return which needs to reflect the end-of-life contractual terms each individual vehicle. Again, experience will reveal what are the items need repairing to avoid additional costs and which ones can safely be left without incurring penalties. Some organisations have considerable additional kit fitted to vehicles and there is an additional de-fleeting process to extract such items for refurbishment to reuse or dispose of as their condition dictates. A brief description of the pre-disposal preparation process should be outlined in the strategy document.

If you are leasing some or all of your vehicles, the leasing company will probably be using as a baseline the BVRLA (British Vehicle Rental & Leasing Association) guide to the return condition for vehicles and will have provided you with a copy of this guidance when taking out the lease. This document has considerably improved and been updated over time, although many operators complain that some definitions and terms, whilst not being vague, still allow a little room for manoeuvre by both parties. Generally, the leasing company will value a long-term relationship with you and want your repeat business, so will be very fair on the charges they levy at return time. Most leasing companies tend to dispose of vehicles through auction, so the charges are intended to allow some repairs to take place beforehand. In practice, for a quick return of their capital, they will probably take a hit on the resale price and let the next buyer carry out repairs. Be aware that some leasing companies charge more at return time than others. As the return process will be a number of years down the line for you, it is worth checking out a company's reputation with your colleagues before signing.

Should a vehicle have had a relatively easy life, hopefully at some time redistributed to a harder working part of the organisation, but still being a relatively good condition, then the strategy should allow for extending the life (and the lease if necessary) of this vehicle for a set period of time. Do make sure it really is a set period of time, by setting a flag in the fleet management system. These extended life vehicles have a habit of taking on a life of their own and perhaps because they are usually fully depreciated, they can be kept on as a useful spare vehicle for far longer than originally intended. That is probably acceptable as long as the vehicle's condition does not deteriorate or maintenance costs increase too far, but a significant number of them can increase your fleet numbers and overheads. It obviously makes sense to transfer such vehicles to a part of the organisation with less demanding work.

9)   How do I make sure our fleet strategy is working? (KPI's)

This section of the chapter will probably make some existing fleet managers who read it shift uncomfortably in their seat. On the whole, as human beings, we do not like being measured. This applies to almost everyone in any field you care to mention, but especially in fleet as there is so much that can usefully be measured. So, wherever it is possible to do so, managers will sometimes do anything other than install the relevant Key Performance Indicators (KPI's) in order to measure fleet performance. The old adage of "what gets measured gets managed", however, truly applies here.

The very simple answer to the question "how can I tell if the strategy is working?" is you will not know, unless you measure the results. The use of KPI's should therefore be incorporated into your fleet strategy and be used on a regular basis to determine the effectiveness, or otherwise, of the strategy. If your performance against the KPI's are improving, hopefully, everybody is happy, if the figures are getting worse, it is an indication to look to the relevant parts of the strategy to see if they can be improved.

The converse is also true, if fleet performance is not being measured effectively then it becomes incredibly difficult to manage and there is a real risk that fleet management becomes an activity that in essence, is operating in isolation from the rest of the organisation, where budgets and expenditure can easily be allowed to get out of control, also leading to a reduction in service levels, a drop in quality or poor value for money.

The way to measure Fleet performance, therefore, has to be by using Key Performance Indicators on a regular basis and regularly publishing them to the appropriate people in the organisation, which, as well as operations, must include senior managers and directors. The latter action is required not only as good practice in order to manage the business, but also so senior organisation personnel should gain confidence that their responsibilities (at least for fleet) under vicarious liability legislation are being met. Effectively, this latter action needs to happen in some format anyway by law, to meet the requirements of corporate manslaughter legislation.

Having dealt with the part that most fleet managers hate, there are now two pieces of good news to impart. Firstly, everything that has happened to IT, telematics and systems in general in recent years means that with minimal effort, KPI's can now be produced almost automatically. Secondly, I would strongly suggest using less KPI's, not more. This is simply because concentrating on up to half a dozen KPI's means they will get followed, managed and support the business. Any more than that and they will almost certainly not all get looked at, perhaps confusing the issue and therefore cease to serve a useful function.

There is also a legal obligation for HGV Transport Managers to comply fully with their O licence obligations, which will require considerable supporting information from the Fleet Manager. Van Transport Managers will also need similar information from the Fleet Manager to give them confidence that their obligations are being met. Regular conversations between all parties within the organisation possessing an interest in fleet and the Fleet Manager will be required in order to manage the amount and frequency of this information.

As an aside, for those of you who have not come across an operator's licence (or O licence) before, I should explain that it is the legal authority needed to operate goods vehicles in Great Britain. The licence is issued by a local Traffic Commissioner (TC) who independently regulates the commercial road transport industry; a TC can take regulatory action against a licence holder if they fail to live up to the promises made on application of keeping good repute and managing drivers and vehicles, including proper maintenance, fully. This applies to operators of all vehicles above 3.5 tonnes Gross Vehicle Weight (GVW) that are used to carry goods on public roads for purposes of trade or business and includes any short-term hire vehicles. It is therefore crucially important to both keep accurate records and stay on the right side of the Traffic Commissioner.

An unnecessary task I most commonly see when doing the rounds are performance figures of many sorts, produced with loving care every day, week or month, maybe annually. When you ask of what use some of the figures are, no-one really knows. I have to say, it does not make consultants popular, as when you point it out, the perpetrators almost immediately know themselves that they have been wasting their time and they are not particularly happy that they needed someone from outside the organisation to point out the fairly obvious. If you feel an impartial view of your processes would be helpful, please contact us on 07771 768080 or email info@thedwconsultancy.com.

The point is, it gets reported because it has always been reported. Probably at some time in the past it was useful, but no more. Therefore, check and regularly review all reports and performance indicators to ensure that the information provided, at whatever level, is relevant and assists with fleet management decisions. If you decide a particular piece of information is no longer useful, do not be frightened to stop producing it. In fact, over the years, I have found the best way to test if a particular piece of information is useful, is not to tell anyone you have stopped and see if anybody asks for it. If they do, you can either explain why you think it is no longer relevant or review your decision. I have to say, in all my career, I can hardly ever remember anyone asking.

I find it also helps greatly if, when asking for administrative assistance to produce a piece of information, you fully explain to the person exactly why they are required to do that particular piece of work. Then, if that piece of information is no longer needed, they are much more likely to raise the issue themselves rather than blindly producing it because "it's always been done that way".

Handy Hint

- Keep your main fleet KPI's that are regularly monitored and publicised to six or less, to make sure they are used and meaningful.

Here is my suggestion for some of the most useful fleet statistics to be reported monthly, or certainly, no less than quarterly. I suggest arriving at a permutation of 6 or less of these general Fleet KPI's that are useful and appropriate to your operation will suit your needs.

- **Vehicle Availability** – number of days (hours in some cases) each vehicle is genuinely available for operational use

- **Vehicle Utilisation** – how much each vehicle is used when compared with availability (above), helping show operational issues and if the fleet size is correct

- **Vehicle Downtime** – number of days (or hours) a vehicle is non-operational due to maintenance and repairs, an important measure of your service provider.

Define how you will record times very clearly, otherwise they have a tendency to "creep"

- **MOT Failures / First Time Passes** – an important and now highly used measure of maintenance provider performance, internal or external; important for OCRS score

- **Vehicle Defects Reported** – high numbers may indicate maintenance issues; also indicates if drivers are carrying out this task when compared with below

- **Vehicle Defects Found** (on service) - numbers may indicate maintenance issues or drivers not properly carrying out defect checks

- **Vehicle Maintenance Cost** – useful to check costs for groups or individual vehicles, may indicate driver or vehicle problems for resolution, or supplier issues

- **Vehicle Tyre Cost** – relatively small compared to maintenance, above, but highly variable; may indicate changes required in tyre or driver management

- **Vehicle Operating Cost** – useful to compare total costs for groups or individual vehicles, assists with future vehicle selection, indicates issues for resolution

- **Fuel Usage** – miles per gallon (mpg or equivalent) - identifies poor driver performance and indicates training requirements; globally assists with future vehicle selection

- **Vehicle Accidents, frequency & cost** – trends are most important here to reduce insurance costs & highlight potential staff training requirements

Other potentially useful Fleet Indicators:

- **Vehicle Service Targets** – the percentage of vehicles achieving their allocated service and inspection times, by location; measures operators & suppliers

- **Vehicle Replacement Targets** – the number of vehicles replaced at their stated time, by location, is a useful measure of the effectiveness of your replacement programme

- **Daily Inspections Achieved** – useful for compliance to keep track of those not completing daily inspections; your target is obviously zero non-compliance

- **OCRS Reports** – those operating under O licence regulations may like to compare their statistics with those available from their Operator Compliance Risk Score – the scoring and banding system used is a little complex, so full details are available here: https://www.gov.uk/guidance/use-the-operator-compliance-risk-score-ocrs-system#scoring-and-bands

---

Handy Hint   👍

- When the 'Vehicle Downtime' KPI (above) mentions there can be "creep", that is understating the situation. Downtime of fleet can have a huge financial effect on the business and measurement can vary enormously; 200% variation is not unheard of. That is largely because the servicing organisation tends to start the clock when the vehicle is made available to them in the workshop and stop the clock as soon as the repair or service is complete. Operations, on the other hand, start timing as soon as they lose the vehicle, so will include travel and waiting time, and stop timing when back on the job, which may be a shift, or more, later. This issue is simply resolved by determining the criteria that will be employed by both parties before starting any agreement.

Top Tips for Fleet Strategy & Planning   ✓

- Your fleet strategy should be a clearly written document, but be reviewed regularly and fluid enough to be constantly updated to reflect any business changes.

- The fleet management strategy should link up directly and clearly with your organisation's other strategic aims and priorities and support their objectives, especially financial and environmental objectives.

- Core to a fleet strategy will be to publish the intended average age of each section of the fleet, along with the maximum age and mileage for each vehicle group, so colleagues can understand when vehicles will get replaced.

- It is really important to declare what Key Performance Indicators (KPI's) you will be using to manage your fleet, why you selected them, how often you will report them, to whom and what happens if they are not met, so there are no surprises for anyone involved.

- Explain how the Fleet Strategy will intersect with other departments such as finance, operations and HR; spell out in clear terms how communication between departments will work to avoid any clash of responsibilities or business decisions.

- For slightly larger organisations, holding user groups are a great way for fleet providers to understand how operations are using the vehicles and vice-versa; there is often a mismatch in understanding between these departments which get resolved by regular consultation.

- Consider producing a brief Service Level Agreement (SLA) between fleet and operations concisely detailing what each department will do for each other – this will help reduce potential misunderstandings.

- User surveys are another good way to find out how well you are meeting the operational needs of vehicle users in your organisation. Repeating surveys at intervals is very useful to measure trends; hopefully improving.

- Always aim to have a logical separation of your fleet listing using sensible differentiators, such that you are always comparing operating costs on a like-for-like basis.

- Conduct a brief but detailed calculation on the optimum economic point to replace your vehicles, for each group of vehicles, once a year if possible, probably budget time, to check you are still replacing at the optimum point.

David's Don'ts ✖

- Don't forget to regularly publish to everyone involved in fleet a clear and regularly updated replacement schedule for the whole fleet – something few fleets do effectively.

- Don't assume all fleet users will read all the updated strategy, policy and procedural documents you produce; they are more likely to file it under "read later", which of course, never happens. Include a clear, brief summary of the changes and don't forget 75% of recipients don't read to the end of an email, so grab their attention quickly.

- Don't forget to include environmental targets within your strategy; how you will be reducing your organisation's fuel use & hence emissions, reducing mileages, mitigating activities and a future strategy on alternative fuels.

- Don't box yourself in with specific targets on alternative fuelled vehicles, allow some movement for price, technology and infrastructure changes.

The Ultimate Guide to Commercial Vehicle Fleet Management

Chapter 4 – Vehicle Procurement

1) *How do I decide when is the most cost-effective point to replace our vehicles?*
2) *How do I manage our vehicle's life cycles?*
3) *What are the benefits of standardising the specification, by group?*
4) *How to arrive at a full operational specification*
5) *How do I take manufacturer and bodybuilder lead times into account?*
6) *How do I negotiate with suppliers to get the best outcome?*
7) *How do I tackle getting approval from senior directors and managers?*
8) *How do I plan and project manage the build process start to finish?*
9) *How do I manage the inspection process during build?*
10) *What other departments should I keep in touch with during the project?*

In chapter 2 we looked briefly about the issues likely to affect vehicle buyers in the next 10 years, such as the onset of autonomous vehicles and improvements in battery electric vehicles, for you to be aware of now, in order to assist in your fleet replacement planning. Later in chapter 6, we discuss the imminent demise of ICE (Internal Combustion Engines) and what potential replacement fuels, for differing classes of vehicles, are likely to replace them. If you are not buying alternatively fuelled vehicles now, you are likely to do so in the not-too-distant future. However, a vehicle is simply a mechanical asset for the business and as such, the rules and guidelines for purchasing that asset will change very little, no matter what the vehicle looks like. Let's investigate the most important guidelines you need to know about how to acquire your vehicles in the most efficient manner.

Too late to change the specification now!

1) How do I decide when is the most cost-effective point to replace our vehicles?

Most Fleet Managers or Fleet Engineers will at some point inherit a fleet with a complete mix of makes, models and ages. The replacement programme and criteria will have been determined by others and sometimes does not even make logical sense, due to the influence of many factors, some of which may not even be visible to an incomer. That is why it is so important to carry out the process of determining a strategy for the fleet, outlined in the previous chapter, especially to identify if what they have inherited meets the organisation's current and future requirements and review whether the current fleet will meet the business priorities and if it is even moving in the same direction.

Having established a feel for the answer to these strategic questions, there is one question that is possibly the most important single financial issue you can decide upon when managing your fleet, namely, that of deciding when to replace. The aim, of course, is to always replace your vehicles at the right point in their life cycle, so as to achieve their lowest possible total lifetime costs. Many fleet operators do not calculate this point and instead replace vehicles at a predetermined point based upon mileage, age or increasing maintenance costs, but generally part of a historical practice, not really well thought through or calculated.

These replacement points are often based on very generalised guidelines, or maybe a feeling that the fleet needs to look fresher than it does, or a few recent maintenance bills were too high. If replacement is based on the latter variable, increased maintenance costs, there is a chance that acquisition may just be occurring at around the right point, but that is still largely a guesstimate for most operators. And for a large number of fleet operators, vehicles get replaced whenever they have cash available. This results in a fleet age profile that goes up and down like a yo-yo and is definitely not the most efficient and cost-effective way to be running your fleet.

First of all, let us deal with the theory. Any number of asset management books or tutorials will tell you that the graph showing when to replace an asset, based on the lowest total cost of ownership, looks like the very clear graph reproduced below. The asset value depreciates in the shape of a nice curve, steeply at first and then flattening out as annual depreciation decreases. The maintenance costs increase gradually over time and naturally rises as the asset, in our case a vehicle, gets older and needs more repairs. You then add in any fixed costs associated with owning the asset, such as insurance, which generally stay relatively static over time, to the other two costs and you get a clearly defined curve. Replacement of the asset should theoretically take place at the lowest point of the curve, or very shortly after, in order to be certain that the minimum total cost point has been reached. Simple.

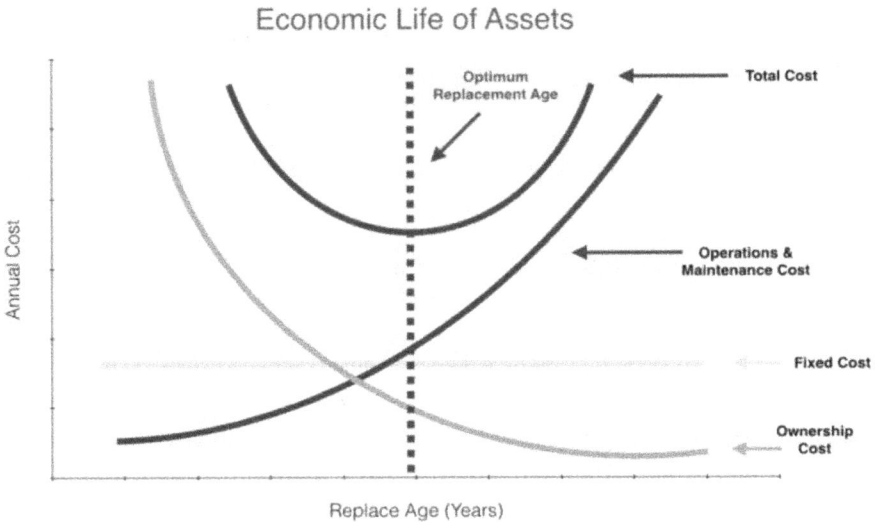

Economic Life of Assets

Image courtesy of: Excess Logic, Asset Management Company, USA & Canada

Unfortunately, all of that is absolutely great in theory. In practice, however, you will hardly ever see nice curves like this in real life. For starters, depreciation plummets like a stone for the first few months and years of a vehicle's life and then flattens out to a gentler curve. In fact, one issue that private vehicle owners can never seem to grasp is that the value of the nice shiny brand-new vehicle they just bought drops drastically the second they drive out of the showroom. If it turns out for any reason that they do not like the vehicle and they try to get the dealer to buy it back, they cannot understand why there are offered many thousands of pounds less than they paid for it, to which the salesperson replies "Ah yes, but you've driven it now!".

Similarly, maintenance costs are never generous enough to rise in a nice gentle curve. Modern vehicles tend to cost very little in the first few months, and even years of life, primarily because of the warranty covering most unexpected costs and because they are now pretty reliable and are built so as not to cause many problems in the first few years. From then on, maintenance and repair costs do rise, but when expressed graphically, it tends to be a much flatter curve in profile than the theory predicts. This is mainly because curves come from time honoured textbooks, reflecting that far more maintenance was required in days gone by, as evidenced by the ever-increasing time between servicing intervals. The introduction of six-sigma and similar quality programmes in manufacturing has resulted in reducing component failure, unfortunately, it has also had the effect of meaning components are dearer to replace when they do fail. In real life, the maintenance cost will rise gently with occasional hiccups in a sawtooth or step-shaped pattern.

This is where a good fleet management system (see Chapter 9) can pay real dividends. Although it is often extremely difficult to pinpoint when one vehicle should or should not have been replaced, the trend is generally a lot more defined when there are a group of vehicles. By averaging the costs across a group of similar specification vehicles, a much clearer picture tends to emerge, less influenced by individual high-cost spikes.

Having said that, even with good records and averaging out costs across vehicle groups, it can still be quite difficult to obtain a clear picture. One way around this conundrum, whether or not you conduct your own maintenance, is to get R&M (Repair & Maintenance) quotations from your dealer or manufacturer (if you buy in sufficient quantities) for a number of varying years of life. Manufacturers' R&M figures possess the benefit of having hundreds or even thousands of the same models on their books. They can almost predict when a particular component is likely to fail, and what percentage of them will fail. Just be aware that some items will not be covered by their maintenance contract, so read the small print and make an intelligent allowance, based on your experience, of what additional expense you should add to give a true picture.

In order to plug in the residual values over time into your version of the graph, probably the best way to obtain them is from the routinely available valuing organisations such as Glass's Guide or CAP (Car Auction Prices) for commercial vehicles. They now use some more fancy algorithms and factors to estimate future vehicle residual values looking at the economics and the desirability of particular vehicles based on previous market data. Every month this is compared against real values obtained at auction or on the forecourt and the predicted figures adjusted accordingly. On top of their figures, you will need to allow some factoring to account for your specific vehicle specification, the value and desirability of the body and equipment, also allowing for any operational factors, such as very light or particularly heavy use.

In practice then, unless you are running high mileage vehicles, or operating in very arduous conditions, you are unlikely to see a dramatic and clearly delineated U-shaped curve as shown in the example above. Instead, you are much more likely to see a long gentle curve where the tail is not sharply rising. This gives the fleet manager a problem, in that the point of minimum expenditure point is very similar for a number of months or even years. In other words, there is not much difference between replacing a vehicle in year six or carrying on to year eight or nine. Part of the reason for this is ever increasing quality in manufacturing, both in terms of the vehicle chassis and body preparation, also increasing the life expectancy of the various components on the vehicle.

So far, we have talked about deciding on the vehicle replacement point due to "hard" factors such as total costs. If it is the case that using such criteria, the vehicle could be run on for a number of years, then other "softer" replacement factors are likely to come into play. Currently, environmental issues are high on the agenda and reduced emissions may be a significant factor in your decisions. Legislation, manufacturer development and customer demand has ensured in recent years that emissions continuously improve year on year. Most medium and large organisations in the current climate declare that their corporate objective is to reduce their carbon footprint over time. That is likely to be a key driver in your choice of vehicle and how often they are replaced.

Image has always been a large consideration and again, improved paint manufacturing techniques or even vehicle wrapping tends to extend useful life expectancy way beyond what used to be possible 10 or 15 years ago. This is obviously countered by the amount of use and damage these vehicles receive at the hands of their users. The higher the mileage, the more likely that dents, scratches and other exterior imperfections become more marked, even if you have been diligent in having most of these repaired during its life. Although these are cosmetic, each vehicle reflects your company standards and image and there comes a point where a refurbishment in any form is not cost-effective.

It is very natural that the older a vehicle then the more likely it is general condition will decline. Of all the items on the vehicle, the driver's seat is the one most likely to show its true age and will probably retain the most component wear, possibly with holes in the cover showing the interior filling. For whatever reason, seats are one of the most expensive items to replace in the interior of a vehicle, although it is possible to get them repaired at a more sensible price. Items like the carpeting and interior trim will probably also have deteriorated and the total environment within the cabin can negatively impact the driver experience, which can in turn impact on productivity or even driver retention. There is a psychological effect on a driver's morale if they know they are "stuck" with a particular vehicle for several years more. All these "soft" factors will therefore need to be taken into account when determining what is the appropriate age and/or mileage criteria for replacing your fleet.

2) How do I manage our vehicle's life cycles?

We have looked above at when might be the theoretical best time to replace a vehicle and seen that it is not as easy as the textbooks would have you believe. We have looked at some potential "soft" issues that might also indicate that replacing a vehicle is a good idea. All you really want to know is: when do I stop throwing money at a vehicle for repair, when the better option is to replace it?

This is where keeping good statistical data on your vehicle expenditure (see Chapter 9 - Fleet Management Systems) is absolutely crucial. The cost benefit analysis will vary from vehicle group to vehicle group and may even vary vehicle by vehicle. The theory identified above is that the optimum fleet life cycle strategy replaces the vehicle at the point when maintenance costs outstrip the financial benefits of keeping the asset. Good fleet management data will enable you to carry out this exercise, however, for reasons of sanity, you probably will not want to be calculating this point all the time.

The sensible method adopted by good fleet managers is to review the issue from time to time. It is worth trying to carry out this exercise once a year, just before budget time or when reviewing the replacement programme, however, I recognise a busy Fleet Manager may not have the time to conduct a full review each year. It would make sense however, to regularly check the ratio of routine maintenance expenditure against capital to help spot any trends and make certain the figures are not moving out of kilter.

However, that means you need an ongoing guide to vehicle replacement that everybody can understand for the day-to-day management of the fleet. You therefore need to decide upon a vehicle replacement approach that meets your current and future needs which is based upon variables that have the most influence on your business outcomes. Most organisations choose to replace based on one of three simple approaches. These are:

- **Replacing Due to Age and/or Mileage**

This is the most common approach which can be seen in hundreds, or thousands of replacement strategies by setting a predetermined age and mileage endpoint for vehicles, such as seven years or 150,000 miles and usually states "whichever one comes first".

Advantages: It is clear and probably the simplest to measure and thus to implement, and in theory, removes subjectivity from the life cycle decision (but see disadvantage below)

Disadvantage: Pure figures of years or miles may not result in the most economic decision as it misses other important factors such as depreciation & reliability. For that reason, I see many vehicles that are over one of the age or mileage limits, but way under the associated limit, so the fleet manager is very happy with reliability or expenditure and, quite rightly, decides it can be kept for longer..

- **Whole Life Cost Analysis**

This approach uses more detailed analysis of individual vehicles total ownership and operating costs. It requires a little bit more detail which need to be defined in the guidelines and includes total life cost parameters such as purchase and depreciation cost, maintenance, repair and fuel costs. Some analysis also factors in downtime and utilisation figures.

Advantages: This approach is more comprehensive and flexible than a straight mileage or time method. It does take account of more specialist and expensive vehicles which are usually retained for longer.

Disadvantages: The analysis requires accurate recording of a number of parameters and some calculations that can vary quite widely and therefore lacks the clarity of mileage or time.

- **Cost Threshold Analysis**

This approach is more often used to decide the replacement of a physical asset such as plant and machinery rather than vehicles, but its use is worth considering as it provides a very definitive point for asset disposal. The asset, in this case a vehicle, is disposed of when a threshold value is reached. Typically, this figure is when annual maintenance costs exceed 30% of a vehicle's residual value. Obviously this percentage figure can be flexed up or down to suit your vehicle mileages and operating factors.

Advantages: This method gives the opportunity to optimise vehicle life whilst keeping maintenance costs to a minimum.

Disadvantages: Requires timely and accurate data to be closely monitored. The excess maintenance trigger point is likely to be passed before triggering a disposal flag, so this needs factoring to the guidelines.

Whichever approach your organisation decides to adopt to arrive at your optimum fleet life cycle strategy, your fleet management system needs to support this strategy with accurate data, presented in the right format, in order to minimise cost of running your fleet. These metrics will vary according to the method chosen and the granularity with which you investigate the figures but should probably include such factors as:

Mileage – a key statistic to managing any fleet is mileage, try to automate this process if at all possible, essential for servicing as well as calculating replacement points.

Vehicle Age – your fleet management system should log its start date and automatically calculate the age of any vehicle, flagging this up at the appropriate point on various reports, including replacement.

Cost per Mile – essential for monitoring each vehicle and each group of vehicles during their life as well as at replacement; costs would usually include fuel, maintenance & repair, depreciation insurance VED & MoT.

Whichever method of life cycle calculation you use, any modern fleet management system should be able to produce, with relative ease, reports to monitor how you stand against your capital budgets and a predicted forward replacement plan, using a variety of the methods identified above. This might seem like quite an effort, but remember this is key to what should be your number one objective, of obtaining the lowest overall cost of running your fleet.

3) What are the benefits of standardising the specification, by group?

Fortunately, there are several things that a fleet manager can do to organise their fleet which potentially saves large sums of money, without costing the organisation anything. One of the most important ways of doing this, which, in my experience, is seldom fully achieved in many fleets, is that of standardisation of specifications. I know from experience this is not conceived as a particularly "sexy" concept, but by standardising a fleet, there are invariably major savings to be made.

Human nature often works against this concept, because every driver and every manager tend to want something slightly different and it is a bold fleet manager who constantly says "no". As a simple example, the average police fleet has around 14 discrete roles across all their vehicles. So, allowing for updated models, you would probably expect to see about 30 differing makes and models in the fleet list, but being generous and allowing for a change of make, or some trial vehicles, say 50. The reality is often 100+ different makes and models, leading to, amongst many other things, hidden on-costs.

As part of your fleet strategy, therefore, you need to declare that you will operate with the fewest number of vehicle configurations that will meet the requirements of the widest range of the various sections, divisions and branches within the organisation. The aim must be to develop a core specification for each specific role, such as mobile service vehicles, small distribution vans, 7½ tonne panel van, and so on. The trick here is for the core specification to cover the maximum number roles, whilst allowing slight variations for a particular need, such as a change in drive axle ratio for really hilly terrain or off-road use. Also, a mobile service van may have the same base specification, but two or three layouts for the internal racking, equipment and workbench to cater for different parts of the organisation. Once again it is important to keep these variations to a minimum by delineating what is truly essential, and what is just nice to have, in the specification.

Many organisations do not believe that standardisation of specifications will have much of an effect on the finances, but trust me, it does. It does this in a wide variety of ways, such as:

- **Increased Buying Power** – bringing together more orders to one vehicle manufacturer and one bodybuilder, with rationalised specifications, can only increase your buying power and reduce prices. Multiple specifications will dilute this effect

- **More Efficient Ordering** - a wide variety of specifications increases the time for order processing and increases the risk of errors occurring during the ordering process. It also increases the communications time and effort between managers, suppliers and administration staff during the whole procedure. Rationalising and simplifying the ordering process will reduce the time involved and result in both financial and administrative benefits

- **Reduced Stock Holding** - standardise vehicle specs directly impact parts costs by reducing stockholding for internal workshops, reducing the stores area and complexity of parts bins, the stock count and reordering time & effort. Prices can be reduced slightly by increased volume throughput of the same items

- **Reduced Technician Training** - internal workshops save time and money by more focused training from fewer manufacturers and less vehicle configurations: instead of individual technicians being sent away to manufacturers' premises, it often now makes sense to invite their trainers to run courses on your own premises thus reducing time and cost again

- **Increased Technician Efficiency** - research shows technician times decrease in almost direct proportion to the familiarity of the operation; by reducing the number of specifications, technicians become more familiar with the same work routines, also becoming better acquainted with vehicle idiosyncrasies and therefore their efficiency is improved, also increasing vehicle availability
- **Reduced Special Tools** - most vehicles have their own special tool requirement, reducing specification complexity naturally reduces this count. Higher volumes could mean that the provision of special tools can be included within the sales negotiations
- **Improved Contractual Maintenance Costs** – the same benefits that accrue to internal workshops will be passed onto your maintenance supplier, to some degree, allowing far more scope for better rates at contract renewal time. Through standard specifications, the efficiency of the work undertaken on your vehicles should also improve, again improving vehicle availability
- **Increased Fleet Flexibility** – standardised vehicle specifications means moving vehicles between depots, divisions or locations due to changes in the business becomes far simpler and easier to achieve. Similarly, good fleet managers will always be trying to balance mileage, age and usage across the fleet - standardised specifications greatly aid this process
- **Improved Staff & Driver Satisfaction** - standardisation reduces the levels of dissatisfaction and complaints from staff and drivers due to an increased perception that they are all being treated fairly. Driver and staff training becomes easier, faster and more likely to be remembered when vehicles are standardised.

Once you understand the principles behind standard specifications, and see the cost benefits for yourself, it will hopefully become almost an obsession to achieve the most efficient fleet specification listing. There are some actions you can take to help the process along.

Firstly, it is essential to centralise the vehicle specification and ordering process. Never let individual depots or departments order their own vehicles or dictate specifications. The benefits outlined above are just too great to allow this to happen. Secondly, when going through the process of deciding which vehicles will be replaced this year, be very clear on distinguishing a driver's, manager's or depot's needs from their wants. One fairly common example is that of four-wheel-drive, often requested to counter the UK winter weather. A quick investigation into the weather stats for that particular part of the world may well reveal that it snows on average only three days a year and is truly icy on another seven. The capital, maintenance and fuel costs of a four-wheel-drive vehicle can be so much higher than a comparative two-wheel drive, that you really need to go some to justify the additional cost, and ten days of bad weather out of 365 just does not cut the mustard – if real off-road driving capability is occasionally required, you could hire if necessary.

Make sure that you review your specifications annually, probably best when also discussing replacements. This makes sure you keep up to date with the needs of the business and you are incorporating the latest technology in your vehicle choices. It is always very easy, but a big mistake, to simply replace on a like-for-like basis. Whilst you are looking at specifications, also take the opportunity of checking the fleet stats for those vehicles. See if there any trends that require investigation. For example, if one particular group of vehicles is suffering a large number of accidents – is it due to the drivers involved or is there an issue with that vehicle? If mpg (miles per gallon) figures for a group of vehicles are down on one depot compared with another, again it could be the drivers, or is there something about the vehicle specification that has caused the anomaly? Look also for peaks in maintenance costs and try to see if there is an obvious cause; it may just be that the specification of that vehicle is not quite right for your operation.

I know I have stated this elsewhere in this book, but it is so important to make sure you involve the staff and drivers in the selection process. If, for all the right reasons, you are trying to standardise specifications and drive it from the top down, you will face almost certain resistance at some point. If drivers decide they have not been properly consulted in the process, they can make life very difficult for you by either treating the vehicle badly or consistently defecting the vehicle, or finding a dozen reasons why it is not right for the job. This is why trial vehicles and the trial process can be so very useful and by careful management, the trial results can often be made to support your preferred buying decision. If drivers are fully consulted and you explain the reasons behind your choice, they will usually appreciate being taken into your confidence and become ambassadors to the cause.

Try to avoid the temptation to arrive at the "lowest common denominator" specification, in other words, to specify according to the minimum case that will cover all eventualities. This may seem to simplify the process but may result in costs nearly as high as the multiple specifications scenario. Instead, you could be more selective by looking at the big picture. If, say, nearly all the fleet take a particular option, which would be difficult or costly to retrofit later, but one or two depots do not. If you believe at least some of those vehicles at those specific depots may be moved at a later date, it may be pragmatic to specify a few of them at any time with that option, which would provide the opportunity to move them later down the track. If you are making these sorts of decisions at buying time, one important tip; always clearly record the reasons for your decision and share them with at least a few others in the organisation, for two reasons. Firstly, you could most unfortunately be run over by a bus tomorrow and secondly, in a few years' time you may not remember why on earth you made that decision.

One important issue that needs consideration with a larger or national fleet is that of the availability and location of your dealer or repair network. You are always as good as the local agent and their manager, so it is really annoying for a depot manager when they have to stick with a national specification, but they just happen to be the one with a really poor dealer nearby. Even when you maintain yourself, there is still warranty, specialist diagnostics, special tools and parts supply to be taken care of. You may therefore need to build in some flexibility in your makes policy to cater for these sorts of difficulties.

4) *How to arrive at a full operational specification*

Very few vehicle operators seem to carry out this very important step. Most organisations buy "more of the same", usually the next model along from whatever is being run now, or something that someone from operations has seen and decides is exactly the right vehicle. Often, someone senior in the operational department involved says "I want one of those", specifying a very specific model, leaving the fleet manager or the fleet department to try and fathom out if this really is the right vehicle for the job. It may or may not be the right vehicle, but you will never know until you have a true operational specification, in other words, exactly what do you want this vehicle to do?

So, however much they complain that they do not have time, insist the users go right back to basics and specify exactly what the vehicle needs to do, who is to use it and how. To help them, provide operations with a checklist tailored to your particular operation, including such items as:

-      Who will drive the vehicle?
-      What role will it perform?
-      Will it carry any passengers? It so, how many?
-      How many hours per day driving?
-      How many miles per week/month/year?
-      What equipment will it need to carry?
-      What load will it carry - (specifically weight, packaging, volume and numbers)
-      What are the variations on loading? (average and maximum)
-      What type of load restraints will be required?
-      Where will it generally be operating and travelling?
-      What types of road in the main? (urban, motorway, or rural)
-      Any known constraints on loading or unloading? What mechanical aids will be used?

The list can be extensive but should be specific to that class of vehicle and your operation.

Most operational managers tend to hate this part of the process with a vengeance, primarily because it involves some hard thinking about things they have not necessarily considered for many years, plus some looking into the foreseeable future to visualise and predict any changes to their work patterns. They will almost certainly need your help and advice in the process. At the very least, if you want some form of useable specification, you will need to provide them with a check sheet containing the sort of questions listed above to remind them what to think about and include in the specification.

The specification for an 8-Wheeled Tipper with Grab will need considerably more consideration than a standard panel van

If we are talking about a slightly more complex vehicle, they may well want some technical help, internal or external, especially if it is a more complex operation or they need more advice about the options available. Talk them through all the variations, options and especially the latest technology which may affect their operation. Even for the simplest operation and vehicle specification, it is worth sitting down with the operational manager and some vehicle users to check exactly what is required. It is so easy to make assumptions at this stage. In the current climate, this process will almost certainly involve a conversation about the suitability of alternatively fuelled vehicles, so be prepared with some data and calculations.

And, of course, the bit that so many managers miss, is to ask the person doing the job exactly what they need and want. This part is absolutely crucial if you want to specify the right fleet and get buy-in from employees and the process needs managing properly. At the very least, arrange for a number of trial or demonstrator vehicles to be supplied. Try to twist the arm of the supplier to attempt to get the demonstrators for as long a period as possible, preferably weeks rather than days. Make sure as many drivers as is practical get to use the vehicle (providing they get enough individual time on the vehicle) and provide them with a check sheet, paper or digital, to prompt them for their appraisal. If your operation, bodywork or racking is more specialist, you may not be able to test the full capabilities of the vehicle, but at the very least you can check its driveability.

Two points to make on the subject of demonstrators and selecting new vehicles. Operators, in my experience, tend to think of a demonstrator as just another vehicle for them to utilise. To the fleet manager, however, they are a golden opportunity, if used correctly, to find out almost everything they need to know about running that vehicle in their own operation. Make sure, therefore, you manage the process carefully and communicate your objectives very clearly to the operators involved.

Secondly, one of the most important functions you can carry out in your role is networking with your colleagues and associates from other operations. Sometimes this can be enjoyable, such as attending an event run by suppliers. Other times it needs investment of your time, such as attending an evening institute event (invariably on a wet, dark winter's evening!). The knowledge you gain from these contacts can be invaluable, including information about other vehicle makes and models, especially new ones, so please do not overlook this method of information gathering.

A word of caution here about the specification process. Everyone and their uncle tend to think it is easy to specify vehicles and many senior managers of transport operations believe they are absolutely brilliant at it, requiring no help in the process whatsoever. However, converting your full operational specification into a physical vehicle build specification is not easy and getting it wrong can have serious financial repercussions for your organisation.

Let's just take one simple example that I see from time to time on heavier vehicles. Many operators using 3-axled vehicles often opt for a 6x4 axle configuration on the basis that they are readily available and give better traction in slippery conditions. That part is true, they do give better traction, however, they are also heavier, meaning less payload, there are also parasitic driveline losses, meaning higher fuel consumption (about 2.5% over the life of the vehicle) and they take more time and money for maintenance. So, unless your vehicle spends considerable time off-road, you will be better off with a 6x2.

This is just one example of the many occasions where, without a full knowledge of vehicle manufacture or operations, a simple decision when ordering can have a knock-on effect for the life of the vehicle. This is when, dare I say it, getting a consultant in with the right experience can really help to make sure all your vehicles are truly fit for purpose and run at minimum cost. (We are, of course, always available and delighted to assist you in the process, please contact 07771 768080 or email dwilson@thedwconsultancy.com).

However, when you have completed this selection process, armed with a true operational specification (not just a buying wish-list) you are already ahead of 90% of most vehicle buyers.

5) How do I take manufacturer and bodybuilder lead times into account?

For some inexplicable reason, in the transport industry, there seems to be a huge desire for operators to buy as many vehicles as they possibly can all at the same time, put them all in a line, take a photograph and get their picture in as many trade publications as possible, saying how wonderfully their business is going. Aside from the difficulties of administration, delivery, undertaking the PDI's, swopping equipment and then the disposal of the old vehicles all at once, which is also likely to depress their market values, it does not aid the manufacturing process one bit. My strong suggestion would be to negotiate with suppliers for the total number and value of the vehicles but then drip feed the manufacture of those vehicles throughout the year.

If you are new to the commercial vehicle buying business, you probably need to understand that all suppliers will give you a range of dates of when you can expect delivery. The first of these will be close to the shortest time they have ever taken to build a particular vehicle or body, requires that no parts are in short supply and is designed to attract you to make a purchase. The second date will be much longer, is probably more true-to-life and represents the longest period they consider they can get away with and still have you buy the product. Then of course there are some suppliers who use a really long lead time like a badge of honour (no names mentioned); in this case you will just have to use all your negotiating powers to get this date down to an acceptable level, or alternatively, go elsewhere. No product is that good. Once a few large buyers go elsewhere, all other things being equal, lead times will magically reduce.

Once you have established all the necessary lead-times you need to become a mini-project manager to make sure everything happens according to schedule. The first step is to produce a realistic Gantt chart which you can follow and update as things go along. Ensure that you include all the necessary lead-times and I would suggest using close to the longer of the two dates given you by the manufacturers. So, for example, if the two manufacturing dates given you are 6 to 12 weeks then 10 to 12 weeks is probably a sensible compromise, but make sure the manufacturer knows precisely the latest date when you want the vehicle. Allow some time between build stages for movement of the vehicle and do not forget ancillary equipment fitting times or processes such as painting or applying vinyl. Many manufacturers will allow third-party installers involved to work in their premises providing their operations are still going on at the same time. Do not forget to schedule in your inspection dates in the process.

Most important of all is to keep operations aware of the delivery dates flowing from the Gannt chart and update them as soon as anything changes. For fairly obvious reasons, fleet managers who are working closely with suppliers to keep vehicles on track, become so engrossed in the latest timetables, that they forget no one else in the organisation has that same knowledge. Many operational managers are very clever at reducing expenditure on a vehicle they know will be leaving them soon. If they know delivery is imminent, they may well be able to keep repair costs at bay. However, if the vehicle does not appear and they have no idea when the replacement is due, you may find those expensive repairs take place as a precaution anyway. Aside from the financial aspect, it is psychologically important to keep operators and drivers aware of when their new vehicle is likely to appear.

Two things to be aware of when predicting delivery dates, especially if there is a lengthy process with a number of suppliers involved. First of all, everyone in your organisation will want those new vehicles sooner rather than later and there will be a huge psychological pressure on you to deliver the goods. So in the example above with a 6 to 12 week window, if you are not very careful, you can find yourself saying the production will be six weeks away, when realistically you know it is more like 10 to 12 weeks. Therefore, my strongest advice is to quote the longest, or near the longest delivery time, and allow a little bit of extra contingency within the plan. Nobody, and I mean nobody, will thank you for quoting an optimistic delivery date and then failing to achieve, whereas if you put in a realistic time and come in early, everyone will be your friend. In addition, you will lose credibility at the sharp end of operations and they will stop try to save money on outgoing vehicles as mentioned above.

Naturally, any plan will reflect the complexity of build and the number of suppliers involved. The associated risk and timeframe for a van that simply needs to be ply lined before delivery, will be far lower than, say, that same eight wheeled tipper chassis that requires a body and grab fitting. The longer the supply chain, the greater the risk and the higher a need for contingency time. When talking to vehicle manufacturers, one of the first items to discuss at any time is "what are your current lead-times?" – find out if they are different for the various models in their range which may have alternative production lines or even factories. Also ask if they are aware of any issues in the future which might extend or reduce these times; most salespersons can be surprisingly accurate about this question. Armed with these times, you can now work backwards to decide when the decision-making and ordering process needs to commence. If long lead times are predicted, explain to everyone involved in your organisation why you need to start early, as they might think you are being over cautious.

Don't forget to add sufficient time into the end of your plan for briefing and training drivers and staff on the new equipment; including chassis, body & ancillaries. Book suitable qualified trainers in advance. Too many operators pass the keys of vehicles costing up to a quarter of a million pounds, possibly fitted with state of the art technical equipment, without proper instruction.

6) How do I negotiate with suppliers to get the best outcome?

There are many, many books, training courses and videos, webinars, all manner of ways claiming to train you on how to be a better negotiator. I am not going to repeat in any detail, any of that sort of advice here. Good negotiating skills can be learnt, generally helped through experience, although there do seem to be a few people who have a real natural talent for it. However, what I would say is that I still meet far too many people who feel that they have negotiated well when they win and the other side loses. My strong advice is to always aim for a win-win scenario, that is; you get the vehicle that you want at a fair price and the supplier makes fair profit, sufficient to be able to support you fully in the future. Indeed, my whole ethos in business has been, and still is, to attempt to build long-term relationships that support both parties when times are good, or, maybe, not so good.

Handy Hint 👍

- In any negotiation with a supplier or contractor, always remember the goal is not just to agree the immediate business, but to develop a long-term trusting relationship that will sustain both your business objectives.

Remember that as soon as you buy more than one vehicle you effectively become a "fleet" buyer. Rather than focus on buying price and discounts, which I see so many examples of, use the fact that you are buying either multiple vehicles or a series of vehicles from the same supplier, to see how much can be included in the overall package. The exact nature of this overall package will vary greatly according to what is important to your organisation. Examples could include such items as an improved or extended R&M (Repair & Maintenance) package, increased discounts on spares or an extended warranty on the vehicle or parts. If you run your own workshops, free or subsidised technician training and free or subsidised special tools or diagnostic tools and updates could be really useful to you. If your maintenance is contracted out, perhaps a replacement vehicle whenever one of your vehicles is off the road beyond a specified time. Using your imagination, there are a raft of items you could attempt to have thrown into the package, depending very much on what is useful to your organisation.

Most dealers and manufacturers in this day and age are operating on slim margins and therefore find it very difficult to lower prices any further, but may surprise you at what can be thrown into the package in order to attract you to buy, simply because it can be a real benefit to you, perhaps giving them the sale, but is not a major cost to their organisation. This is where good negotiation comes into play – instead of always buying on price alone, spend some time investigating what this particular sale means to the supplier and what other benefits their organisation may be able to bring to the table.

This is also the point where some hard work may be needed when considering the short list of buying options. There is no substitute for going through the details of each quotation to check what is on offer, what is included in the offer and what is at additional cost. A simple spreadsheet or matrix to compare costs, benefits and choices can be of real help here to clarify what is on offer.

I have already said I will not repeat the huge amount of basic advice on negotiating that is available elsewhere, but before we leave the subject, it is worth reminding you of some of the key points to remember when specifically negotiating vehicle or vehicle supplies purchase:

- Draw up a list of the key considerations you need to bear in mind when setting the objectives for purchase negotiations for your organisation with your suppliers; decide what you are, or are not, prepared to negotiate or compromise on. Set these out in writing before the meeting to help clear your thoughts. These probably will include:

    o   Maximum prices.
    o   What value for money means to you.
    o   Delivery timescales.
    o   Payment terms & discounts.
    o   After-sales service and maintenance arrangements.
    o   Quality standards and management.
    o   Lifetime costs of the vehicle or service.

- The key is to establish your preferred outcome whilst remaining realistic - if you are not prepared to compromise, the negotiations will not get very far. Try to consider what offers your supplier could make and decide in advance what you are willing to concede or compromise on. For example, you decide that you could pay full price, but only in exchange for a fast turnaround, as rapid delivery would be worth a lot to you.

- Make sure you are talking to the right decision-making personnel at the outset, do not waste time trying to negotiate with people who still require permission to agree.

- This may seem strange to those new to vehicle purchase, but remember the timing of negotiation on anything connected with vehicles can be all important. Sales departments are still required to meet targets by the end of the month, quarter or year (do not forget their financial year may run differently to yours - another fact to check beforehand). The best terms are often agreed on the final few days of the month.

- Conversely, some of the worst terms and deals are struck by public sector organisations desperate to spend the remains of their capital budget in the last few days of their financial year. I appreciate how difficult this may be, but in such a case, try to anticipate if any money may be left in the coffers and pre-negotiate a deal earlier in the year, without actually signing, until the money is definitely available.

- It is crucial to consider what offers the supplier is likely to make before any discussions take place and to think through how you will respond. This avoids making decisions 'on the hoof' and being surprised; you will no doubt get better at anticipating likely replies with experience.

- Of course, getting the best possible deal in the short-term will be important to your standing in your organisation, but remember a good relationship will help you get further prices reductions or other benefits, such as priority delivery. Never underestimate the value of good will.

- If the supplier is relatively small and you represent a considerable purchase, your negotiation leverage may be quite high, but do be careful not to erode your goodwill, it could damage service levels, the supplier could drop your product or, in extremis, go out of business, so do tread carefully. Remember, although vehicles are expensive, there can be a lot more money in the downstream part of the business, so getting a good price on parts and servicing can represent much better value than a high initial discount

- Many negotiators, (including me in my early days!), forget the huge value in conducting basic research into a potential supplier beforehand, to help understand how important your business is to them and hence your bargaining power. There is really no excuse for not doing this now, as so much information is available from the internet – but make sure you also talk to some of your colleagues, who they are already supplying, to help gain useful intelligence.

- In terms of negotiating power, a supplier who is in a monopoly or near monopoly position will have the advantage; however, if the supplier has competitors, or is a new entrant to the market, or is trying to fill production capacity, you will be in a stronger position and more likely to strike a good deal to help increase their market share – try to find out as much of this sort of information beforehand. Consider how you will use your strengths and also how to counter any of your potential weak points.

- Decide who you will need to support you – most likely someone from purchasing and someone from finance or accounts. The larger the contract, the more senior support you will need and it helps to match seniority with their sales team, so find out who will attend the negotiations from the supplier beforehand. Have a short pre-meeting to brief your team on all your considerations so far and what your strategy will be – it helps to have a confident and combined approach; you really do not want your finance director challenging one of your decisions during negotiations.

- During all your price comparisons and negotiation, be very wary of discounts. It can feel really good to be getting a very high discount but that may be on a very high base price - always check and compare the net prices, that's what ultimately counts.

- If you have enough negotiating power, use your own terms and conditions which your organisation will have checked and be comfortable with. If you have to accept your suppliers' terms and conditions you will need to check them very carefully and may often require legal advice.

- Always commence negotiations by clarifying the points you and the supplier are both happy with, ask the supplier to restate their offer discounts and payment terms to clarify for everyone involved

- Don't introduce the points on which you have concerns or the ones you are prepared to compromise on too early in negotiations, stay for as long as possible on the positive points you can both agree on. This keeps discussions on track – an amazing number of people want to commence by talking about the issues that they disagree on, which can only have a negative effect on proceedings.

- If negotiations, for any reason, need to be continued later, always follow the initial meeting <u>immediately</u> with the key points of the deal that have been agreed in writing and especially any assurances given during the discussions. These can be quickly reiterated at the start of the next meeting to remind everyone how much agreement there is, and that those particular issues do not need to be discussed again

- Try to keep matters factual and avoid discussing too many items that cannot be checked up on; do not be swayed if you suspect the other party is introducing any element as part of a negotiating tactic – if you do not feel happy at any stage, have a break, or even agree to reconvene at a later date until after you have checked some facts or thought through the issues.

- One item that many vehicle buyers are apt to accept without much question are features that do not necessarily have any value to your organisation. If so, ask if they can be removed and wherever possible, the price reduced. Even if they can be removed but there is no price reduction, there is a minor shift in the phycological balance of power, as you have taken something out of the calculations; strange but true. If the item really cannot be removed, treat it as an unwanted free gift.

- Ensure any necessary checks on the supplier such as a credit check and any reference checks (always undertake these fully) have been carried out well before negotiations commence. You may well be able to get assistance from other departments in your organisation to undertake these. It is so important to not go ahead until these checks are finalised, especially if you are going to need this supplier for any long-term arrangements.

Handy Hint 👍

- To keep discussions positive, always start any negotiation by clarifying the items on which both sides agree, leave matters on which you have concerns, and ones on which you are prepared to concede or compromise for later on. During any pause in negotiation or at the conclusion, always confirm the agreements in writing, as soon as practically possible.

---

7) How do I tackle getting approval from senior directors and managers?

Once you know when to replace your vehicles and you have established an operational specification, you have then worked that into a physical vehicle specification, obtained a variety of quotations and negotiated a final deal; at some point, you will have to gain the approval of whoever has control of the purse strings within your organisation.

There is a definite art to getting that approval. You will probably have to present to a couple of Directors, or the board, or a perhaps a budgetary approval committee. My strong advice here is that less is almost always more. Most decision makers are really not that interested in the details that you have probably been struggling with for months. And to be honest, you do not really want them to be – their job is to deal with the high-level strategy, not the minutia of detailed vehicle specifications. They just need to be convinced that you have done your homework, the operators are happy, the vehicles will be fit for purpose and they represent best value for money. Hopefully, you will have been keeping key directors or managers informed of progress during your investigations and calculations, so there will not be any major surprises. Be aware that this part of the process also acts as a double check that there are no longer-term organisational plans that you may not be privy to, such as a proposed changes to a depot network. Describing your future fleet plans to senior management should uncover any issues of which you need to be aware.

At some stage in the run-up to this point, possibly as long as 6 to 12 months ago, the finance department should have asked you how many of your vehicles you estimate you will replace in the coming financial year and how much that is likely to cost the organisation. That exercise will involve matching the current fleet list against the agreed criteria of mileage and age, extrapolating both, and estimating which will exceed these figures in the coming year. In addition to that calculation, you should have contacted all your senior operating managers asking them if they believe there are any vehicles in the fleet they control that are not being fully utilised which they would like to return. Unsurprisingly, that will generally be hardly any. In addition, establish if there are any other vehicles that they consider are in urgent need of replacement, whether or not meet the agreed replacement criteria, which will normally be considerably more than returns.

A little bit of a juggling act will come up with a list of vehicles for potential replacement and an estimated budgetary capital expenditure. The outline of this list should always be circulated to operating managers so that they are fully aware which vehicles are intended to be replaced and are able to add any recommendations for the replacement. It also primes them to try to keep any major expenditures down on an out-going vehicle.

The actual presentation should be relatively simple. You need to outline the current profile of the fleet, identify which vehicles require replacing and by when. I would then suggest showing the extrapolated cost of running the selected vehicles on for a further year, matched against the probably increased finance costs of the new vehicles, but considerably reduced R&M costs. In an ideal world, there would be a running cost saving from new vehicles, but as the finance costs are likely to be considerably higher than the previous vehicles, this may not be the case. In which case, other softer justification factors will need to come in to play, so for example, a few photos of some of your worst condition vehicles may help your case. A key factor to be demonstrated here is reliability. Although vehicles are far more reliable than they used to be, the operational penalties for late delivery or not attending an appointment can also be higher. Figures showing an increase in unplanned breakdowns and their cost to the business can also help the decision process.

Your objective should be to leave the meeting having received clear approval for all the vehicles you plan to replace, leaving you free to progress the next stage of the buying process. What you may get is a series of questions, some of which you were unable to answer at the time, that the decision makers require you to investigate and report back. This is why keeping the senior personnel informed of the bare bones of your initial findings and negotiations is very helpful, as is a mass of homework beforehand, hopefully anticipating their queries. There may also have been a recent shift in financial priorities, so part of the expenditure is approved, with the remainder held until later in the year. Try to anticipate the potential direction of this meeting beforehand by keeping your ear to the ground, so you are comfortable with whatever result you get in the decision-making process.

One very minor, but crucially important point here, please learn from my earlier mistakes. Once you have gained financial approval to spend part or all of your capital budget, my advice is to get it spent quickly, or at the very least, get the orders in place as soon as possible. Early in my career, I made the mistake of thinking if the money had been earmarked for my capital budget, no-one could take it away from me. How wrong I was! I soon learnt that many other competing organisational priorities could suddenly appear, and that permission could disappear as quickly as it arrived and with it my potential spend. That also generally had a knock-on effect so that maintenance figures were almost certain to rise in the next year.

Handy Hint 👍

- When presenting to senior decision makers, less is definitely more; present only what they need to know to make high-level strategic decision, stay out of the minute detail which they do not need to know. Spend any capital approved as soon as practically possible.

8) *How do I plan and project manage the build process start to finish?*

Let us be brutal about this subject. If you are acquiring more than a handful of vehicles then the only way of managing this process well is to partly become a project manager yourself, using some of their useful techniques. One of the most important ways to achieve success is to constantly check that everything is happening according to plan. If your organisation is large enough, you may be able to delegate this responsibility, but I suspect most fleet managers will be undertaking it themselves. There is a huge temptation for a busy fleet manager, with many other priority tasks taking their time, to assume that all suppliers in the chain will deliver on the declared date. In addition, many manufacturers will not tell you when they have problems because they are "hoping" to resolve them before the due date.

So by constantly, but very quickly, keeping in touch every few days you can anticipate any issues, work with the suppliers to get them resolved and keep other people down the line informed so that they can plan appropriately. In other words, employ a "no surprises" policy right throughout the chain. This takes a little bit of time and effort, but the dividends are well worth it. However, it is obviously really important that you do not become a complete irritation to your supplier. It helps if during each phone call or contact you can give them some little piece of information which will be of use, thus making it a two-way process of benefit to both of you.

During the project management phase, your Gantt chart will literally become your most import roadmap to success. Update this constantly with the results of all your discussions and record any date changes immediately. Other people within the organisation probably do not need to see all the details of this chart, however, sending a simplified version of important changes, with much of the detail redacted, is very helpful to anyone involved with Fleet. If you do this, as ever, do make sure any changes are identified somehow, so that busy people do not to spend time trying to decide what has changed from the last version.

One additional word of caution here; I have seen a number of people using fairly complex project management software for vehicle purchases who get carried away with the technicalities of the system. If not careful, you can spend an awful lot of your time updating and adding detail to the system and not achieving the end objective of an on-time vehicle delivery. My advice with project management software on vehicle build is, as with many things; just stick to the basics.

One other factor worth considering and talking to purchasing (or whoever handles contracts in your organisation) prior to ordering is to include a small penalty clause within the contract in case of non-delivery by a certain date. A lot of caution is required here. The penalty cannot be so large so as to drive your supplier away, or so small that it is of little or no consequence. It also needs to address the issues of risk, so the supplier needs to be confident there are not too many factors outside of their control which would cause the penalty to be employed. This clause is especially useful if you have visited the factory or workshop and decided that another customer may just be getting priority before your build – it will help to keep the mind of the supplier focused on your vehicles. If you require the vehicles in order to meet the start of a business contract for your organisation, then you may wish to seriously increase the penalty and perhaps offer some sort of incentive for early delivery.

9) How do I manage the inspection process during build?

If at all possible, before placing the order, try to visit the appropriate plant or factory in order to see production for yourself. You need to do this as part of your due diligence anyway, but look for the efficiency of the operation, the quality of the build and also what other vehicles are being built and the time taken. All other things being equal it is normally good to see a good mix of customers going down the line as a predominance of one customer probably indicates they will have priority over anyone else, including you. Factor in regular inspection visits during production in order to check progress. If you are really too busy to visit, find someone else to do it for you, but this process is really important.

If you do not inspect regularly during production (obviously the number of visits depends on the complexity of build), then any issues picked up on final inspection will invariably result in a delay of some sort whilst the vehicle is reworked or new parts obtained. However, if you have conducted one or two inspections during build, any problems picked up at that point stand a good chance of being repaired or replaced in parallel with the final vehicle build, thus meaning that delays are eradicated, or at least, kept to a minimum.

This is where your previous work will come into its own. By insisting on an operational specification and then producing a vehicle specification to match the requirement, you will have thought through all the detailed points of the build, discussing them with vehicle, body and equipment manufacturers, so refining the specification, piece by piece. Make this specification as detailed as necessary, without going overboard, but lay it out in logical sequence to aid later inspection. The manufacturer's own specification to you, may lack sufficient detail, but you will need to put in just enough detail to make sure you get exactly what you want. This is an art that you will get better at with experience.

On inspection, simply work to the specification. Go round the vehicle in a logical sequence, checking each detailed point. Most importantly, assume absolutely nothing, check every item. As ever, immediately after any inspection, get the key points in writing and back to the supplier without delay so they can take any necessary action. A crazy tip, and it is not always possible, but if you take someone with you for the inspection, perhaps an operator with a vested interest in the vehicle, they can drive on the return trip, leaving you free to dictate notes whilst fresh in your mind. Train travel offers similar benefits.

Do not forget that all vehicles will require a PDI (Pre-Delivery Inspection) which should cover all aspects of the vehicle before going into operation. It obviously needs to ensure the vehicle is technically ready for operation and safe for drivers and operators to use, but should also pick up on the little items that, for whatever reason, have become out-of-kilter during the build process. This inspection needs to be carried out properly, but does not usually take too long unless it is a very complex build specification. This item is often rushed or missed, so ensure you negotiate times and dates for PDI with your supplier and, of course, allow time in your Gannt schedule. This is really crucial when a considerable number of vehicles are coming to completion nearly all at once (another reason to avoid this occurrence).

If you are new to vehicles, vehicle production and commercial vehicle body building, do not worry; just remember everyone has to start somewhere. Do not be frightened to ask questions of any supplier – they will invariably be happy to educate you into their manufacturing materials and techniques. Also remember, like any industry, the vehicle industry delights in acronyms and buzzwords as shorthand, but I am sure in some cases, just to appear clever. Again, just keep asking until you understand. The important thing to the supplier is that you fully understand your operation, so you can answer questions such as where to position items in the cab or body. If you are new to your operation, spend the first few weeks and months in your new role learning as much about it as physically possible. Try to go out with some of your drivers to see how the operation works, you can never ask enough questions.

10) What other departments should I keep in touch with during the project?

Briefly then, here are some suggestions of the people in your organisation you should be talking to during the procurement process.

Possibly the most important people to talk to, but often overlooked, is operations. Even if you are keeping regional managers at a senior level fully informed of progress and naturally assume that this will filter its way down to depot and driver level, do not assume that is always the case. If you want drivers and staff to look after your vehicles and treat them well, part of the deal is to keep them involved in the replacement process. In so many organisations I visit, fleet replacement has become a black art where vehicles just appear at intervals with little or no explanation and not necessarily much discussion about the vehicle being replaced or the new vehicle arriving.

I believe that many fleet managers fear that by informing staff at all levels of the vehicle replacement program, it could give rise to a barrage of questions or requests about the incoming vehicles. That can sometimes be true, but the benefits of good communications with the users far outweigh the slightly increased hassle of a multitude of questions. You may also find some questions are really helpful, as it may uncover something that you had previously overlooked! It often takes a little bit of time to make sure everybody involved is aware of what is happening, especially if anything in the program changes, but I guarantee it is well worth the effort.

Finance should be involved at every stage of the process. From devising the capital budget through obtaining quotations, gaining approval, and finally supplier payment. One important point here is that whatever terms the payment you have agreed, make absolutely sure finance keep to it - do not allow any internal issues to delay this process. If you want to sustain a good long-term relationship with a supplier, it is absolutely critical to make sure you pay them on, or preferably before, the due date.

if you have a procurement department, always involve them fully in the process right from the beginning. A good procurement team can add massive value, especially with things like parts or service purchasing. Although you will probably want to keep control of most of the process, using procurement to place the orders will reduce your administration stress and may also cover off items of a legal nature that you perhaps had not thought of.

Quite often the fleet Department have their own administration team, or a shared administration with other departments. Making friends with both finance and procurement can often help relieve all the administration associated with buying.

At the lighter end of the commercial vehicle spectrum, especially if vans are being taken home, you will probably need to inform HR of the details of any new vehicles, not least for tax purposes. You may wish to grant them access to personnel and vehicle data held on your fleet management system, which could usefully save duplicate administration. As ever, make sure you follow your own GDPR (General Data Protection Regulation) procedures with such information.

Top Tips for Vehicle Procurement ✔

- The actual point where figures show when to replace a vehicle does not always match the theoretical one; the graph is likely to be flatter, longer and be stepped, not a smooth curve. It is worth checking where the replacement point is, by group of vehicles, at least once a year.

- As well as 'hard' cost facts, you are likely to have to use 'soft' factors such as emissions, image and condition to help you decide when to replace vehicles.

- Measuring whole life costs is the best way to determine when to replace, but for practicality, you will probably still declare a mileage or age limit on each discrete group of vehicles.

- Standardisation of specifications is one of the most important ways of reducing fleet costs and helps massively at replacement time.

- Good purchasing negotiation is both an art and a science, which you can learn and improve with experience; make sure you research your supplier fully and think through likely responses before negotiations.

- Make sure you brief senior decision makers on the progress of negotiations before presenting final figures for approval.

- Good project management during the build stage is essential; keep in regular contact with all your suppliers to ensure they are on track; allow time for inspection throughout the process.

- Keep other departments in the loop throughout the project; attempt to use their skills and administration to assist your efforts.

David's Don'ts ✖

- Don't forget to involve drivers and operations very early on in the replacement process in order to get full 'buy-in' from them throughout the project.

- Don't be tempted to publish the shortest quoted lead-time for production; declare a realistic one and then move heaven & earth to make sure suppliers stay on track, through good project management.

- Don't forget to allow sufficient time for new vehicle inspection throughout the build process.

- Don't let operations dictate makes and models; insist they provide you with a full and detailed operational specification which you can then convert into the right vehicle for the job.

The Ultimate Guide to Commercial Vehicle Fleet Management

Chapter 5 – Commercial Vehicle Finance & Funding

1) *What is the best way to finance our fleet?*
2) *What are the alternative options to buying outright with cash?*
3) *When applying for funding, what are the four key criteria to decide?*
4) *What is a finance lease and what are its advantages and disadvantages?*
5) *What is an operating lease and what are its advantages and disadvantages?*
6) *What is contact hire and what are its advantages and disadvantages?*
7) *What is hire purchase and what are its advantages and disadvantages?*
8) *What is contract purchase and what are its advantages and disadvantages?*
9) *What issues should I take into account when trying to decide how to fund my vehicles?*
10) *What do I need to know about commercial vehicle insurance & self-insurance?*
11) *How can I reduce my organisation's vehicle insurance premiums?*

1) *What is the best way to finance our fleet?*

One obvious key decision to make when operating your own vehicle fleet is how you pay for it. The transport arena, excepting a few niche sectors, has been a low margin, low barrier to entry sector for as long as I can remember. That means margins are tight and choosing the correct model for financing the fleet is crucial, possibly making the distinction between operating at a profit or a loss. At the very least, it can make the difference between being financially comfortable or always having to struggle at the end of the accounting period to make ends meet. There are obviously many financial issues to take into account and many factors to juggle in order to arrive at the most economic methods to finance your fleet.

What we are talking about here is effectively asset finance, although a very specialised area of asset finance. Whichever method is used to finance your vehicles can also essentially be used to fund any asset used within your business, so can include trucks, vans, cars, trailers, tippers, tankers, specialised bodies, cranes and workshop equipment, albeit that the tax treatment of each asset class may be very different, leading to widely varying whole life costs.

If you cannot immediately afford to buy your assets outright, financing gives you access to the equipment and assets you require now and allows the cost to be spread over time, although there is obviously a charge for doing that.

Personally, I always buy my vehicles outright and so do almost half of UK fleet operators. This may not be the most advantageous way to finance vehicles in terms of cash flow, corporation tax or VAT, but as a method of funding, it has one massive advantage. Should anything happen to the business, and the effects of Covid-19 is a prime example, the vehicles cannot be taken away, or at least, not due to non-payment of rental or leasing charges. According to the BVRLA (British Vehicle Rental & Leasing Association) 2020 industry survey, an incredible 44% of commercial vehicle operators agree with me and fund their new vehicles (including second-hand) outright by cash purchase. For commercial vehicles, unless other factors play a hand, it is also generally the cheapest method for the organisation over the life of the vehicles. For company cars, contract hire is probably more tax efficient due to VAT recovery.

There would seem to be, at least up until the present, a cultural issue in the United Kingdom, in that many transport operators, especially those with larger trucks, tend to wish to own their own fleet, rather than pay for the use of those same vehicles. One thing that going through Brexit and the Coronavirus issue has taught us is that flexibility is now more than ever key to managing your business. Buying outright with organisational cash is not only the cheapest method generally, but also maximises flexibility.

Buying a Commercial Vehicle may require more than just a Piggy Bank

However, there is no getting away from the fact that using cash to buy what is essentially a depreciating asset may not be the best financial decision for the business, especially if that same cash can be used elsewhere in the organisation to generate a better rate of return. Also, the figure for outright purchase hides the real story, as not all of these cash payments are genuinely "free" cash, but may be made with borrowed money, probably at favourable rates from a bank. However, if this is the case, it obviously makes sense to check that your bank rate cannot be beaten by a lower lending rate from your leasing company. Even if your organisation is cash rich, do not dismiss borrowing or leasing completely. Generally, the rate of borrowing for public sector fleets has been very low for a long time and more recently, the rate for private sector borrowing has also stayed low, but is unlikely to stay that way for too much longer. That needs to be taken into account when making financial decisions that will impact your organisation for five years or more into the future.

2) What are the alternative options to buying outright with cash?

If not buying outright and alternative sources of finance are required, there are four main options, with a couple of additional variations available to most operators. To me, when investigating these options, they always seem very understandable at the start, but soon become incomprehensible to the non-financial person, as each option has varying "for and against" criteria, which get more and more complex the further you examine them. Trying to balance off the various factors becomes increasingly difficult and finance providers always talk as if you should know and understand all the complexities involved. By now, you should realise that I am not a financial expert and although I can negotiate with the best of them, I always seek expert independent advice when making strategic decisions on how to acquire vehicles, especially regarding tax and VAT implications, and so should you.

I would therefore suggest that you do not rely solely on the advice of your finance product provider, as they often will have their own preferred solution, generally due to the way they are funding the deal. Usually they will do this, quite naturally, in order to maximise their return by concentrating on what they do best. Nor can they ever fully know your tax situation or be in a position to advise you on it. Providers also vary in the range of products they offer; some may only specialise in a narrow range of options. Their advice therefore needs checking out by your own financial department or your accountant or financial advisor, but be sure that they too understand the full implications of the figures, any liabilities incurred and the risks involved in the detail of the small print presented. Asset finance and especially vehicle finance is a specialist area and really needs people who understand the field and the effects of variations over time on vehicle residuals.

Most important of all is that you do not select a finance method through habit, because you have "always done it that way". Whenever you are coming up to a major purchasing project, use it as an opportunity to check out the marketplace and assure yourself that you are using the best finance route possible. Also, there are no rules that say you can only use one way. Your finance advisor may voice an opinion if every vehicle is acquired differently, however, if, say, you required a group of vehicles specifically for a three-year contract, they may well suit a different finance product to your normal seven-year replacements.

Whilst we are mentioning the picture in seven years' time, it is worth pointing out that every purchasing choice outlined in this chapter has been around for a considerable time, has been well refined and developed over that time and is available today. However, there are potential changes coming in how we buy vehicles which will start to accelerate quite shortly. Starting logically in the private car sector, there are providers entering the market, including OEM's (Original Equipment Manufacturers), offering new operating models such as new car subscription services which replace traditional long-term purchase or leasing arrangements with more flexible monthly contracts. These combine insurance, maintenance and other costs into an all-inclusive price, usually accessed online. This suits those who want full-time access to a vehicle but the flexibility to change models or 'pause' their usage.

For private buyers, manufacturers particularly like these models as these schemes represent an opportunity to maintain relationships with customers and take back control from on-demand platform providers, who have been growing massively in recent years. The rise of on-demand services is almost certain to grow further with the introduction of autonomous vehicles and a consequent decline in vehicle ownership, particularly in urban areas. It is easy to see how these models appeal to many urban car users, who no longer see the need to own a vehicle.

At the moment, there are few models of this sort for commercial vehicle operators due mainly to the way vehicles are used. However, I suspect the financing and acquisition of commercial vehicles will not stay in its current format for much longer due to the economic impacts of the need to de-carbonise, along with the introduction of autonomous vehicles and alternative fuels. The finance industry suggests that there will be far more "pay-by-use" schemes which can also be employed in the commercial vehicle arena. There is already considerable innovation being employed in logistics business models, such as peer-to-peer logistics platforms and blockchain, along with technology driven models for last mile deliveries such as drones and pods. All this development means that future methods of distribution will not stay in their current format for too much longer and acquisition methods will almost certainly have to keep pace with these changes.

For the time being, however, your choices are mostly limited to existing business models. In order to assist you in being able to make some strategic decisions about how to acquire your vehicles, let's first unpack the benefits and disbenefits of buying a commercial vehicle outright when compared with a financed option.

So firstly, we can state that some of the key benefits of buying a commercial vehicle outright, as distinct from leasing or hiring are:

- Buying outright will generally save you money in the longer term, with less regular outgoings.

- Owning outright gives you the opportunity to convert or adapt a vehicle at any stage to meet the needs of your business as they change, without having to gain acceptance from other parties (providing the changes are legal, that is); however, both Hire Purchase and Lease Purchase contracts should allow adaption of the vehicle.

- You have complete flexibility over mileages; in contrast, although contract hired vehicles have no mileage limit, you will have to predict the mileage for a leased vehicle at the outset and if it changes during the period, make alterations to your contract and monthly payments or potentially pay a surcharge, sometimes hefty, at the end of term. A well-negotiated leasing deal, however, may allow you some cash back if mileages are below expected.

- You can go for a more bespoke solution at the outset; generally, you may have to "make do" with a leased vehicle as it stands and you are restricted to a large extent in what you can do with it, as you will inevitably have to give it back, in an appropriate condition, after a set period of time. If the vehicle is not in the agreed return condition, you will be charged a figure to represent the loss of sale, however, a fully owned vehicle in the same condition will also lose value, so in theory at least, this aspect largely balances out.

- Buying a commercial vehicle means you can adapt it fully to your operation and achieve the most appropriate vehicle specification for your specific needs. However, most hire purchase, lease purchase or leases with conditional sale will allow the same.

- You will generally be able to deduct the full cost of a new commercial vehicle from your profits before tax using your Annual Investment

Allowance, again you can do the same with hire purchase, lease purchase or leases with conditional sale.

- Unlike company cars, for commercial vehicles purchased through a business, you can generally claim 100% tax relief in the year the vehicle is acquired, again you can do the same with hire purchase, lease purchase or leases with conditional sale.

- You can claim back 100% of the VAT incurred on purchase of your vehicle, but do not forget you will have to account for VAT on the sale of the vehicle; again this applies to hire purchase, lease purchase or leases with conditional sale.

- Owning, rather than leasing, should generally result in lower insurance premiums. I have to say I have never fully grasped the reasoning behind that fact, but that's how it is.

- You have an asset with a value, albeit a depreciating one, which you can realise, if necessary, at any stage of the vehicle's life without further payments to the leasing company. Although if you let the vehicle run on too far, you may of course have to pay someone to take it away! In contrast, there is a cost to the early return of a leased vehicle, higher at the start of the term.

- You will not face unexpected end-of-life charges, a real benefit for some operators. However, as mentioned above, if well negotiated at the start, these charges should be no more than the lessor's loss of sale proceeds, which you would also suffer yourself if you bought outright. Unfortunately, many operators complain of excessive end-of-life charges, and there are ways to improve vehicle sale proceeds if the process is entirely in your control.

In contrast, some of the key benefits of commercial vehicle leasing or hire purchase (or any similar method of acquisition) are:

- It is suitable for operators who do not need ownership of the vehicle but just require the use of the vehicle for a set period – it has to be said that this is the way the world is moving regarding mobility, although most transport operators still retain the historic model of vehicle ownership.

- Leasing or Hire Purchase can be a tax efficient form of funding that protects cash flow by spreading the cost of the vehicle over its economic life.

- If you decide you still need of the vehicle at the end of the lease, it is often possible to extend the lease for a secondary period.

- Leasing or Hire Purchase avoids most upfront costs as normally the deposit will equate to a small number of monthly payments – useful for new businesses or start-ups to preserve cash flow.

- Currently, when ownership of the vehicle remains with the lessor, this keeps it off the balance sheet for most smaller transport organisations, excepting those that already account under IFRS (International Financial Reporting Standard), such as international companies or PLCs (Public Limited Company).

- You can generally offset rentals against your tax liability, although this may not be as beneficial as writing off the cost up front if you buy outright

- If you are a smaller operator, there is no need to worry about potential trade-in costs

- There is no need to concern yourself about depreciation costs, these are taken care of in the rental payments. If depreciation massively increases during the period, that is generally the responsibility of the lessor

- You can usually choose a maintenance option where the lessor bears the cost of routine maintenance and repairs, avoiding most unforeseen costs, keeping outgoings relatively static – maintenance costs for an owned vehicle will naturally increase over time. Bear in mind though, you will probably be overpaying in the first half of the contract.

- Depending on the finance model chosen, Leasing or Hiring can sometimes offer more financial flexibility than buying a vehicle outright, choosing terms such as the deposit, the repayment term, and optional lump sum final payment to keep your monthly repayments low. You may also be able to vary your monthly payments to match seasonal variations in your cash flow.

3) *When applying for funding, what are the four key criteria to decide?*

Possibly a good way to approach the finance puzzle is to prioritise and decide for yourself the answers to four key criteria questions; this should rule in or out a number of the available options. These questions are:

Firstly, do you want to own the vehicles at the end of the period?

If Yes; choose Hire Purchase, Cash or possibly Contract Purchase.

If No; then an Operating Lease, Finance Lease or Contract Hire are probably your options.

Secondly, do you wish to pay VAT up front, or monthly during the leasing period? If paying up front, you can usually reclaim VAT in the next quarter

If monthly, choose Finance Lease or Operating Lease.

If up-front, then Hire Purchase, Contract Purchase, Finance Lease or Cash is for you.

Thirdly, do you want the liability relating to the vehicle contracts to appear as debt on the balance sheet?

If Yes; choose Hire Purchase, Contract Purchase, or a Finance Lease.

If No; then you need an Operating Lease, Contract Hire, or buy Cash.

Note that since the inception of finance regulation IFRS 16 in 2019, international or publicly quoted organisations must show **all** leases on their balance sheets. The idea is to help avoid disparity between companies owning or just using assets. Not having to declare vehicles on the balance sheets means an organisation's financial position appears stronger than it actually is. It is likely that after 2022, most companies will have to declare all their assets on the balance sheet, so this issue would no longer be so relevant when leasing.

Lastly, there is the more complex question of tax relief and capital allowances

For the full Annual Investment Allowance and/or Writing-Down Allowance, use Hire Purchase, Contract Purchase, Conditional Sale or Cash.

Most other options will allow tax relief against monthly payment, as described below.

It is easy to forget that with all purchases except cash, you do not actually own the vehicles during the leasing period. Also remember, if you wish to ultimately own the vehicle, there are likely to be settlement fees at the end of the leasing period for Hire Purchase or Contract Purchase.

Similarly, unless you take out a maintenance package, the on-going maintenance of the vehicle remains your cost for every option excepting Contract Hire. For all methods of finance, it will remain your legal and contractual responsibility to keep the vehicle maintained to manufacturer's recommended standards, the difference will be who pays the bill to the servicing agent. Of course, if it is a heavy vehicle on your O licence, you still have to comply with your legal responsibilities to maintain the vehicle, so remember you also need access to timely reports on all the maintenance work carried out.

So, having prioritised which type of funding would probably suit your organisation, let's examine the advantages and disadvantages of the most widely used options available to you when seeking finance for commercial vehicles. I have tried to list them in some form of logical order in order to aid understanding.

4) What is a finance lease and what are its advantages and disadvantages?

Finance Lease

In this, possibly the most basic finance scenario, the operator takes the risk of the residual value of the vehicle, so the asset will appear on your balance sheet, however, perversely, you will never own the vehicle. You can elect to run the vehicle on after the end of the agreement at a peppercorn rate or sell the vehicle onto a third party keeping most of the proceeds. As you are essentially hiring and never own the vehicle, you cannot claim capital allowances, so a finance lease will suit a business that has already used up their annual allowances.

Advantages: The quoted monthly repayment fees should be reduced to reflect the fact that the finance company will claim capital tax allowances. Also, this method of financing the vehicle results in a low initial outlay as VAT is paid monthly and can be reclaimed, whilst the whole of each rental payment can be offset against tax, rather than just interest as is the case with some other options. You can elect to vary the monthly repayments to suit your own seasonal business patterns, thus helping cash flow. As with some other finance methods, a balloon payment at the end of hire will reduce monthly payments.

Disadvantages: It could be said that a finance lease gives you all the costs and risks of running a vehicle without ever gaining ownership. Monthly fees cover the full cost of the vehicle plus any interest charges involved. The vehicle has to appear on the balance sheet without the benefit of owning the asset, and there is also the risk of asset values falling during the agreement period, which then effectively becomes the operator's responsibility.

5) *What is an operating lease and what are its advantages and disadvantages?*

Operating Lease

This method differs from the Finance lease above in that the lessor takes into account the vehicle's estimated residual value in the calculations for monthly payments. This again means the operator never owns the vehicle, however, in effect, the operator is only paying for the depreciation of the vehicle during the period they use it.

Advantages: Once again VAT is paid monthly, so there are no upfront payments and therefore low initial charges, whilst the entire monthly rental is again tax deductible. Currently this method of finance is classed as off-balance sheet as the finance company takes the risk of the residual value of the vehicle. As the rental period on an operating lease is generally shorter than the life of the vehicle and only depreciation for the period of rental is taken into account, the monthly costs should now be cheaper.

Disadvantages: Once again the operator does not have an asset at the end of the period, so there are no capital allowances for this method of finance. Rentals will be higher during periods when residual forecasts are low.

6) *What is Contact Hire and what are its advantages and disadvantages?*

Contract Hire

Effectively contract hire is an operating lease (as above) but often with repair and maintenance included, although non-maintenance packages are available. It is a well-used route to obtaining vehicles, generally for periods from 1 to 5 years, having a fixed monthly bill, apart from any user-generated charges, to aid cash flow. Other fleet management services can be included within the contract hire fee, again aiding budgets and cash flow, often very suitable for smaller businesses.

Advantages: Contract periods can often be set to match customers' operating requirements, thus making this method of finance relatively easy, if you should wish, to match operating contracts also removing the problem of off-loading vehicles at the end of a contract. There are fixed monthly all-inclusive costs with fixed interest rates, currently reported off-balance sheet, so this option is good for operators who are risk-averse and like to know what their expenditure will be each month with few surprises. Once again, the monthly rental fee will be tax deductible with no upfront costs. Some suppliers also offer an open book "profit-share" (usually 50/50) arrangement on unused fees for items such as maintenance, tyres and benefits from vehicle resale.

Disadvantages: Although having fixed monthly fees and covering most of the cost, this option can be more expensive than purchase as, if desired, it often includes more services and also transfers the risk to the lessor. This can also make it quite expensive to cancel a contract mid-term unless the facility to do so has been built in the start, obviously at an extra cost.

7) What is Hire Purchase and what are its advantages and disadvantages?

Hire Purchase

This is the first finance option we have looked at so far where the ownership of the vehicle can transfer from the supplier to you at the end of the contract, for a small fee. In effect, the finance company buys the vehicle on behalf of the customer and hires it to them for the period. Some accountants would describe it as an agreement to hire with an option to purchase. Conditional Sale is similar to Hire Purchase where it is already agreed that you will purchase the vehicle at the end of the term. After an initial deposit, ongoing monthly payments cover the total capital cost of the truck, plus interest and any fees.

Advantages: As you will have the option to own the vehicle at the end of the contract, full capital allowances can be claimed. Helpfully, if you feel that interest rates are going to rise in the foreseeable future, repayments are normally specified at a fixed rate for the whole of the contract and no VAT is charged on them.

Disadvantages: The residual risk on the vehicle resides with the operator and VAT is payable as a lump sum at the start of the contract. Hire purchase liabilities will appear on the balance sheet. Only the interest element of monthly repayments is allowable against tax.

8) What is Contract Purchase and what are its advantages and disadvantages?

Contract Purchase

This option is very similar to hire purchase, but in the same way that an operating lease differs from a finance lease, the lessor takes account of the residual value of the vehicle, therefore you are effectively paying just for the depreciation of the vehicle during the period of use, not the total value of the asset, so rentals are lower. At the conclusion of the contract period, you can either return the vehicle to the supplier or pay a final "balloon" payment to buy the vehicle outright. The former makes sense if residual values are low, the latter is advantage if the residual value is now higher than the original estimate, so benefits the user either way.

Advantages: To me this can be one of the most advantageous methods of commercial vehicle finance in that it gives maximum flexibility for the period of the loan. Monthly payments are lower than hire purchase (but not lease purchase) and there is no VAT on them, which is not of major significance to most operators. At the end of the contract, you can either return the vehicle, or buy it and continue to run it, then selling it later at your convenience, ensuring a largely risk-free disposal route. Full capital allowances are available.

Disadvantages: Although monthly payments may be lower than hire purchase, total costs could be higher because there is an element of transfer of risk, i.e., the residual value is underwritten to give you flexibility at the end of the lease. VAT needs paying upfront and only the interest element of monthly payments can be offset against tax. As for hire purchase, these vehicles will appear on the balance sheet.

9) What issues should I take into account when trying to decide how to fund my vehicles?

If you have decided on a funding option, you obviously need to decide where to obtain the money from. In years gone by, many fleet organisations, especially SME's would naturally turn to their bank, or at least a bank. That seems to be less common recently, primarily because the banks seem more risk averse to lending and have made the process more difficult by asking for more regular reviews and charging higher rates. It may also not make sense to use up your available lines of credit with your bank on vehicles, especially as they may be used to finance other assets, but perhaps not commercial vehicles, or to finance other areas of the business.

Vehicle manufacturing finance arms have the benefit of a good knowledge of the market and they should be well placed to quickly assess your risk and creditworthiness. They also have a route to market for used vehicles, thus exercising some influence over residual values, especially important for contract hire and operating lease rates. Interest rates will probably be in line with the overall market, but residual prices may be slightly keener than some other lenders, making prices slightly lower. If going through dealers, always check the market thoroughly. A mystery shopping exercise I conducted for a university a few years ago gave one set of interest rates almost double the lowest from the same manufacturer, but through a different dealer.

That leaves a big market in contract hire and vehicle leasing specialist companies, usually backed by large banks or finance institutions. They keep rates low by borrowing in bulk cheaply off their parent company. They obviously possess a full knowledge of the market and often have deals available if you are perhaps prepared to accept a fairly standard vehicle specification. Their associated repair and maintenance contracts can often be very competitive as they can negotiate good workshop rates through bulk buying, which can be a useful benefit to smaller operators. A word of advice here; sometimes the negotiated rates from the workshop are of more significance to the supplier than the quality of repair – check which workshops will be maintaining your vehicles and do some background checks with other operators using those repairers before signing.

For completeness, it should be mentioned that there are other ways of funding vehicle acquisition, however, banks, vehicle manufacturers and leasing companies described above are the 3 main sources that the vast majority of operators turn to. There is one other way of providing vehicles which can be exceedingly useful at certain times during an organisations' life: that of short-term hiring or rental. There is obviously a financial premium to be paid for this flexibility, however, occasionally, some very good deals are available making prices not too distant from longer-term finance. When hiring, try to make sure that payments are scheduled in line with your organisation's income stream to smooth cash flow and be aware that for the few months before the Christmas peak, many hire vehicles are spoken for as long ago as the previous Christmas.

Handy Hint 👍
<ul><li>If part or all of your operation are HGVs and you possess an O licence, don't forget that hired HGV vehicles count towards your total vehicle compliment for the specified operating centre – make sure you do not exceed capacity. With the introduction of on-line reporting facilities for most operators, you would be well advised to inform the Traffic Commissioner as soon as you hire the vehicle.</li></ul>

The availability of money depends very much on the state of the economy and the financial climate, obviously quite difficult at the current moment (2021). Whichever lending route you choose, be aware that lenders will want to examine the business case and the reasoning behind the facility, also looking carefully at your balance sheet and your current and future contracts and revenue earning potential. They will obviously also have to conduct a full credit check. As with purchasing property, the level of deposit will reflect the economic uncertainty at the time and the perceived level risk for the lender, so as ever, shop around. Also be very aware that interest rates, which have been very low for an unprecedented length of time, are likely to rise in the near future. If possible, therefore, factor in increased charges into your business plan, or attempt to lock-in low interest rates for the foreseeable future.

New businesses or those with inconsistent profits and those considered as high risk will find it harder to find finance organisations willing to lend to them. They will be exposed to increased scrutiny and may find they face harsher contract terms than a comparable organisation with consistent profits and a good track record over a number of years. For longer lease periods or those deemed to have a higher risk, the level of deposit may increase; the good news is, of course, that this will bring down monthly repayments. However, I would advise you not to treat your finance provider as just a commodity; you are not just trying to find who will provide the most money or at the cheapest price. Instead view it as a long-term partnership with someone who can provide added value to the organisation and become a trusted partner over time.

If you are looking for finance for more than just a few vehicles, you will need to present a proper business plan to your investors. There are many examples of good template plans freely available, not least on the internet, but try to find one that enables you to cover just the critical key business issues, such as:

- o   the outline business concept
- o   the current and projected finance figures
- o   any equity involved
- o   how much you need to borrow, and
- o   how that will benefit the organisation

You will need to find a template that suits your business needs and presents the right figures in order to convince potential financiers. Include a little about the organisation structure and personnel and especially why your organisation is a good investment. For a business plan, less is definitely more; just include the very basics, do not go into too much detail. Finance experts need to understand the risks involved, they do not need or want 'war and peace', in fact that is highly likely to be counter-productive and could well result in rejection.

Remember that your finance provider needs to be convinced that the potential rewards of the investment outweigh any risks they are taking by loaning you the money, so they will need to be convinced that your intended market is sound and that the project will be efficiently managed. If your organisation's management team is also investing in the project in any way, that tends to help. They will also want to know the best and worst-case financial scenarios and potential returns from each.

Past performance showing you have previously achieved projected figures will also help greatly.

One option that has not been mentioned so far is that of refinancing. In this case you have to own your fleet already and the finance house will buy the vehicles off you and then lease them back to you. This method is generally and unsurprisingly called "sale & leaseback", thus releasing capital into the business for other uses. Repayments are normally calculated to be in line with the expected income streams generated by the leased vehicles, thus making this a relatively painless way of raising additional capital for the business, providing, of course, real income matches or exceeds your predicted figures. This is not an option to be taken lightly as there are obvious risks and costs involved, but it is a useful option when undertaken for all the right reasons.

Another option that has not been mentioned is buying second-hand vehicles. The main advantage of buying a used vehicle is that you avoid that large chunk of depreciation in the initial months and years – the rate slows down considerably over time. The downside is, of course, that you lose the associated period of warranty that goes with the early years and although you should have records, you will never know exactly how the vehicle has been driven or looked after. During periods where there is a glut of used vehicles, it is a buyers' market, you generally control the negotiations. When there is a shortage of second-hand stock, as now, prices rise and you may have to accept a less than perfect specification. Buying second hand also tends to take more management time in terms of finding the right specification at the right price. Once you have selected your vehicle, you can finance it using many of the finance options available for new vehicles.

Whichever financing method you choose, whatever level of service provision you select, make absolutely sure at the outset that the responsibility for everything on the vehicle is clearly laid down in writing. Check the small print and if you do not like anything, re-negotiate it and confirm in writing before leasing the vehicle. So, for example, make sure that the responsibility for issues like:

- o roadside breakdowns
- o road user charges
- o tyre replacement & repairs
- o windscreen & glass
- o vehicle inspections
- o MoT preparation
- o vehicle presentation and repairs
- o vehicle servicing history
- o mileage limits

are all laid out clearly in the contract. Do not assume anything – always clarify such points in writing before taking on the vehicle – mistakes here can be very expensive later down the line.

Similarly, the return condition for any vehicle must be specified in the contract and is usually based on the BVRLA (British Vehicle Rental & Leasing Association) Fair Wear and Tear guide which sets out end-of-life standard terms and conditions. These have been refined over the years and are fairly well used throughout the industry, generally being fair to both sides and clearly recognising that an amount of fair wear and tear will always take place on any vehicle and increase over time. When hiring for a shorter period, I strongly suggest that you take pictures of all sides of the vehicle when collecting, as some hire companies seem, shall I say, a little forgetful of the original condition of the vehicle when charging you for any defects found at the end of the rental. I see drones are now being used by rental companies to take aerial pictures of the vehicle before and after rental, to add another bit of technology to the mix.

Handy Hint   👍

- When leasing any vehicle that will be returned, unless you have a suitable mileage pooling arrangement, the fleet manager should start monitoring mileage figures from day one so that if necessary, you can move vehicles around to average out the figures or re-negotiate mileage terms early. Operators seldom notice mileage differences and it is amazing how quickly mileage variations can build up, such that by the time you notice, it is too late to take any action and penalties can result.

If buying outright is not for you, when deciding which finance option route to choose, you also need to consider exactly what the vehicle will be used for. If it is a construction vehicle for example, used in a harsh environment, possibly a leasing agreement which expects the vehicle to be returned in good condition is not the right choice for you. Also, consider how much additional investment is involved in the vehicle and if it needs significant additional work carried out. If so, you should probably lean towards, say, a contract hire option rather than a finance lease, as the former is more flexible than the latter and could be a better option for a vehicle that is customised and still in good working order at the end of the period.

Lastly, do seek advice on your current and likely future taxation position. Your organisation needs to understand what is their right choice for tax purposes, in terms of owning or just using your vehicles. For the next few years at least, you also need to decide if you want the assets shown on your books.

10) What do I need to know about commercial vehicle insurance and self-insurance?

Really, commercial vehicle insurance should be simply entitled "risk management" because that is precisely what it is all about. Unless you deposit a large sum of money in the form of a bond with HM treasury, (and unless for some reason you just cannot obtain insurance elsewhere, I really cannot see any logical reason for doing so), you have an obligation under the Road Traffic Act to carry insurance covering the legal liability for injury to other road users and damage to their property. Partly because of increased premiums, but also because various governments have gradually, but consistently, seen fit to increase insurance tax as a great way of increasing revenue, there has been a real increase in self-insured fleets in recent years. In reality though, this means offloading the third-party risk to an insurance company and then manage all other risks yourself. The risk of obtaining a multi-million-pound third-party claim is just too great for most organisations to bear, so externalising this part of the equation makes so much sense.

In effect, self-insurance is simply a risk management tool, whereby a calculated pot of money is set aside by the organisation in order to compensate for any potential future internal claims. These losses are the result of own-fault incidents resulting in damage to the fleet's vehicles which cannot be recovered from any 3rd party. Future losses can be fairly well defined from previous history, which is simply what an insurance company will do, but adding their own profit level and fees on top. Self-insurance requires some well-defined internal rules to be set up over who pays for what and some good administration to keep accounts on track.

However, most fleets, especially small and medium sized fleets, still take the traditional approach to insurance, paying for fully comprehensive cover with the insurer taking on all of the risk, excepting an agreed excess, for every at-fault incident. The insurer pays both for repairing fleet vehicles and for any other 3rd party vehicle or property involved in an incident. Importantly, this includes any third-party injury claims, which are generally the most expensive part of vehicle insurance. It has the benefit of being simpler to manage and off-loads most of the administration of handling claims onto a broker and insurance company.

The process of deciding whether to self-insure and move from fully comprehensive becomes easier and more logical as the fleet size increases. Third party risks can account for at least half the annual premium, with another 25-30% going to other fees, made up of administration costs, insurer's profit, broker fees, reinsurance fees and government levies, leaving the rest as the cost of own damage to the fleet. So you can calculate the risks of own damage losses happening and measure against the premium you are paying to insure for that risk; if the cost of paying your own losses will be lower than the cost of insuring against those losses, then it makes sense to self-insure. At the very least, such a review may result in you increasing your excess figure, which can have a very beneficial effect on premiums.

If you decide self-insurance is for you your organisation will require an increased awareness of insurance processes, claims handling and risk management, which is why this method is more suited to larger fleets and organisations that have the appropriate resources and controls to manage the administration. Most fleets have been undertaking a risk improvement programme in recent years in order to improve their public image and reduce insurance costs. However, if self-insuring, you receive the financial benefits of such a programme almost immediately, whereas using the traditional route, you will have to wait for your insurer to reflect the improvements in reduced incidents over time through lower premiums. One thing to remember if you have been self-insuring, is that it can be a little more difficult and expensive to get back into fully comprehensive insurance again due to the lack of an insurance-based record.

Increasingly, self-insured and some traditionally insured fleets are working with accident management companies who take over the responsibility for handling at-fault claims by collecting the information and details of the incident, sourcing a replacement vehicle, assessing the damaged vehicle and handling any personal injury claims. They then arrange and chase repairs through the provider of your choice and recover costs, dealing with any legal implications from the accident through the at-fault parties' insurance provider. However, as ever, this field has become very competitive in recent times and it has become so important to select the right provider to avoid excessive charges or poor service. As with many other areas in fleet management, if you are considering using the services of an accident management company, it is really important to gain references, then look at the terms and conditions for different suppliers, side by side, to compare costs for the same activities and query anything you do not understand or charges that look excessive.

11) How can I reduce my organisation's vehicle insurance premiums?

For medium to large fleets, the single biggest factor in determining their insurance premiums is their claims history, usually taken over at least three years. Everything you do regarding insurance, therefore, should be done in order to keep that record as clean as you possibly can and importantly, reducing over time. Insurers will be particularly looking at the frequency, number and total cost of your claims. For small fleets, they tend to look more at individual driver records, especially their age and experience. For all fleets, overall mileage is a key factor.

However you are insured, there are a series of tried and tested measures you can take to reduce risk and improve your accident history, thus improving premiums. I cannot really prioritise them for you, as their effectiveness depends very much upon your operation, your insurance company and to an extent, your drivers, but they all work. Different insurance companies can take a very different view on the level of risks in your fleet and reflect that in your premiums (which is why it is so important to shop around).

So, in no particular order, the key issues to look at when attempting to reduce your insurance costs are:

1) **Camera Technology** – cameras have probably been the insurer's number one technology favourite for many years, primarily as a weapon against the rising tide of fraudulent claims. I think they overdid the reductions in premiums a few years back, which were not matched fully by reductions in incidents, but they now have far more experience of their potential. Forward facing cameras provide valuable data for promptly defending claims or swiftly settling at-fault claims. Rearward or side facing cameras are particularly effective at reducing the costs of damage claims. The monitoring effect by management also has a beneficial effect on driver behaviour which should help reduce incidents and claims.

2) **Driver training** – Insurers really like to see evidence of effective and targeted driver training programmes, especially defensive training. It is important for employees to know and see that you are monitoring incidents and taking appropriate action such as training, wherever necessary. Monitor training in parallel with your incident records to measure how effective the training has been. Where incidents look avoidable, or involved excess speed, or are repeated, make training mandatory and keep a watching brief on that particular driver for a period of time, letting them know you are doing so.

Chapter 8 on Telematics explains more about how effective the technology is in aiding and supporting the whole driver training process.

Chapter 11 on fuel management details some techniques on reducing fuel consumption by improved driving behaviour, which coincidentally, just happens to have a very direct relationship on reducing vehicle accidents.

3) **Risk Management** – it pays to work with your broker and your insurer as interested, but involved outsiders, to assist in analysing your claims history in order to highlight areas for improvement. Carry out risk assessments of all parts of the operation where incidents have happened in the recent past

and produce a plan of how to reduce the risks of future incidents. Once again, just the act of reviewing the figures can have an amazing effect on results.

4) **Young Driver Risk Management** - The shortage of commercial vehicle drivers in the UK means that many organisations have to accept drivers of all ages. However, it is well known that insurance companies take a dim view of young drivers, purely due to their very poor statistics on claims. Work with your insurance provider to restrict your use of younger drivers until they reach 25 years. Perhaps use them on smaller, lighter weight vehicles until they reach a stated number of years' service with you, or use additional tracking and a top speed limit. It is usual for most policies to dramatically increase the excess for young drivers.

5) **Limited Top Speed** – some organisations have elected to take a few mph off the legal limited top speed including a number of van operators, mainly for the reason of saving fuel. However, operators with such a policy in place state their drivers often report a psychological effect of not having to try so hard when driving, making them more relaxed and reducing incidents, which insurers love. This is not always an easy policy to get past directors but may be well worth trying.

6) **Telematics** – the fact that there is a whole chapter on Telematics in this book speaks volumes. Insurers like the fact that vehicles are constantly being monitored and can report by exception when entering or exiting areas they should or should not be in. Using Telematics fully to monitor and improve driver behaviour will considerably reduce incidents with resulting reductions in premiums. This technology is often combined with cameras, so the telematics can often pinpoint infringements and the cameras provide suitable evidence.

7) **Increased vehicle security** - for high value vehicles or loads it may be worth looking at security trackers which are hidden and have back-up batteries and often have more than one method of transmission to help find stolen vehicles. If any of your vehicles are not already sufficiently alarmed, consider fitting additional alarms, however, only if vehicle theft has proved to be a problem for your operation. If your location is a problem, there are many ways of improving the security of your depot and parking, such as better fencing or lighting, which should have a direct effect on premiums; again, best to work with your insurer to find out which interventions have the greatest financial effect.

Top Tips for Finance & Insurance ✓

- If cash flow and reserves allow, buying outright is generally the cheapest and safest way to acquire vehicles for your organisation; recognise, however, there may well be better uses for that cash, giving a better return, elsewhere in the organisation.

- If going for a leasing or finance option, shop around and evaluate the market fully; rates can vary enormously between similar suppliers.

- Always get independent financial advice on finance contracts and your Tax and VAT position before making a final decision on purchase.

- If you include maintenance in your finance contract, always check the quality of those repairers before signing the contract.

- Conduct an evaluation into self-insurance; if the figures stack up, make sure you have the administrative capability and expertise in place before starting.

- Evaluate your main insurance risks and put an action plan in place as soon as possible to reduce them; review at quarterly intervals.

- Telematics coupled with cameras are probably the most effective interventions to help get your vehicle insurance premiums down.

David's Don'ts ✗

- Don't enter a finance agreement without checking the small print fully; make sure that all vehicle activities and responsibilities are clearly laid out – refuse to sign until everything is clarified.

- Don't use an accident management company without a full review of their Terms & Conditions and a full check on their referrals.

- When presenting your business plans to finance organisations, don't go into chapter and verse, stick to the essential figures.

The Ultimate Guide to Commercial Vehicle Fleet Management

Chapter 6 – New Technology and Alternative Fuels for Commercial Vehicles

1) *What is the background to alternative fuel for Commercial Vehicles?*
2) *What are the primary alternatives to the ICE (Internal Combustion Engine) and emerging technologies available to you now and in the foreseeable future – how will they develop over the next decade?*
3) *What are the basic advantages of alternative fuels for fleet use?*
4) *What are the basic disadvantages of alternative fuels?*
5) *What new and emerging vehicle technologies are already in existence, available now and how are they likely to be developed further in the future?*
6) *What other new vehicle technologies should you be aware of that may appear in the next ten years?*
7) *What are some of the potential pitfalls of new technology to be aware of, now and in the future?*

It is worth mentioning here that every country has their own way of dealing with emerging technology, with their own infrastructure, often their own version of the legislation and their own future plans. Generally, these will be focussed in order to benefit their own industries as suppliers and also their consumers, of course, supporting their own transport industry. However, as much of new technology effects everyone around the globe in a similar fashion and most of us recognise the need to reduce our environmental impact, the majority of the following comments are applicable around the world, but some points mentioned obviously reflect the situation specifically applying here in the UK.

1) What is the background to alternative fuel for Commercial Vehicles?

There are currently a number of alternatives available to the petrol or diesel engine; most are being developed like crazy at the moment and their supporters will all tell you that their way is definitely best. Trying to predict which energy sources will be the winners for transport over the next ten years is a tricky game. The truth is, whatever I say, in ten years' time things will have moved on considerably and we will have adapted to whatever changes take place over the period. That is why you can find so many wonderful predictions, articles and scenarios in newspapers, the trade press, pod casts, TV and radio interviews, saying that the transport world will turn to all electric, hydrogen, gas, nuclear or whatever. I have to say there is occasionally a substantial lack of knowledge and hence responsibility on behalf of the persons or organisations making these predictions. The fact is that at this juncture, nobody really knows the full picture, although some routes are much more likely to happen than others.

During my spell working for the government sponsored Knowledge Transfer Network as the transport expert within the Location and Timing arena, we must have seen at least a hundred presentations from academia, start-up companies or big business predicting "the very next big thing" in the satellite and telecommunications business. Nearly all of them looked good, with definite benefits for the user, there was often impressive and clever technology being utilised and you could see the end user wanting to adopt whatever was on offer. Of those 100 +, I suspect only between five to seven actually came to market in real life and you can probably find many of them, in some format, as apps on your mobile phone right now.

The reason why the other fledgling ideas, some of them really clever, inventive and useful, never came to fruition is simple. They had to be fully commercially viable so the sales offering had to make sense and the business model must also be right for all the businesses involved in the supply chain, so everyone has to be making a profit, or at least getting a business benefit at some stage. In addition, as we are talking about completely new technologies in a changing world, the technology has to be developed, standards written so that everyone can use it, legislation might have to change, accompanying technology may need to be developed, all in parallel with infrastructure changes, societal changes and any other changes that the inventors and developers anticipated would happen. That is a big ask and a long and torturous journey, which may or may not happen as predicted, in the right sequence over time. It is like a horse race, where first one horse is ahead, then another, and like horse racing, it is very difficult to predict the outcome, else we would all be very rich!

Many other factors come into play when considering alternative energy technology for transport. Very early in my career with Ford, I attended a meeting where a really senior executive from Ford of America said quite emphatically "we are just five years away from mass production of hydrogen vehicles - hydrogen is the future fuel of the world".

That was over 45 years ago and sadly hydrogen has been five years away from production for all my career and probably still is. Yes, there are a small number of production vehicles in existence and Japan & California have a small infrastructure in gestation. However, there are some good reasons why, without additional technology breakthroughs, it is not likely to extend much further in the very near future.

Hydrogen Power is already here, just not yet Commercially Viable

It takes massive amounts of energy to extract hydrogen in the first place, it is not so easy to store, transport and distribute, and is only 35% efficient at converting back into propulsion energy, more inefficient than some other useful fuels, like diesel. So, yes, it is fantastic at reducing environmental pollution at the tailpipe, however it will not do much for decarbonising the planet as a (relatively) inefficient power source, unless surplus green power becomes available in large quantities. Having said that, it is a front runner for HGVs over the next ten years as it is one of the few fuels that has the energy density available to replace diesel. The problem is, you will find any number of commentators ready to say that hydrogen is the fuel of the future, but until we find the ways to get over its inherent problems, I would suggest it remains an outsider. To get the technical details on hydrogen and other alternative fuels for transport, rather than excited headlines, look at a blog on the subject written by David Cebon here:http://www.csrf.ac.uk/2020/12/electricity-or-hydrogen-economy/

Possibly the most sensible advice to be found on the subject of transport energy came from a really clever person called Sir David MacKay, Chief UK Government Scientific Adviser on Climate and Energy, who very sadly died of cancer in 2016. One of the most sensible presentations ever made on energy was by him in a TEDx talk in 2012 – find it here:

(https://www.ted.com/talks/david_mackay_a_reality_check_on_renewables?langua ge=en#t-6646). Amongst other topics, he looked at the subject of biofuels, which at the time many people were saying was the way forward (some said the only way forward) for transport. He conducted a very rough calculation on a single carriageway road, carrying only cars with average fuel consumption, travelling at average speed, 80 m apart and asked how much land alongside the road would be required to grow biofuel to keep these vehicles moving? The surprising answer was a strip of land 8 km wide.

So, a four-lane motorway would require 32 km of land alongside it in order to fuel just cars on the motorway. If you then add all other forms of transport, including HGVs and contemplate the whole of the United Kingdom covered in huge network of motorway and dual carriageways corridors for just growing biofuel; logically, this suggests that biofuel as our prime transport resource is also an outsider. Sir David MacKay did not propose that any one energy source was the solution to the problem of decarbonising transport. What he did say is that we really do need to have grown-up discussions on the way forward based on the real facts and statistics available to us right now and not just lobby groups proposing that their vision was the only way forward because of certain advantages their fuel type.

Handy Hint 👍

- When calculating whether the finances for alternative technology vehicles add up, use very rough ("back-of-the-envelope") figures first, extracted from sources such as government websites to check if the vehicle is viable. If it is, then progress to the detailed calculations.

So, given this ever-changing and unclear scenario, how can operators plan their future vehicle purchases for the next ten years or so, if no particular fuel can be seen to be the favoured technology to use? For anyone buying or replacing a vehicle fleet, they face huge question marks regarding the infrastructure, service arrangements and residual values of an alternatively fuelled vehicle fleet. And it is not just fuels that operators have to grapple with, a number of new vehicle technologies have appeared in the last ten years and it is really tough to know where it will go in the next ten years.

Before switching to an alternative fuel, in order to check if the right decision is being made, operators need to consider 'hard' factors such as:

- The base vehicle cost, with grants and discounts applied
- Infrastructure change costs, with grants, if applicable
- Maintenance & repair costs over the life of the vehicle
- Expected resale values (obviously the best estimate for newer technology)
- Fuel availability, both at base and en-route, now & in the future

- Total distances involved, now & in the future
- Typical routes with average mileages and the effect of a new fuel
- Factor in any financial effects of changes in load capacity
- Factor in any financial effects of changes to the operation
- Whole life vehicle cost profile, amortising any infrastructure costs

Going through the above process, especially the total life cost profile, should give a clear indication of the cost of such a move to the organisation. Currently, vehicles such as battery electric will likely be dearer to buy, but cheaper to run, meaning their total life costs will be comparable, with possibly some infrastructure or operational costs to take into account.

Once 'hard' factors are accounted for, then 'softer' issues, such as a cleaner working environment, public image and benefits to the planet can be added to the mix and discussed fully by decision makers. The important point here is to make sure all costs and effects are factored into the equation, so there are few surprises downstream.

Given that there is so much information out there, some conflicting, how do fleet operators make sense of it in order to make a decision on future vehicle purchases? The following is the best estimate scenario I can muster based on all the information, statistics and evidence currently to hand.

2) *What are the primary alternatives to the ICE (Internal Combustion Engine) available to you now and in the foreseeable future – how will they develop over the next decade?*

Let's not beat about the bush – despite what politicians and environmentalists will have you believe, the diesel engine is with us for some time to come, certainly for HGVs where there is currently no real viable option, mainly due to the energy density of diesel fuel. In other words, it is the most viable fuel for carrying heavy loads and do not forget the diesel engine has been the most efficient mass-produced ICE (internal combustion engine) for around 130 years. For this reason, manufacturers will continue to make steady improvements of the diesel powertrain, in terms of efficiency & emissions, although research efforts are of course, now majoring on alternative fuels.

At some stage, Euro 7 emission regulations will come into force, the most likely date currently being around 2025. If the UK wish to continue selling into Europe, it will have to follow these regulations. The introduction of Euro 7 has been delayed primarily by the VW diesel fiasco, when regulatory authorities realised they really must utilise real-world measuring of emissions, not just rely on test results. We have also reached a point where the demand for low Carbon Dioxide, low Particulate Matter, and low Nitrogen Oxide each place very conflicting demands in technical terms on engines and especially diesel engines, so it is no easy task to decide what the new lower targets should be.

Cities around the world are also making their own individual demands on what emission levels they require and there is the added complexity that at these very low levels, measuring these pollutants is no easy task, either in the operating engine or on the test bed. A move towards the integration of emission standards is expected, and hopefully the gradual introduction of global, rather than the regional standards, that have sprung up in recent years, the latter making vehicle specifications both difficult and expensive for operators and manufacturers alike.

Incentive schemes for road freight transport operators are likely to continue in order to encourage and support operator investments in alternatively fuelled vehicles. Unfortunately, although the basis for the incentive is usually backed by sensible scientific advice, the actual implementation will be politically driven. It is then almost impossible to estimate what or how much these incentives will be, when they will be applied, in what format and for how long. Experience shows they have a habit of drying up at inconvenient moments, due to political priorities or changing financial imperatives. However, they must be factored into the buying process, providing whole life costs are also taken into account and the incentive does not become the prime reason for operating that type of vehicle.

Systems of taxation that were based largely on vehicle ownership or the type of propulsion energy used, have moved towards taxation systems based upon environmental performance and the type of vehicle used. This principle will continue to apply to all road vehicles, including commercial vehicles. Politicians will not wish to slow the advance of electric vehicles, but will be faced with a massive drop in revenue from current fuel duty, so some form of charging by use is extremely likely to be introduced, although a road user tax in the UK is seen by politicians as the road equivalent of a poll tax, the introduction of which helped to bring down the Thatcher government in 1990, so a smarter alternative will have to be found to make it more politically acceptable.

Despite a recent spike in oil prices, due to the economy restarting after a lockdown, which followed an all-time low price for a number of years, experts believe that oil prices are likely to rise steadily over the period, mainly driven by political and producer's commercial action, rather than by supply and demand. Efforts to decarbonise the electric power generation grid will certainly continue through the decade. Rapid decarbonisation of the power sector will be required to satisfy increased demand as the transport sectors become further electrified. This has to be achieved by increasing the share of low-carbon energy sources, particularly renewables, with a corresponding reduction in the use of fossil fuels.

Worldwide, renewables now produce around a third of power capacity. Capping greenhouse gas emissions from fossil fuel power stations by installing Carbon

Capture & Storage (CCS) is playing an increasing role globally and it is claimed that it even has the potential to generate 'negative emissions', removing CO_2 from the atmosphere. This is being combined with bioenergy technologies for power generation. In the short term a shift from 'dirtier' coal to lower-emission natural gas helps to reduce power plant emissions, but of course needs to be replaced, primarily with renewables such as wind and solar power.

Measures to prepare the electricity grid for increased usage by road transport vehicles, including commercial vehicles, are already being taken and will increase in the next decade. Long-term electricity production plans must obviously take into account the increased demand from electric vehicles. Along the way, there are many challenges that need to be overcome due to the growth of renewable energy, giving rise to considerable grid integration costs and extended planning requirements.

Currently, when intermittent resources are at a low point, the power market responds with conventional substitute resources, but in a decarbonised future, those options will not be acceptable or available. The UK has already started to recognize this and is looking at battery energy storage and distributed resources as two possible options, so the energy contained within electric vehicles is increasingly seen as playing a part in this scenario. The sector is too small to be playing a significant part at the moment, but this will change in the foreseeable future.

In parallel, the technology behind improved battery technology and improved charging technology will continue to improve the usability of electric vehicles, meaning increased conversion rates from ICE. Although improvements in battery technology have been happening for 100 years or more, the global effort behind R&D (Research & Development) in this area is currently staggering, resulting in ever-increasing battery capacity and decreasing charge times. There are also substantial efforts underway to remove the more toxic and rare components of batteries, making them more environmentally acceptable. It is really important to remember that at the moment the environmental footprint of a new electric vehicle is considerably higher than an equivalent ICE vehicle, and represents a large proportion of its lifetime carbon footprint, although they are annoyingly still continually described as "clean".

Obviously, the wholesale adoption of electric vehicles will not happen until the infrastructure improves and many operators report current difficulties in getting improved supplies to their premises. However, the cost and performance of batteries is perhaps the biggest factor in the acceptability of electric power for commercial vehicles. Currently, the move towards electric vehicles is often driven by a demand either from the customer or a local emission reduction initiative, but as the storage energy density and cost (i.e., watts per £) and recharging time reduces, so will the uptake of electric commercial vehicles for business reasons, particularly as they extend into heavier weight ranges.

It is evident that regional and local deliveries, especially urban delivery, will increasingly move to electric battery-powered operations, as the infrastructure and battery design is improved. As an important aside, at the time of writing, Oslo has recently commenced a trial which is testing wireless charging for electric taxis. Plates in the road top up the battery every time the vehicle comes through the taxi rank. This means, if the trial works, that the taxis stay virtually fully charged for most of their working life. Unsurprisingly, there is a slight efficiency loss (around 10%) for the convenience of mobile charging, offset by removing the need for the "downtime" of charging the taxis. Using this method could mean that vehicles with the right duty cycles have more than one driver and are utilised for 24 hours in the day.

Advanced testing of electrified long-distance transport is likely to continue, including via the electricity grid, most likely from overhead catenary wires or perhaps a more advanced form of wireless charging. This type of solution does not really allow for incompatible systems from country to country, so road infrastructure authorities, especially across Europe, will have to be seen to be working together in testing and development in order to unify standards and technologies that can be used by the different types of vehicles involved. In parallel, a suitable cross-border finance mechanism will have to be developed in order to allow infrastructure development for the long term, if electric long-distance transport is to be introduced before the end of the decade

Current Biofuel Research & Development, with continuous advances, will operate at the periphery of alternative transport fuels and will become a relatively small part of the solution, but is highly unlikely to ever become mainstream due to the need for increased food production and competition for land use. The technological development of advanced biofuels is expected to speed up, probably aided by a long-term legislative framework which could include incentives, such as quotas or CO2- based fuel taxes.

In order to explain these last comments, let's unpack the current Biofuel situation a little further:

Biofuels are produced from renewable organic materials with two main types used in UK vehicles: bioethanol and biodiesel. Bioethanol is an alcohol generally made from corn and sugarcane, mainly used in cars, whereas biodiesel is made using vegetable oils and animal fats and generally a recycled material, but both offer an alternative to the non-renewable crude-oil derived fuels of petrol and diesel. Biofuels tend to be seen as a short to medium-term solution to traditional fuels as we move towards a probable world where electric vehicles are the norm.

Importantly, Bioethanol is largely classed as carbon-neutral, as any carbon dioxide released is arguably removed from the atmosphere by the crops themselves. Biodiesel, however, recycles otherwise unusable waste products, such as animal fats and cooking oil. Very roughly speaking, depending very much on the source of the fuel and the processes used in production, biodiesel cuts CO2 emissions by around 75% whereas bioethanol reduces emissions by up to nearly 50%. It has to be said that some experts are challenging those figures and suggest that not as much CO2 is absorbed by the plants and more is produced in the growing process, making the process less environmentally friendly than claimed.

Biofuels are mainly used in the UK mainly as part of blended fuels; petrol and diesel that is blended with a certain percentage of biofuel to make them more environmentally friendly. Unleaded petrol from UK forecourts used to contain anything up to 5% bioethanol, whilst regular diesel includes anything up to 7% biodiesel. Only around 3% of UK vehicles run solely on biofuels, with cooking oil derivatives currently the most popular. There are no real issues in using current blended fuels, however, in order to increase our contribution to global emissions, the UK government has recently consulted on the introduction of a 10% ethanol blend (E10), generally supplied throughout Europe and has now introduced it to the UK, late in 2021. Operators need to be aware that this potentially may cause problems on some older vehicles, as it is more aggressive on seals and components around the engine, so need to check that their vehicles can run on the higher blend. (Visit https://www.gov.uk/check-vehicle-e10-petrol for details). As well as providing a use for organic waste products, blended fuels produce fewer carbon emissions, meaning the higher the percentage of biofuel, the less carbon emissions produced.

It could be argued that biofuel is already fairly widely used in the UK in blended fuels. In Brazil and Sweden, however, vehicles are available that run on 85% ethanol which in theory, could happen in the UK in the next decade. Given the scenario described earlier in this chapter of how much land is required to produce biofuels, many simply see biofuels as a stopgap solution, hence the lack of major investment so far. Following the government's announcement to ban the sale of all pure ICE small vehicles by 2030, biofuels look fairly certain to be overtaken by electricity when it comes to road transport, certainly for lighter vehicles.

Generally, most biofuels cost less than fossil fuels, depending on the current price of crude oil and the tax regime applicable at the time. This reduction in price needs to be tempered by the knowledge that the lack of availability or accessibility to fuelling stations will effectively increase costs, depending on relative locations & distances. Generally, Biofuels are slightly less efficient than their fossil counterparts, so actual fuel consumption increases.

Continued steady improvement in the gas powertrain is likely to continue, along with the development of biogas capacity for use in commercial road freight transport, prioritising such production methods as methane producing digesters. For completeness, there is a technology called GTL (Gas to Liquid), which converts natural gas to liquid fuels, such as kerosene. Although the resulting product is cleaner than fuel derived from crude oil, it is still a fossil fuel so does not really have a future in a decarbonised world.

A section of transport is already running on gas, often utility vehicles based in cities and urban environments, as the fuels burn much cleaner than petrol or diesel and therefore pollute the environment less. The most utilised forms being CNG (Compressed Natural Gas), LNG (Liquified Natural Gas) and LPG (Liquified Petroleum Gas). The last one, LPG, is not actually a natural gas, but is instead obtained by distilling oil and is made up of butane and propane. It is stored in a liquid state at low pressures of around 10 bar. CNG is a type of natural gas and is stored at room temperature at high pressures between 200 and 250 bar. LNG is a liquid gas stored at -162 degrees, thus reducing its volume by around 600 times. It also has the benefit of being odourless, colourless, non-toxic and non-flammable and due to its higher energy density, is also useful for providing longer ranges between fill-ups.

All these gasses are similar, but treated differently, having different operating regimes, differing advantages and disadvantages, especially in terms of cost and consumption. Providing tax regimes do not alter too far, they are generally cheaper than conventional fuels. However, aside from cleaner burning, the big advantage is that they produce around 30% less CO_2 than conventional fuels. The big disadvantage, of course, is that they are still fossil fuels and therefore are only really useful in the transition stage of decarbonising transport. There is also a big handicap in that methane often gets released in the production process of fossil gasses. In environmental terms, methane has 28 times the global warming value of CO_2, which tends to neutralise any benefits of burning cleaner.

Hybrid vehicles are an excellent mid-term transport solution, much misunderstood and often mis-used on the wrong duty cycles, such as steady-state motorway running. Hybrids effectively return considerable previously lost energy when decelerating back as stored power to be used again when needed. Formula 1 cars show just how clever these systems can get when required and a lot of effort is put into the design and refinement of the system. Hybrid energy is also likely to contribute more to long-haul transport in the future, including the use of on-demand hybrid systems to provide auxiliary power around the vehicle, when needed.

3) What are the basic advantages of alternative fuels for fleet use?

There is a huge mass of information out there on future transport fuels, some of which conflicts, depending on the source and what axe they have to grind. In order to assist in the decision-making process for future vehicles, I have very briefly synthesised the pros and cons of the main various alternative fuel options, as far as I know them:

Main points of differentiation and advantages:

Biodiesel

- Produces fewer carbon emissions and harmful particulates than standard diesel.
- Availability is much lower than diesel, but it retains the option of filling up with standard diesel when required.
- Biodiesel is more energy efficient in its production than petroleum products
- Better fuel costs than regular vehicles.

Ethanol

- Mixture of petrol and a propellant derived from grain.
- Needs conversion from a pure petrol engine.
- Emissions-friendly fuel.

Hybrid

- Combination of mainly petrol or sometimes diesel and electric power.
- Electric battery (or equivalent device) stores energy during driving and slowing – most suitable for continuous changes of speed, where waste energy can be harvested, saving fuel costs.
- Plug-in hybrid batteries can be charged through cheaper grid electricity – vehicles with short journey cycles use less or no hydrocarbons, but retain range capability when required.

Hydrogen

- When derived from water, it is fully renewable.
- Exhaust environment-friendly, dispenses water back into the environment.
- Good energy density therefore little or no range anxiety.
- Zero emissions at the tailpipe.

Battery Electricity

- Much cheaper to run (currently no effective fuel duty – likely to increase).
- Cheaper to maintain (fewer moving parts).
- No tailpipe emissions, although currently grid power still 50% fossil based.

o When so equipped, can supply back to grid at peak times, balancing demand.

Bioenergy from Food Waste helps decarbonisation

4) What are the basic disadvantages of alternative fuels?

Biodiesel

o More expensive to produce than regular diesel.

o Where not recycled, reduces land available for growing food crops.

o Large-scale, mainstream production would use vast amounts of land.

o Slight increase in maintenance costs due to increased oil changes.

Ethanol

o Ethanol contains less energy than petrol, so delivers less mpg.

o Very limited supply of ethanol fuel blend as E85 or E100.

o Some experts suggest that emissions from fossil fuels used in producing the grain, exceed the ethanol's own emission benefits.

Hybrid

o Higher capital costs.

- o Slightly higher maintenance costs (two power sources).
- o Some doubts about the longevity of the storing battery – however, many hybrid vehicles of 10 years age or more still have operating battery capacity.
- o Hybrids are heavier due to the motor & batteries, so the right operating duties are crucial - not suitable for steady speed operations.

Hydrogen

- o Cost-effective mass production has proved elusive for many years.
- o Additional transport & delivery safety issues over petrol or diesel.
- o High production energy requirements.
- o High loss conversion back to electricity.

Battery Electricity

- o Higher upfront capital costs, likely to reduce over time
- o Limited range, likely to increase over time
- o Availability of recharging points is low, increasing somewhat now
- o Time to recharge can be long; reducing over time or with more expensive fast charging but still interrupts journeys and delivery schedules significantly

5) What new vehicle technologies are already in existence, available now and how are they likely to be developed further in the future?

Having talked about the many possible fuels we may be using in ten years' time; we also need to consider the advances in vehicle technology that have occurred in recent years. The driving factor behind technologies in this group is nearly always safety. They are generally advances in the sophistication of how vehicles respond, often introduced when someone asks the question "wouldn't it be good if ......?"

These advances nearly always appear in very much the same way; after R&D and testing is completed, they are first introduced into top-of-the-range vehicles as a very expensive and much-discussed option, later becoming more widely available on more, perhaps all, models in the range, usually as a much less expensive option. Finally, the technology becomes a standard fit item on all vehicles in the range and becomes incorporated in the list price of the vehicle. By then, manufacturers and buyers have determined that this new technology has now become the new "norm" for that class of vehicle. The speed this happens depends on lots of factors, not least what other competitors offer in the same area and the stage of a particular model in its life cycle.

You can group the technologies that already exist on vehicles in a number of ways. For starters, there are ADAS, (Advanced Driver Assistance Systems), often with semi-autonomous capabilities, normally using AI (Artificial Intelligence) within increasingly complex electronic systems, generally in the form of technologies that assist the driver. These have been creeping into vehicle specifications over the last ten years or more and are still being heavily developed.

These technologies have been developed by vehicle manufacturers as added features to help sell their vehicles, whilst at the same time giving them valuable research and development experience. This experience and feedback will aid them greatly in their ultimate goal to be leaders in the race to deliver autonomous vehicles. Most of these technologies are already familiar to current drivers.

These technologies include such items as:

- Automatic-braking sensors & systems – these can take over from the driver if they do not notice potential risks or are not braking hard enough in a given situation, or apply the brakes if the driver has not noticed a hazard for any reason.
- Lane adherence and change sensors & systems – alerts the driver to wandering or reduces potential to change lanes when a vehicle is in their blind spot.
- Blind spot sensors & monitoring – useful on all vehicles, but perhaps most useful and most prominent for HGVs in left turn situations.
- 360-degree cameras – used as additional information and blind spot reduction.
- Adaptive cruise control – keeps vehicles a set distance apart and reduces stress on the driver.
- Telematic systems that remember routes and terrain - improved technology to anticipate hills, traffic and other road features, sometimes changing gears on AMT gearboxes.
- Self-parking capabilities – more often found on cars, but a stress reducer, especially for drivers not very familiar with their vehicles and a low-speed collision reducer.

As this sort of technology become available more widely, there will be an additional, possibly surprising effect, in that the focus of driver training in the future can be expected to shift away from merely taking straightforward actions, towards properly reading, using and reacting to ADAS features. This happened to some extent when ABS brakes were introduced and many drivers did not fully understand their operation. Be aware that increasingly, ADAS technology is also becoming available as a retrofit option. A number of academic studies suggest that the cost benefits from reduced accidents and incidents fairly rapidly outweigh the cost of supplying and fitting. These are further items that will require trials and testing as the financial benefits will vary considerably from fleet to fleet.

There is another group of new technologies which one can see simply as on-going natural advances in vehicle design and become part of the ever-increasing complexity and sophistication of a modern vehicle. Whilst the technology will be developing over time, in this group, they are not a necessary development for autonomous vehicles. This group includes technology such as:

- Virtual mirrors (camera & screen) – replacing increasingly large and expensive mirrors, reducing blind spots and the potential for damage, as well as drag and wind noise.
- Digital rear-view mirror for vans (showing enhanced rear views) – acting very much as a driver aid to help reduce slow speed incidents.
- Under vehicle cameras (for blind spots) - modern vehicle design tends to reduce the ability to position the vehicle precisely when manoeuvring.
- Increased driver monitoring for response, lack of attention, onset of sleep or illness – DDAW (Driver Drowsiness Awareness Warning) - these can take control of the vehicle if necessary, - likely to be introduced on all new vehicles under EU regulations between 2022 and 2024.
- Alcohol Interlock Facilitation (AIF) – the driver has to breathe into an alcohol monitor to start the vehicle - likely to be introduced on all new vehicles under EU regulations between 2022 and 2024; although they have been in use in the UK on some PSV (Public Service Vehicle) operations for some time, and available as an accessory.
- Intelligent Speed Assist (ISA) – uses a speed sign-recognition video camera and/or GPS-linked speed limit data to advise drivers of the current speed limit and automatically limit the speed of the vehicle as needed - likely to be introduced on all new vehicles under EU regulations between 2022 and 2024. This technology produces an interesting response in most drivers, who almost universally hate, or certainly dislike, the idea until they try it for any length of time. Surveys then tend to show considerable driver acceptance and reports of feeling much more relaxed at the wheel.
- Intelligent glass – manual or auto tinting of glass, likely to be increasingly utilised on direct vision vehicles with large glass areas, useful for helping to keep vehicles cool, reducing air-conditioning use and hence power consumption.
- Intelligent headlights – after 100 years or so, this is at last likely to eliminate the need for a dipped beam by blocking out the part of the beam pointing

at on coming vehicles and able to better illuminate potential hazards and corners.

- On screen displays – largely a spin-off from the aeronautical industry, they have been around for some time but not yet widely offered or adopted, useful for reducing the driver's need to take their eyes off the road.
- Intelligent tyres – greater data feedback to alert drivers and management to issues plus the ability to change pressure whilst travelling, reducing the need for constant checks and giving the ability to improve grip and traction for differing road surfaces whilst on the move.
- Turning assistance – generally helping the driver with blind spots or judging the speed of other vehicles – this last one will, of course, also be of significant use in developing autonomous vehicles.

This second group of technologies will all continue to be developed into the next decade until such time as autonomous vehicles can be sold in any quantities, when research will be focussed on improving technologies for autonomy and therefore reduce effort spent on driver aids.

All the technologies mentioned here present no major issues when buying vehicles, apart from increasing complexity, as they should all be fully supported by the manufactures and updated when necessary. The buying decision will be a moderately simple one of affordability; so, does the safety or advantages of the particular option warrant the extra expenditure at the time of buying and will it positively effect residual values or maybe reduce incidents? These sorts of choices have faced vehicle buyers for many years. Most fleet buyers will probably wait for the second wave of availability, after any initial bugs have been ironed out, prices have dropped significantly and the option in question is more widely accepted and available across more of the model ranges.

6) *What other new vehicle technologies should you be aware of that may appear in the next ten years?*

Predictive vehicle technology that informs the owner when the vehicle needs servicing or inspection has been around and in limited use by some fleets for the last decade or so. What is very likely to happen in the next decade, sooner rather than later, is that this technology becomes mainstream and standard in use. It will also go much further and carry out things like automatically conducting some of the current daily driver vehicle checks, then more importantly, depending on mileage and condition, the vehicle technology will be able to estimate its current performance, flag up any issues to management and with authority protocols, set up repair appointments in real time with allocated service agents and inform users of any safety hazards linked with a malfunctioning vehicle or recalls.

More advanced Predictive Vehicle Technology will become more common place. Artificial intelligence (AI) and machine learning (ML) will also feature heavily in the future of the commercial vehicle industry. Predictive capabilities are already becoming more prevalent in vehicles. Manufacturers are applying algorithms that use data to automate the process of setting up a vehicle, including a vehicle's application preferences. Vehicles are becoming IoT (Internet of Things) devices which can connect to external IT sources to alter commands, changing the user interface. All this technology is generally available now, but is not so readily used due to the standards and legislation that needs to support it and also the worry by manufacturers and government agencies that systems could be "hacked" by criminals and others with evil intent; therefore, the security of such devices needs to be very high indeed before releasing to the general population.

It is likely that there will be continued revision of EU weights and dimensions legislation and related type-approvals, along with general safety rules, allowing further flexibility in vehicle weights and dimensions on the grounds of both environmental performance and road safety. Hopefully, this should create possibilities for increased carrying capacity, provided that infrastructure-related performance standards are still met, including turning-circle, vehicle width and axle (weight, number and type) requirements. Despite our leaving the EU, these weights and dimension revisions are also likely to be reflected in the UK.

The general trend of more aerodynamic vehicles and cabs should continue in the forthcoming years and carry on through into autonomous vehicles, which will also benefit equally from such design changes. It is likely that weight and dimension regulations will accommodate any improved vehicle designs to allow for technology advances and improved aerodynamics of complete vehicle combinations. Certainly, the introduction of Euro VI regulations, with the accompanying equipment this involved, made space very tight on many vehicle chassis. It will not be possible to keep adding to the equipment required on vehicles for ever without some relaxation on dimensions and possibly weights.

Trials of Truck "Platooning", where a number of vehicles are connected wirelessly and led by the driver of the lead truck, are still in progress in the UK and the EU, although delayed by the pandemic. The general initial feedback is that it does give some level of fuel saving, improves the use of road space and the drivers involved feel safer than expected pre-trials. Drivers have only had to interrupt in about 2% of cases by changing speed or direction, mainly due to someone cutting into the platoon's road space. Results are a little more mixed in the UK, where higher congestion means savings and practicality are perhaps not as great as on European roads. If the technology is to go ahead, the implementation of the EU regulatory framework would probably allow truck platooning on all major European roads by around 2025 or so. However, this could be a useful first step towards the use of fully autonomous commercial vehicles.

On that last subject, the biggest technology change in the next ten years will undoubtably be autonomous vehicles. As mentioned before, existing technology, such as reactive cruise control, has been moving that way for some time. Tesla unfortunately muddied the waters somewhat by claiming they had produced a fully autonomous car, but it only effectively reaches level 2 autonomy (see levels of autonomy below). Other vehicle makers claim to be able to achieve level 3, but choose not to manufacture in that format. Full autonomy is the big goal for all vehicle manufacturers, so the process will be commercially and technically driven, but requires allowing by legislation. Further developments in regulatory frameworks should enable progress in vehicle automation to take place within the decade.

This need explaining a little more. The Society of Automotive Engineers (SAE) defined 6 levels of driving automation ranging from 0 (fully manual) to 5 (fully autonomous). These have been largely adopted by most manufacturers operating in the autonomous arena. Briefly these are defined as follows:

Level 0 – No Automation - A human does all the driving

Level 1 – Driver Assistance - ADAS (Advanced Driver Assistance System) on the vehicle can sometimes assist a human in steering and braking or accelerating, but not simultaneously

Level 2 – Partial Automation - ADAS on the vehicle can control both steering and braking or accelerating, simultaneously under some circumstances. A human must pay full attention by "monitoring the driving environment" at all times, also performing the other driving tasks

Level 3 – Conditional Automation - ADS (Automated Driving System) on the vehicle can perform all aspects of the driving task under some circumstances. A human must be available to monitor the environment and be ready to take back control whenever the ADS requests, or it is required. In all other circumstances, a human performs the driving task.

Level 4 – High Automation - ADS on the vehicle can perform all driving tasks and monitor the driving environment – essentially, doing all the driving in certain circumstances. A human need not pay attention in those circumstances, but be available to take control.

Level 5 – Full Automation - ADS on the vehicle can do all the driving in all circumstances. Human occupants are now only passengers and never need be involved; driving is then optional.

In essence, many vehicles are already at level 2, with some others capable of level 3, although not manufactured in that format and legislation does not allow this level in many areas of the world. Level 4 is available under test conditions, or in very limited areas where legislation allows. A review by Consultants McKinsey & Company in

2017 concluded that the overriding blockage to producing level 5 vehicles in the next ten years would be software development. The hardware is already largely available, however the issue for autonomous vehicle software is the range of environments that a human can cope with, that a computer has to mimic. This is (relatively!) easy in urban conditions, where street furniture and limits such as clear markings are available. However, imagine being in an open landscape when heavy falling snow wipes out most easily recognisable road features. Then imagine tackling this same landscape at all hours of the day or night with the consequent varying light levels. The software has to tackle the mass of information coming from sensors in these scenarios and many, many others.

The problem for legislators will also be manyfold. Firstly, how will the change period, when some vehicles are autonomous and some driven, be handled. There are also problems for semi-autonomous systems where a human is present and the system hands back control to the driver for any reason – if the human has not been paying attention, by the time they reassess the driving environment, it may be too late. Secondly, as mentioned, will be the conundrum of how to prevent undesirables 'hacking' into vehicle systems, causing them to undertake unintended manoeuvres or actions. Fully autonomous vehicles will leave yet another problem for operators as to how to reorganise their workforce, along with existing policies and procedures, often currently led by the role of drivers. There are also some jobs routinely currently undertaken by drivers, such as vehicle inspection and administration that will have to be carried out elsewhere.

However, there are signs that the major automotive manufacturers are speeding up the process by collaboration with global giants such as Amazon, Google and Microsoft, who in turn, have already invested heavily in developing the software and hardware for robotics and autonomous vehicles. Many countries, such as Germany, also see the benefits of autonomous vehicles and are assisting the process with grants, infrastructure and legislation changes.

Although many industry commentators may not agree, there are four other important dynamics that I believe will put autonomous vehicles on the road, in some format, before the end of the decade. Firstly, most countries, including well developed countries, have horrendous road accident and death records, largely brought about by human error. These can be almost eliminated by fully autonomous vehicles, along with the benefit of reducing the associated costs to infrastructure repairs, emergency services and the health systems. Second is the commercial gain for the winners of this race. In a relatively short period of time, most motorists and transport operators in the developed world will wish to move to autonomous vehicles from their current machines and, by the way, they will also need to be fully decarbonised. Thirdly, drivers will now become passengers and able to undertake other functions whilst on the move. Providing this does not merely mean increased time commenting on social media, it should result in major productivity improvements. Lastly, the current constraints on driver's hours would also be eliminated, meaning vehicles could operate almost 24 hours a day. These industry drivers are so attractive to so many parties that the pace of development cannot fail to increase dramatically in the coming decade.

7) What are some of the potential pitfalls of new technology to be aware of, now and in the future?

Some of the newer technology features existing on vehicles today such as blind-spot warning systems and collision avoidance systems have allowed drivers, especially relatively young or inexperienced individuals, to get complacent behind the wheel. Instead of using their eyes and mirrors, they start to rely more and more on the technology. Despite how useful these advances can be, it cannot reveal all that their own eyes and senses can. In addition, despite careful setting up, technology such as nearside blind spot sensors have a habit of issuing false warnings, which through human nature, start to become ignored. And to counter that problem is the opposite one of sensor failure, where no warnings are issued at all. There is not space to comprehensively examine the subject here, except to remind you to include the subject fully in your driver training, in order to alert your drivers of the potential pitfalls and dangers of overly relying on technology.

Currently the most likely alternatively fuelled vehicle in any fleet will be battery electric, especially at the lower end of the weight range. The early adopters of this technology tended to be local authorities, generally to demonstrate to the public that they were going "green", or commercial enterprises that also wanted to demonstrate their environmental credentials to customers or shareholders. Unfortunately, in their keenness to get the vehicles in service, the charging structure was not always fully thought through before purchase.

The power requirements for one or two trial vehicles were probably easy to accommodate, but then as the numbers of EV's on the fleet started to increase, the limits of power supply for the site were often reached, more quickly if rapid charging with much increased power requirements was involved. Upgrades could then become eye wateringly expensive. Please learn from these early mistakes and make sure charging requirements are always included in the overall project plan, making due allowance for future growth. Also be careful of plans for "smart charging" and "load management" where vehicles have to obtain power at certain times of the day from shared charging points. They may place potentially unworkable constraints on your operation or extend charging times, situations that are just not necessary for ICE machines. And for vehicles that have to be taken home for any reason, there are still few easily workable solutions to the on-street-parking whilst charging situation.

Once away from base, any operator currently considering alternative fuels needs to investigate the refuelling infrastructure now and whether the proposed investment in infrastructure for the near future will take place as planned, especially if this has been anticipated within your business case for the new technology. There are some very grand and optimistic predictions on what will be available to support each fuel in the near future. If you were to add them all up, there would be huge over capacity in terms of energy supply, so it is unlikely for them all to be correct. My take on predicted infrastructure improvements is to look at how long it has taken to get to the coverage existing today for any particular energy source and extrapolate from there. If the claimed future rate is now double, treble or more the previous performance, ask very carefully where this additional development and particularly funding, is going to come from. If the funding is from the government, please be careful if counting on it for your plans, as we have seen how, regarding vehicles, political will waxes and wanes with other priorities, as do government grants and funding.

Pretty key in any plan for alternatively fuelled vehicles is to have a robust back-up plan for what happens if vehicles run out of fuel and there are no local supplies available. A comprehensive breakdown service should be part of the contingency plans, with tight timeframes and plans for alternative deliveries for goods and services provided by each vehicle. However, you can also take into account how reliable modern vehicles are, so with sensible journey planning, adequate refuelling or recharging regimes, it should only be occasional driver error or the odd unforeseen technical problem that causes a glitch in the usual cycles.

Most operators already using alternatively fuelled vehicles, generally battery vehicles, and to a lesser extent, hybrids, generally seem to feel that providing they have the range and weight capabilities at least close to that claimed by the manufacturer, apart from the capital cost, they are very happy with the performance and pleased for their organisation to be doing their bit for the environment.

Providing that is, the vehicle does not develop a fault. That seems to be where the problems begin. Despite all the media and political talk, these vehicles are still some way from being mainstream, so finding nearby dealerships and technicians that have had the requisite training and perhaps more importantly, the relevant experience on particular models, can still prove a little difficult. However, in the last 6 - 12 months or so, the feedback from these same operators has improved, so it would seem that resources in these new technologies is at last increasing. Before purchase, spend some time investigating the service agents you will be using. Don't just take the headline information, such as how many trained technicians they possess, try to carry out some background research with colleagues already using these services; how have they performed – how quickly are vehicles returned to service?

In the recent past, some manufacturers have sometimes been a little slow in providing resolution to technical issues, such that many operators using alternatively fuelled vehicles often had at least one non-operational vehicle parked up, for weeks rather than days. Again, this position seems to be getting better as the total numbers of new technology vehicles increases. Whilst considering the technical aspects of such vehicles, generally battery electric, you need to include considerable time and possibly cost in educating your workforce about the health and safety issues of a new fuel, such as high voltages around the vehicle and how to cater for them.

Drivers will also need educating on the differences of driving a vehicle with alternative fuels – some suppliers make light of the differences, but they require different driving techniques. Battery electric drivers undertaking longer distances will need to be introduced to the concept of scheduling potential time-consuming refuelling stops in their journeys. This sounds self-evident, but some of the training currently in use assumes a level of understanding from staff, who may well need additional help. Some exponents of battery electric vehicles will recommend many actions to improve vehicle range, such as warming up the vehicle in the winter whilst still being plugged into the mains and not using heated seats whilst on the move. These actions are one way around any range anxiety difficulties, but I struggle with new operating conditions that take away some of the benefits that today's drivers have come to expect. If these sorts of regimes are required to extend mileages, make sure they are fully discussed and agreed with staff and unions beforehand to avoid any animosity towards using the vehicles.

To counter possible technical issues encountered on any alternatively fuelled vehicle, it makes sense, if possible, to include clauses in the purchase agreement about the availability of the vehicle. In other words, specifying the uptime required. In order to guarantee uptime, some level of back-up vehicle provision will almost certainly be required. This has the obvious effect of pushing the downtime risk involved back onto the vehicle provider and incentivises them to repair the vehicle more rapidly than would otherwise be the case. If, for any reason, this cannot be guaranteed, then the accompanying risk needs to be factored into the buying decision for those concerned in the decision-making process.

Top Tips for New Vehicle Technology ✔

- Any new technology for vehicles, including alternative fuels, require everyone in the chain to make a profit, or a business benefit, in order for it to work.

- Before investing, carry out research on the available background facts and figures for any new fuel or technology and don't rely on any grand predictions on performance from the exponents - check performance with existing operators.

- Development of driver aid technology will continue until the introduction of autonomous vehicles; the buying decision remains one of balancing benefits against costs.

- ADAS (Advanced Driver Assistance Systems) such as adaptive cruise control and automated braking will be improved and integrate seamlessly into autonomous vehicles.

- Diesel, with improved emission controls, is likely to remain the primary power source for HGVs, supported by Hydrogen or some form of Electricity.

- Vans are likely to become increasingly battery electric as their range increases, weight decreases and the charging infrastructure improves.

- Predictive vehicle technology will eventually automate some of the current manual vehicle checks and self-automate much of the repair administration processes.

- Biofuel and Gas will remain useful cleaner transition fuels in the move towards full decarbonisation of transport.

David's Don'ts ✖

- Don't count on predicted infrastructure improvements from a provider, carry out your own homework on how rapidly it has grown up to present; check where any new finance or development is coming from.

- Don't rely 100% on grants or reductions in tax to justify the purchase of an alternatively fuelled vehicle, these are likely to be withdrawn at short notice in the post-Covid, post-Brexit world. Similarly, electricity prices for electric vehicles are unlikely to remain relatively low for too much longer.

- Don't forget to include time and effort for staff training, both technicians and drivers on new technology vehicles.

The Ultimate Guide to Commercial Vehicle Fleet Management

Chapter 7 – Bolt-on Commercial Vehicle Technology

1) *What non-manufacturer equipment is available for my vehicles?*
2) *What items do I therefore need to consider fitting?*
3) *What do I need to know about reversing alarms?*
4) *What do I need to know about reversing aids and sensors?*
5) *What else do I need to know about fitting cameras?*
6) *What do I need to know about dash-cams & rearward facing cameras?*
7) *What do I need to know about GDPR and cameras?*
8) *What do I need to know about nearside sensors & turning alarms?*
9) *What do I need to know about on-board weighing devices?*
10) *What do I need to consider when fitting any additional equipment items?*

1) What non-manufacturer equipment is available for my vehicles?

In the main, the equipment we are talking about in this chapter is primarily fitted for safety, for example, nearside sensors, or forward-facing cameras. Excluding items like cranes and fridges, up to, say, 10 years ago, there was not much need to fit much additional equipment to a commercial vehicle. Anything you really wanted could all be specified and supplied by the manufacturer or bodybuilder, although aftermarket equipment was still available and sometimes cheaper or even better, for some functions.

For a long time, there has been additional safety equipment available on the market, for example, a rear bumper that applies the brakes when it touches a physical object. This feature was adopted by many safety-conscious fleets, however, never really achieved full mass market appeal, such that it did not became a standard fit. There has also always been a number of commercial vehicle owners who wish to customise their vehicles, which, although they can sometimes end up looking rather garish, is par for the course. My only objection to fitting these accessories is when it has a fairly obvious detrimental effect on fuel economy, or even in a few cases, safety.

In most other cases, if the owner had a specific liking for a particular piece of equipment they would supplement, or even replace, a factory fitted item. More recently, we started to see useful pieces of additional technology equipment come on the market such as satellite navigation, which tended to progress faster from third party suppliers than manufacturers, who, mainly because of longer lead times, would invariably follow a proven trend, a little later in the cycle. Either way, sat-nav's have now become almost a mandatory fit item.

Additional equipment is also fitted by operators for reasons other than profitability or pure compliance to legislative requirements. Many operators really want to be seen as leaders in the transport industry in terms of decreasing their environmental impact, not just in the fuels they are burning, but by decreasing the likelihood of an accident or the effects on the public when they do interface. Good operators also want to be seen to improving the welfare of their drivers and staff.

Even more recently, we now have a major trend of vehicle specifications being determined by regional governments, such as the plethora of additional equipment which operators are required to fit and register in order to travel and deliver into London. Further items may be required in retrospect, such as exhaust treatment to meet revised air quality and pollution limits. Although national and international regulations are far easier to manage, the trend of local legislation shows no sign of abating in the near future. All this means that, whilst it used to be relatively straightforward to specify and purchase a commercial vehicle, now the subject has become far more complex and interrelated.

2) What items do I therefore need to consider fitting?

Well, unless you are fitting any of these items to meet contractual or legislative needs, the short answer is, you probably do not have to fit any of them. So, decisions on fitment will be taken, in the main, as part of a cost-benefit analysis or as part of a safety or environmental initiative. Spending a little more time than usual on compiling the risk assessment on this area would be really beneficial in order to point you in the right direction, certainly as far as safety is concerned. There is, however, usually a fairly clear economic benefit in fitting safety equipment that does have the effect of reducing the number of incidents that your fleet incurs. Quantifying that benefit is perhaps not so easy.

There is a plethora of equipment that can be fitted to increase the security of the load which in turn helps protect drivers and staff when driving or loading and unloading. There is not space to go into the subject in detail here, however, the government have provided some extremely useful advice, in a mix of formats, which is worth referring to at: https://www.gov.uk/government/publications/load-securing-vehicle-operator-guidance/load-securing-vehicle-operator-guidance .

Also thinking about another aspect of load security, to help reduce and manage theft and avoid the issue of stowaways, the cameras discussed below, mounted internally or externally can greatly help prevent theft, damage, and avoid stowaways with consequent fines.

Similarly, there is ample evidence that the development of commercial vehicles in general, but HGVs in particular, means that there are considerable blind spots left for the driver, even if using all the mirrors fitted. Operators wishing to improve this situation, especially in urban environments where the issue becomes acute, will wish to purchase the most appropriate vehicles possible and fit the right equipment to alleviate the problem. Leading the field in terms of trying to reduce these blind spots and especially the effect of the blind spots is TfL's (Transport for London's) 'Direct Vision' initiative, put in place this year (2021). Once again, there is not space to discuss all the required equipment or the standard of vehicle required to comply, however, full details can be found here: https://tfl.gov.uk/info-for/deliveries-in-london/delivering-safely/direct-vision-in-heavy-goods-vehicles

One early comment to make about cameras, which is usually appreciated by users, is that they now become a really useful accompaniment to an on-board telematic system. Telematics will often alert an operator to a specific piece of driver behaviour, which without cameras would normally require a conversation with the driver to understand the background to the event. By using cameras, especially with live or near-live data transfer, the reason behind a particular event can often be established without ever disturbing the driver.

I should just sound a brief word of caution here. A few years ago, an airworthy Air France Airbus A340 sank with all hands in the mid-Atlantic, mainly due to one sensor failure, but more importantly, due to the number of alarms going off in the cockpit, which seemed to completely confuse all three of the pilots. We have already reached the point where the poor driver of a vehicle is often surrounded by a mass of indicators, instruments, screens and alarms and is supposed to make sense of all this incoming data while still safely driving the vehicle through an often busy urban environment. There is a real case to be made here, that in terms of information, then often "less is more". Please think very carefully before adding yet another alarm burden to your busy drivers' day.

3) What do I need to know about reversing alarms?

Statistics show a disproportionate amount of damage and accidents occur whilst vehicles are reversing. For example, the HSE's (Health & Safety Executive's) own website https://www.hse.gov.uk/ reports that nearly one in four deaths involving vehicles working in the transport arena, occur during reversing. This is especially true in the construction industry, which is why nearly all construction safety codes require assistance for vehicles reversing in and around their premises. Your own historic insurance and accident statistics will probably confirm the dangers of reversing vehicles.

If alarms are fitted, it is quite important to make special mention of them within your driver training programme, so as to attempt to alleviate the "blue light" syndrome, sometimes found by emergency service drivers, of believing you are virtually immune from accidents when the siren is sounding. Make sure drivers understand that the responsibility for a reversing manoeuvre remains with them at all times, no matter what else is going on. And please do not forget to remind them that some people may be deaf!

As reversing alarms have become near ubiquitous, it almost feels like they are a legal requirement, but that is not the case; indeed, they are illegal for vans under 2 tonnes gross vehicle weight, which comes as a surprise to many operators. In common with quite a number of transport issues, although reversing alarms are not mandatory, if an incident should occur where an alarm is not fitted, the HSE may take a dim view of this occurrence and would most likely want to see a risk assessment backing up the decision not to fit a reversing alarm.

Having said that, the HSE themselves recognise that alarms are of limited value in some workplace environments due to the level of ambient noise, other alarms in the vicinity and the general volume of traffic or noise, meaning that pedestrians become ambivalent to alarms in general.

In practice, this means you should carry out risk assessments on the dangers involved in reversing your vehicles and that will probably result in your organisation deciding to fit reversing alarms in most cases. Your risk assessment should take account of the frequency and difficulty of the manoeuvres involved, within your own particular operations, of reversing your vehicles. Your assessment should also include a brief review of your organisation's historic damage and accident records to evidence whether the level of reversing incidents would indicate fitment should take place.

Any technical solution to an issue such as reversing should be thought of as perhaps the last line of defence. So, in common with all other transport related risks, you should attempt to reduce or remove them within the operation before fitting alarms. This is best done by conducting a proper risk assessment on reversing and it is always a good idea to rank the locations and type of operations involved against the number of incidents. Your own depots are likely to feature highly in the ranking as that is where all the vehicles congregate and manoeuvre most often. Undertaking a depot review and employing revised traffic techniques such as one-way systems, improved parking and loading bays or clearer signing, lighting and linage may sound pretty basic, but may actually prove more effective than just fitting alarms.

In recent years, alarm manufacturers have moved away from pure tone alarms towards "white sound" or broadband alarms which operate over a wider frequency, can be heard more easily over background noise and their direction is easier to distinguish in the ear of the beholder. Manufacturers are currently vying with each other about which is the best type of noise, also adding clever features such as volumes that adjust to the level of background noise. In general, of course, the more features your alarm possesses the dearer it will be to fit.

One decision that must be made if fitting alarms is how to turn them off. Night-time deliveries will almost certainly require alarms to be silenced. This can be done by a simple switch, however, not unnaturally, drivers often forget to turn them back on again. Some operators wire them into the sidelight circuit, turning them off when the lights come on, but this would seem to negate the purpose of fitting alarms in the first place as the dangers often increase with darkness. With competition between manufacturers, many other night-time solutions are available, such as self-adjusting alarms, low noise night-time alarms, or increasing the brightness of associated flashing LED lights when the sound is off.

Another decision to take if you are running artic vehicles is to decide where the alarm should be fitted, either on the unit or the trailer itself. The trailer is the most obvious mounting place in that it will present the sound at the very rear end of the vehicle to pedestrians and other users, however it will require additional wiring to connect to the tractor. Fitting the tractor with the reversing alarm is a lot simpler and means that the vehicle can give warning when coupling to the trailer, but is of considerably less use when the whole outfit is reversing.

As a last comment on reversing alarms, it is probably not a good idea to assume that a commercial vehicle's standard mirrors, even with class V and VI fitted, will be sufficient to take care of all reversing activities. Fortunately, you do not have to fit alarms if it is not "reasonably practicable" to do so, however, as they are relatively cheap and easy to fit, there cannot be too many cases where that would apply. If you should decide not to fit reversing alarms, your risk assessment should state why you think they are not necessary in your case. If you determine there are risks involved, but alarms may not be solution to your particular problem, then perhaps fitting some other kinds of reversing aids may be the answer in your case.

4) What do I need to know about reversing aids and sensors?

Reversing alarms above, are obviously intended to alert any personnel within the vicinity of the vehicle that it is about to manoeuvre in a different direction. However, this is not necessarily a complete answer and there are a number of aids available to assist the driver, other than having a 'banksman' or deputy to assist in the reversing process. There are three commonly used reversing aids in operation in many commercial vehicles.

Possibly the most well-known, generally the cheapest and simplest is an ultrasonic system. It is simple inasmuch as it is the system most easily recognised by drivers, being fitted to most cars on the market currently. In commercial vehicles it differs from cars in that a car sensor will probably operate within a range of one and a half metres from the rear of the vehicle, whereas trucks and larger vans need a longer range of around 3 m.

The second commonly used reversing aid is a radar system. It is similar to, but differs from, ultrasonic, in that the range is generally longer, perhaps up to 10 m, giving more time for the driver to react. Last, but not least, there are an ever-increasing number of reversing cameras, linked to a screen within the cab, such that the driver can see exactly what is going on behind the vehicle. A reversing camera is usually one of the first cameras to be fitted to any vehicle, primarily because of the dangers involved in reversing a larger vehicle.

If the number and difficulty of reversing operations within your fleet warrants giving drivers additional help, then you are probably going to make a decision to fit one or more of the reversing aids available on the market. This is where, yet again, it is really important to carry out a thorough risk assessment of this operation. The outcomes of the risk assessment should really drive the decision to fit additional equipment.

So, what are the pros and cons of the three aids outlined above?

Ultrasonic systems are well understood by drivers as they have probably use them in their own cars. It is important when fitting the system sensors to find the right height and angle to mount them to the rear of the vehicle, to give the best impression of what is around the vehicle to the driver within the cab. The most difficult part of fitting and the most important to get right, is to mount the outermost sensors mounted correctly, in in such a way as to give the driver the best possible indication of what is alongside the sides of the vehicle without issuing false alarms. Some installations can also visibly appear really well fitted, often being flush or nearly flush with the rear bumper.

Exactly as a car ultrasonic sensor, there is normally a display mounted on the dashboard which is usually colour-coded or with a digital readout. Probably more useful is an associated audible alert that gets more excited as an object gets closer to the vehicle, finishing with a solid tone at under around 300 mm. As ultrasonic reversing systems are relatively cheap, they are a useful device for alerting drivers to objects in their vicinity in the large blind spot behind them.

In comparison, radar reversing sensor systems provide a very similar audio and visual picture within the vehicle cab of objects in the blind spot. Whereas ultrasonic sensors use sound waves to detect physical objects, radar uses electromagnetic waves to do so. This means that environmental variables do not affect radar measurements quite the way they do ultrasonic sensors, so actions like cleaning the radar sensor, in theory, are not required.

Radar also suits vehicles that may require a longer detection range to give advance warning of objects entering the vehicles proximity. They are particularly common on refuse vehicles where reversing down narrow streets lined with cars is almost obligatory. Radar sensors are easier to hide behind plastic bodywork making them a more sophisticated fit. Radar systems tend to be slightly more expensive than ultrasonic as the range, sensitivity and shape of the detection field is variable and programmable, in some cases being sensitive to the speed of the vehicle. There are also some more expensive radar systems in the marketplace, which, if desired, can incorporate automated vehicle braking.

Reversing cameras on vans and trucks are being seen in increasing numbers, in a similar way to cars. The logic is simple, in that the general advice of having somebody on hand to guide you when reversing is great in theory, but not always useful in practice. Prices tend to reflect both the quality of the product and the features provided. One of the major issues with cameras is keeping the lens clean, so the daily driver check is an ideal time to carry out this action, making sure suitable equipment is available to clean a high-level camera lens. The monitor picture really does deteriorate quickly when road spray film covers the lens. More expensive cameras may have a built-in lens cover, only opening when in reverse or alternatively, some systems have a lens wash-wipe device. If night-time deliveries are required, you will probably need infra-red lighting to go with the camera. It is important to check the lowlight performance of the camera and monitor before buying, as performance can vary greatly and is not necessarily linked to price.

Monitors come in varying sizes and generally speaking, the larger the better, however, as mentioned earlier, it is getting more and more complex to find a suitable space within the cab, so take that into account when specifying. Positioning the monitor is also more important than just finding a spare space, as the image has to be in a logical position for the eye and easily visible to the driver, whilst not blocking his or her exterior view. The use of the monitor should also be compatible with use of the rear-view mirrors, or indeed rear-view cameras on the latest vehicles. Split screens perform a useful function, however, be aware that if they are showing multiple directional views all at once, they can upset the coordination of the viewer (remember the Air France Airbus incident).

Manufacturers are constantly adding more features such as on-screen graphics, most providing line markings and guides that help the more inexperienced drivers to park or manoeuvre sensibly. Van drivers are also catered for with a number of neat camera monitors incorporated into the vehicles' interior mirror, again only visible when in reverse gear. This option is great for security purposes and reduces equipment clutter in the cab.

Typical Side Camera Mount

5) What else do I need to know about fitting cameras?

When selecting equipment for your vehicles, it is usually worth knowing what other operators value. A fairly recent survey (March 2020) investigating the use of cameras, conducted by Commercial Motor in conjunction with Motor Transport magazines, (https://motortransport.co.uk/blog/reports/in-cab-and-forward-facing-cameras-a-look-at-how-the-technology-is-used-and-deployed/) showed that the feature operators valued most highly was the camera and video quality of on-board cameras, nearly 75% thinking it was very important. This was closely followed by automated instant capture and playback and the capability of the video storage. Live viewing was considered very important by 42% of the respondents and the ability to integrate with other telematics at 41%.

When considering where to mount cameras, be aware that those mounted at or around bumper height get very dirty, very quickly. Before fitting, especially at the rear of the vehicle, check where dirt is accumulating. You will probably find there are some specific low-pressure areas where the dirt is attracted. Try to avoid these and stay in the higher-pressure areas where road dirt is not such an issue.

Reversing cameras on trucks and larger vans are generally mounted fairly high up and angled downwards which gives a view of the rear of the vehicle, which helps give context to the driver as well as better showing the area behind it. In keeping with alarms, cameras fitted to trailers will require compatible connections with the tractor, although some operators are electing to fit wireless transmission for the pictures at extra cost. Once a reversing camera is fitted, most systems will have an option to expand fitting of additional cameras and views, eventually arriving at an effective 360-degree view.

Be aware that camera technology obviously has some limitations. When the vehicle moves from very dark areas to much brighter ones, it can often take a little time for the system to adjust and the driver is therefore blind during that period. Generally, the more expensive the camera, the shorter this period. Drivers who have not had previous experience of a particular system may find a little difficulty in accurately judging heights and distances until they acclimatise. Similarly, many fleets cannot afford to fit the whole fleet all at once, so some systems are more up-to-date, or they trial a number of systems on different vehicles. If drivers move from one vehicle to another, using a different camera system, perhaps mounted slightly differently, they again take time to acclimatise, so obviously, try to standardise your fitted equipment as much as possible. As with other additional technology fitted to the vehicle, allow sufficient time for driver training to take place.

6) What do I need to know about dash-cams & rearward facing cameras?

Possibly one of the most contentious pieces of technology currently in use is that of the rearward facing camera mounted within the vehicle cabin. Commonly called safety cameras, or similar, these are typically mounted in conjunction with a road facing camera, so as to give the context behind what is being seen internally. A video of the cab interior is not particularly helpful on its own without knowing exactly what is going on at the same time outside. These two views are often backed up with a number of other external views from other cameras. These types of cameras and recordings can be incredibly useful in reducing false claims and proving that your drivers are not at fault in an incident, as well as having a safer driver training role in improving driver behaviour.

Evidence shows that along with telematics data, this technology has the benefit of significantly reducing road incidents and accidents through increased driver feedback, often coupled with appropriate training, and simply the fact that drivers know they are being monitored produces a beneficial effect on their driving performance. Unfortunately, unions and drivers can, quite naturally, often take an opposing view and feel that cameras could be fitted as a means to penalise them, as well as becoming yet another method of monitoring their performance or behaviour, leading to a feeling of distrust.

Early engagement with unions and drivers is therefore key to the successful implementation of this technology. It should be emphasised to staff, drivers and unions that the video recording technology is being installed to protect drivers by providing accurate evidence to dispute false or fraudulent claims. However, it is really important that any statement issued by directors or management to that effect, must be backed up by visible action, so in essence, to use a common expression, you must 'walk the talk'.

Coaching sessions arising from evidence of poor driver performance should be dealt with sensitively and should be seen to be operating fairly across the board and not just picking on specific offenders. Disciplinary action should really be used as a last resort, as your drivers must feel they have been treated equitably and that this technology is there to benefit them, not chastise them.

7) What do I need to know about GDPR and cameras?

Most importantly since the introduction of GDPR (General Data Protection Regulation) and the associated rules concerning the storing and handling of personal data, it is imperative to get the storage, processing and management of any video footage generated by the system correct from the outset. Operators will need to identify a specific person as their data controller, ensuring that any video-based data captured is necessary for their road transport business in order to monitor their vehicle performance, driver behaviour and encourage a high standard of road safety.

The operator, through the data controller, should be able to demonstrate that there is a legitimate interest in gathering any such data used and delete any footage that does not meet the declared criteria. Getting this process correct is a key component in getting buy-in from staff and the unions. It is best to adhere to whatever rules you have agreed on the storage and use of this data and not change your mind at a later date. You should also demonstrably be seen to be getting a business benefit from the use of this data to justify your reasons for keeping it in the first place.

Most of these recording systems generate pictures, or flag up video footage, by exception. In other words, they record specific images when an incident has happened or when sensors say an incident may potentially have occurred. Given the density and complexity of modern traffic flows, especially in urban areas, it needs to be clearly understood at the outset that these systems can generate vast amounts of footage. That may mean taking up considerable time of one or more members of staff, depending how big your organisation is, or it may make sense to outsource at least part of the reviewing function externally.

If you take the latter route, please do not forget that you are still fully responsible for your organisation's GDPR obligations. This means you must make drivers aware of exactly how cameras and the data generated is being used in their vehicle. You must also make clear the justification keeping this data, who will have access to it and for how long it will be stored.

You must gain your staff's consent to the images being used by including a simple statement to that effect in all new employee contracts and incorporate an addendum to existing employees' contracts, giving them a route to take if they severely object. However, of course, an individual's concerns must be taken into account, but on their own they cannot be allowed to dictate an organisation's policies. Lastly, it is important to respect the drivers' privacy, so for example, arrange for cameras to be turned off during rest periods, unless they are being used for security purposes, but in that case the driver is unlikely to be in the cab. Remember that the regulations require that the amount of personal data your organisation may hold should not be "excessive in relation to the purpose or purposes for which they are processed".

Data from camera systems which record video are covered by GDPR rules, excepting cameras which are only used to view blind spots and are not being recorded. This means that anyone recorded by a camera system must be aware of its presence, which includes the driver, the public and anyone else that may come into the vicinity of the vehicle such as customers. Unless not practical, probably the easiest way to achieve this is to fit warning signage displayed prominently on the vehicle, including interior signage for cameras in the cab or load areas. It should also make clear where audio recording is being used. If you decide such signage is not practical in a particular situation, you should record a risk assessment detailing why not and what steps you have taken to minimise the risk of unintended data capture.

8) What do I need to know about nearside sensors & turning alarms?

There has been a huge increase in front corner and side proximity sensors and alerting systems in recent years, largely due to operator recognition schemes and their Direct Visions Standard, originating from TfL in London. Generally, these are ultrasonic in nature, usually fitted in groups of four and operate very similarly to reversing sensors, except the output of the sensors is coordinated along the sides of the vehicle and around the front nearside, specifically to alert the driver to pedestrians and cyclists within the typical vehicle blind spots.

Very similarly to reversing sensors, they will have monitors within the cab, generally colour coordinated, typically showing green, amber and red to indicate the closeness of the obstacle. They will also have an audible alert to the driver, the urgency of which increases in line with obstacle's closeness. Some versions apply the brakes if the system thinks collision is imminent. These systems are generally supplemented with a waterproof external speaker alarm, mounted at chassis or near head height, designed to warn pedestrians and cyclists that the vehicle is turning left, which sounds when the appropriate indicator is activated and they are detected within the vicinity.

My concern with all this technology is that the bodies that insist this equipment is fitted and also some of the transport managers that have fitted it, think that is "job done" and these vehicles are now protected from incidents. I conducted a straw poll of around 200 drivers using these alarms a few years ago, to try to ascertain the best equipment to fit and not one of them declared their system was good. The best response I received was "not too bad", the worst regularly ripped the wires out, due to disgust from the sheer number of false alarms they received from letter boxes, rubbish bins and other pieces of street furniture. I am reliably informed the performance and especially the calibration of these systems has significantly improved more recently, but I still remain to be convinced, so please do not think this equipment is completely fool proof and I suggest regular surveys of your drivers to check the equipment is performing as required. Include testing the correct operation of these sensors in your maintenance and inspection schedules and include their operation as part of your daily checks.

9) What do I need to know about on-board weighing devices?

On-board vehicle weighing devices have been employed in transport for many years and have changed little over that time. The basic mechanicals are still fairly similar, however, the way the data and information is presented has moved forward considerably. The use and installation of this kit has remained relatively expensive, so the devices are not universally adopted. However, for vehicles with variable loads that often need to get towards maximum vehicle weight in order to make a profit, on-board weighing can pay for itself fairly quickly by maximising carrying capacity, whilst avoiding prosecution and protecting O licences from being found to be running vehicles overweight. It also avoids those fraught journeys to try to find a local weighbridge to check weights.

Generally, an on-board weighing solution consists of three sets of components. Firstly, the sensors, usually mounted on or around the axles. Secondly a vehicle unit, the clever part which calculates and presents the weight of the vehicle, usually split by axle, and lastly the interconnecting wiring harness. Weight information used to be simply displayed to the driver and recorded within the vehicle, now modern technology means that data can be transferred via wireless handheld displays, on-board printers, data loggers and can also be transmitted in real time to the back office or wherever desired, usually by GPRS (General Packet Radio Service, meaning Cellular Communication). Transferred data can also include time and a GPS (Global Positioning System) location to give context to the declared weights.

The specific technology to select for on-board weighing applications is generally guided by the type of vehicle being used, in particular the method of loading, the vehicle suspension type, along with the desired accuracy of the weighing solution. Most sensible operators do not assume the indicated weight is always correct and allow a small margin of error to ensure they stay on the right side of the law.

The three main sensor types used for on-board weighing are firstly a load cell, generally being the most accurate and mostly found on vehicles with steel-sprung suspensions. The second type of sensor is an Air Pressure Transducer (APT), unsurprisingly found on vehicles with air suspension. This second type has the advantage of generally being the cheapest of the three, but the disadvantage of being the least accurate and requiring more frequent calibration. The third type of sensor is a strain gauge, probably in the middle of the other two as far as accuracy is concerned.

Properly calibrated and used, all three sensor types can achieve an accuracy within 5%, with load cells being most accurate. Depending on operating conditions, for a relatively low desired accuracy, re-calibration need only take place every two years. For accuracies better than 1-2%, calibration periods of no more than one year should be considered. What is important, but is not always considered by operators or the driver, is that for reasonably accurate weights, the vehicle must be parked on a level surface with the engine running, wheels straight, and the brakes released, in order to release any forces held by the vehicle chassis and suspension. Equally, if the load is liquid, there has to be sufficient time for any movement to settle to avoid mis-readings and trust me, that can be an unbelievable amount of time!

An On-board Weighing Device can save trips to the Weighbridge

10) What do I need to consider when fitting any additional equipment items?

Each individual type of technology will have its own particular issues on fitting, but there are some common matters arising which we can outline here.

Weight – thankfully, this does not often become a real problem as most of these devices use solid state electronics and their design has been refined over time so as to minimise their weight and size – this issue only really becomes a problem if you are fitting considerable amounts of equipment, but it makes sense to do the sums when calculating tare weights and maximum carrying capacity. However, it does become a more serious issue when considering vehicles at the lighter end of the weight range, where small weights are a much higher proportion of the total vehicle weight. So, if we are talking about lighter vans, already with some equipment fitted, often carrying one or more passengers; these possess increasingly sensitive gross weight limits due to a gradual and continuous increase in unladen weights, mainly due to increased safety features. Do therefore allow for the weight of any additional equipment when calculating your margins on these weight-sensitive vehicles.

Fitting Location in the Cab – Many organisations have an increasing number of screens and other devices needing to be fitted inside the cabin area; you really need to give their location some thought, so occupants remain safe in the event of an accident. As a quick piece of education, I suggest rapidly trawling through the internet to have a look at videos shot inside a vehicle cabin when an accident takes place. You cannot really fail to be surprised by the way the driver, and especially any passengers, flail around due to the forces impinged upon them – and the reach of their head and limbs is also astounding.

You therefore need to mount this kit within easy reach of the driver, in order to be able to operate or read the equipment. However, it must also be mounted out of harms' way, or at least offer some sort of protection, should the worst occur – not an easy task. Luckily, most fitting agents should be able to give you some advice on safe positioning. Do not be tempted to think that if your rules state "no passengers", you do not need to worry about them. There are times, such as a maintenance check, when another person has to be in the vehicle cabin, they also need to be protected, even for very short periods. Also be aware that non-driving information should not distract the driver from their prime objective, controlling the vehicle.

Fitting Locations on the Vehicle

During the purchasing process, try to select equipment where the sensors appear well protected from the transport environment. Wherever possible, sensors and cameras should be flush fitting or as near flush with surrounding bodywork as possible, with protective housings to avoid damage. Quality, although possibly more expensive, often pays dividends here, as cheaper alternatives generally suffer more damage and hence associated repairs. As with most other things connected with commercial vehicles, a good indicator of the quality of the systems you are using is the warranty period offered. Fairly obviously, good quality systems tend to offer longer warranties. This should become apparent during the selection process and taken account of when buying. Although obvious, it has to be said, if you are attempting to meet the latest Direct Vision standards, any additional equipment fitted must not obscure the standard direct vision through glass panels or mirrors already fitted on the vehicle. Nobody said running a fleet of vehicles was easy!

Maintenance: this is a clear issue from the outset – these pieces of equipment all need inspection to determine that all aspects of their systems are still working and the kit is in good order – usually problems occur at the sensor end or from cameras positioned in exposed locations. The difficulty is that the periods recommended for inspection for each item of equipment will probably be different, so you need to determine a suitable inspection period when everything can be carried out at the same time and then work it into your inspection schedules.

At the same time, do not forget to add a brief check of the equipment functionality to your daily inspection sheet for your drivers so that faults get corrected early. In fact, if you are registered for one of the operator recognition schemes, you may fail simply if the inspection of ancillary equipment is not clearly noted on your daily check sheets. As mentioned above, many camera lenses and ultrasonic sensors will need cleaning, daily in the winter months, generally less often in better weather. For cameras mounted high on the body, either automated cleaning, a cleaning device or access will be required by the driver. One of the advantages of radar type sensors is that in theory, they do not need cleaning.

Allow a little extra time in the daily checks to inspect, clean and adjust any of this additional equipment as necessary. This type of equipment will not actually stop the vehicle operating and often was not fitted to the vehicle from new, so there is a feeling in the minds of staff that it is not absolutely necessary to the running of the vehicle. I have therefore noticed a tendency for some operators to leave any repairs to defected equipment for a later inspection or service. However, I would suggest that the last thing you need to encounter is a serious vehicle incident where it turns out sensors on a particular vehicle have been inoperable for any length of time. Additionally, the DVSA (Driver & Vehicle Standards Agency) have made it clear that whatever additional safety equipment is fitted to the vehicle, they will determine that it should all be working in order to be declared a fully roadworthy vehicle.

Fitting Quality: it is really important that when fitting any additional equipment to a vehicle not supplied by the vehicle manufacturer, take care that the supplier and fitter follow completely the vehicle manufacturer's recommendations and guidelines, usually published as a set of instructions in a body builder's manual. This is particularly important with any electrical accessories which must only be wired into specified points in the vehicle's wiring loom in order not to interfere with the CANbus operation or any 'life and limb' items. It is wise to obtain something in writing from your supplier to the effect that they understand and have fully complied with these guidelines.

Training and Spares: your drivers and technical staff will also require training in order to understand the equipment, even when you still have to bring in external specialists for some or all of the repairs. In order to keep your vehicles on the road, it pays to carry a sensible number of spares of replaceable items for each system you are using and hold in stock, an important issue to negotiate with the supplier when purchasing. There can often be delays in procuring spare parts for a number of these systems and carrying suitable spares helps keep downtime to a minimum.

Of course, the big drawback to maintenance and training is the amount of time it takes. Training can be scheduled and carried out as part of the overall installation project, but it takes time to get everyone trained properly, so allow for this when considering fitment, also making sure you capture all of your staff. There is something about transport staff that means 90% of the staff involved are usually trained relatively quickly and then somehow, capturing the last 10% seems to take months and months.

Weather Proofing & Quality

Commercial vehicles often operate in some quite harsh environments and have to deal with the vagaries of the British weather. Nearly all the equipment we are talking about in this chapter will require input from either sensors or cameras. The water Ingress Protection ratings (IP) for each piece of equipment is therefore an important factor in your purchasing deliberations. Look for as high a test IP number as possible; so in very general terms IP 67 will give you reasonable waterproofing protection, IP 68 has considerably improved weatherproofing, whereas IP 69 will be resistant to water ingress from equipment such as a pressure wash. Those of you that have used pressure washers will know that the moisture seems to have the ability to get in everywhere, so this latter standard is quite impressive.

Look carefully at the design of the equipment. You want it to be effectively a 'fit and forget' item, so check the design shows an ability to withstand the level of shock and vibration it will receive on your vehicles and has been tested to show resilience. Have someone handling your maintenance look at the equipment from your selected supplier that you intend to fit, to check that components will be easily replaceable, with common connectors of high quality and modular installations wherever possible.

Top Tips for Bolt-on Commercial Vehicle Technology   ✔

- The main reason for fitting additional equipment to new and existing vehicles in the last 5 years has been the massive expansion of local regulations and standards for commercial vehicles operating in specified areas.

- Try to keep the number of alarms or screens in the cab to an absolute minimum to avoid overloading the driver; mount screens out of harm's way and in a logical layout to avoid confusing the eye.

- If reversing alarms are not being fitted as a matter of course, conduct a specific risk assessment into reversing to ascertain if they are required.

- Depending on the results of your reversing risk assessment, consider fitting one of the 3 aids available, ultrasonic, radar or cameras.

- If fitting forward and rearward facing cameras in the cab, involve staff and unions in trials and discussions early on; be sensitive about how you deliver any resulting driver training, ensure it is fair and equitable.

- Regularly check that the calibration of nearside sensors and alarms is still set up correctly and the driver is not suffering from excessive false alarms.

- On-board weighing devices are still relatively expensive, but payback is quite rapid for the right operations.

- Go for the highest weather-proofing standard you can afford to reduce later repair issues.

David's Don'ts   ✖

- Don't fit additional equipment to your vehicles unless a) you have to meet local delivery regulations, b) your risk assessment requires it, c) a cost-benefit analysis suggests it, d) your organisation requires it for environmental or safety reasons, or e) your customer/s insist on it and f) for other legal reasons.

- Don't fit cameras anywhere on the vehicle in a low-pressure area or where road dirt accumulates – simply check where dirt always builds up now and avoid that area.

- Don't fit too many camera varieties across the fleet, after trials, try to stick with just one make & layout so drivers get acclimatised; when updates occur, ensure all drivers are trained in any difference.

The Ultimate Guide to Commercial Vehicle Fleet Management

Chapter 8 – Telematics

1) *What do I really need to know about Telematics for commercial vehicles?*
2) *How does Telematics actually Work?*
3) *How do you know whether to fit Telematics to your fleet or not?*
4) *How do you select either a factory fit system or after-market?*
5) *What information do you require from your system?*
6) *How do you select a system from the large number of telematics suppliers & how do you select the best system for your fleet?*
7) *What are the basic costs, pros and cons of the various ways of buying systems?*
8) *What improvement results would it be realistic to expect for your operation?*
9) *How do you get the best out of your Telematic system for the minimum management input?*
10) *How can you combine telematic data with your fleet management and other systems to improve data quality and reduce manual input?*

1) *What do I really need to know about Telematics for commercial vehicles?*

Whatever the prime purpose of running your fleet of commercial vehicles, using telematics software is certain to benefit your services, improve your operations, along with helping the day-to-day management of your vehicles and staff. Most importantly, it will provide data that can assist in planning and reducing your overall costs. Compared to an organisation without telematics, it can provide a paradigm shift in customer service, providing both management and end users with up-to-date and accurate progress reports, resulting in substantially less operational queries which automatically improves performance. Businesses that use the reports fully, invariably report significant bottom-line savings in running costs like fuel and insurance, whilst also achieving slightly less direct benefits, such as reductions in maintenance and increases in productivity.

However, it has to be said that in the past, many company or organisation directors and managers have been reluctant to introduce the technology, sometimes through a suspicion that the necessary investment in time and money will fail to deliver a sufficient return. Equally relevant, is the fear of drivers and unions labelling it as 'big brother' or a 'spy in the cab'. It is true that benefits such as fuel savings will be relatively easy to sell, as it is easy to demonstrate how it will impact the company's bottom line. Others benefits such as improved customer service or improved duty of care are slightly more esoteric, but equally valid.

Virtually all Telematics Systems rely on good signals from the Global Satellite Network

The organisation will also benefit through greater operational efficiency as vehicles will be better managed and over the longer period, suffer less accidents and become less prone to breakdowns. Telematics is increasingly being used to keep track of vehicle servicing needs and instantly report on faults diagnosed by the system, whilst also flagging up errors instigated by the actions of drivers. But in order to get the best from any system, be aware that it is no good just collecting data. It has to be analysed, understood and then used as a tool for obtaining performance improvements; it will not happen of its own accord.

However, when implementing telematics, I cannot emphasise enough how important it is to give full consideration to the feelings of drivers and vehicle operators, who sadly, often get forgotten in the process. The high value of operational savings that are available from using telematics tend to cloud all other judgements. In fact, prior to the advent of telematics, many drivers really enjoyed the day-to-day challenge of achieving a set of targets without significant intervention from anyone else. Now they are clearly visible to scrutiny at any time by anyone with access to the technology, which, if not addressed at the outset, can detract somewhat from their job satisfaction.

There is no getting away from the fact that how a vehicle is driven contributes directly to the cost profile of a vehicle. Transport managers often try to ignore this fact due to the current shortage of high-quality drivers, but in general, smooth, considerate driving always gives the best results to both the vehicle and other road users. Poor driving, through rapid acceleration, harsh cornering, or unnecessary hard braking for example, will, over time, always lead to excessive fuel consumption, increased maintenance and unfortunately, an increased accident rate and therefore increased insurance costs. Those poor performing drivers, often in liveried vehicles, do nothing to promote a good corporate image.

Sensible data, fed back to managers allows them to make really accurate decisions about routes, times, delivery regimes, potential poor driver behaviour and how the vehicle and driver are performing against expected targets. This allows managers to make informed decisions and take action to correct problems that left alone, would result in increased costs, a loss of performance and hence, for the private sector, reduced profits.

Herein lies the first and major problem with telematics. The systems can provide so much information that it is literally a full-time job trying to analyse all the feedback and even more of a task knowing just what to do about it. One issue that telematic providers do not always seem to fully appreciate, is the amount of time that their systems can suck out of a transport manager's day, and how many other, more urgent issues will divert their energies.

Directors often feel the difficult part of the process is the investment decision, however, most managers know that is only the start of the process. In order to make the investment worthwhile and to maximise returns, fleet managers have to act on the information created by the telematics. The data by itself delivers nothing; it is only actions that achieve results.

For that reason, telematic providers have not really altered the basic functionality of systems that much in recent years, but what has changed greatly are the methods of reporting. A host of more useable dashboards, reporting suites and apps have sprung up in order to help make their product and their systems more useful to the operator than the competition.

Many businesses forget to extend the use of telematics to other departments, where some of the data may well aid their activities, for example, the finance department may benefit from reporting on mileage, or the data can assist in producing invoices and quotes for customers. Engineering could benefit from vehicle analytics and HR from performance reports, showing how much time drivers are spending behind the wheel and monitoring both the health of the driver along with the vehicle.

When researching telematics, you can often find dire warnings about data ownership and data security. It is true that some Telematic providers take the view that your data is actually theirs for them to do what they like with on a commercial basis. There is an ongoing debate within the industry about exactly who should own this data, so it is essential to establish that simple fact at the time of purchase and have it written into your contract.

Other warnings about GDPR and telematics are best taken with a pinch of salt. It is quite likely that if you are collecting data concerning vehicles, drivers and staff, that at some point personal data may get included in the package. Some staff and their unions may get vexed about this fact, but if you apply all the appropriate GDPR data handling protocols and principles, use it for business purposes only, and apply all the usual security measures over personal data, it should not be any different to other data used by your organisation.

For commercial vehicles, it is important to understand early on that there are effectively two types of telematics. Both use standard satellite technology to track the vehicle, one uses CANbus to tap into vehicle systems and produce a wealth of information about the condition of the vehicle and how it is being driven. The second, usually cheaper, version does not have CANbus, but do use ever-more clever algorithms and calculations, probably adding in an accelerometer to the system, so it can provide significant driver behaviour performance data. However, the cheaper, basic version will never be able to provide such things as fuel usage or the more detailed information on the vehicle, used for full driver management and training. As the more expensive connected option will also be getting data from many sources, it is more likely to give a complete picture of what the vehicle is doing at any given time.

It is also worth pointing out here that the allowable tolerance for manufacturers on CANbus fuel consumption reporting is +/- 5%. That is quite a margin when we are looking for a few percent savings. However, fuel flow measurement generally comes from the engine management system and the good news is that whatever the error today, it will be virtually the same tomorrow, so it is perfectly acceptable to work on trends in performance and use actual fuel purchased as the real guide. Some systems even allow for correlation between reported fuel and actual fuel used (from forecourt fuel pump readings) over time.

One less tangible benefit from telematics that is often forgotten in the decision-making process is that it enables fleets to make continuous improvements in their performance. Without telematics, it is unfortunately a given that most driver training, however effectively it is delivered, gets gradually forgotten over time and drivers will often revert back to old, less efficient habits. This performance trend has unfortunately been demonstrated to be true by countless academic exercises investigating how long the effects of training last over time. Properly used and with the correct feedback, telematics allows improvements to continue over time and become 'hardwired' habits.

2) How does Telematics actually Work?

This explanation can get very complicated and customers sometimes get confused by the separate elements of such a complex system, involving any number of suppliers, so let's keep this as simple as possible.

The basics of any system is that data is collected by a telematics device, often referred to as a "black box", fitted in some way to the vehicle.

For commercial vehicles, these are often either incorporated in the base vehicle electronics or hard-wired in by a separate provider. Other, more mobile devices are sometimes sold which can be moved from vehicle to vehicle, sometimes tapping into a data port to obtain information from the vehicle.

What virtually all systems have in common is a GPS receiver that will receive satellite positioning information enabling it to track the exact position and speed of the vehicle, the same as the sat-nav in your car. It is worth noting here that contrary to general opinion, satellite signals are very weak indeed, so can easily be blocked or "bounced" when in cities with tall buildings, known as "urban canyons". Vehicles can therefore "disappear" for short periods of time, for example in underground or multi-story car parks.

More importantly, signals are very susceptible to interference or "hacking", which has not really been much of a problem to date in the UK, but will become so if, for example, any kind of tolling or road user charging ever comes into being. Providing secure positioning data will also be a crucial factor in the progress of autonomous vehicles, as one of the first things an autonomous vehicle needs to know is exactly where it is at any given time.

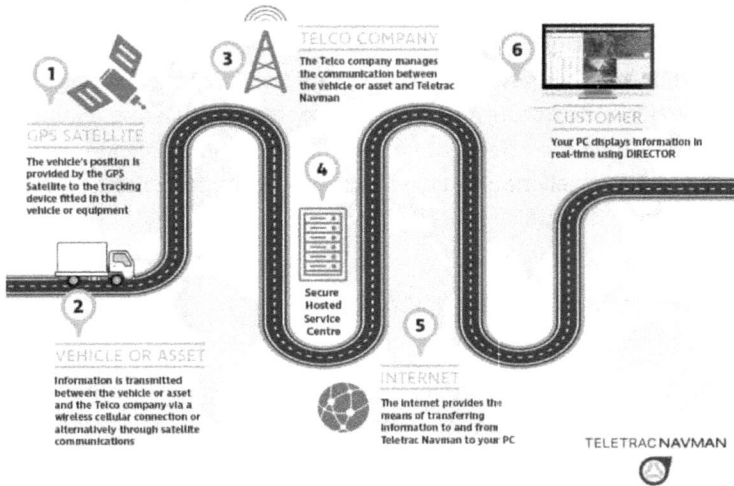

Infographic of vehicle data transmission – Source - Teletrac Navman

Often the black box will include an accelerometer, measuring the g-force produced by the vehicle, both fore and aft and usually side (cornering) forces and possibly vertical forces. All this data is collected together, along with any other data required to be gathered, (for example the temperature of the load, which would require additional sensors), and sent as a package, usually by GPRS (the mobile network) to a data centre.

How the data will be viewed or transmitted to the operator depends on the functionality of the system, but will normally be viewed through a fleet management software portal, on a secure website or app. More recently the portal will generally be accessed remotely in the cloud, but potentially may still be on a customer's hardware.

All this background technology and systems have been developed over many years and all providers use similar technology – they all use the same satellites and signals, for example. What does change from one supplier to another, is the way this gathered information is reported on and displayed and that is the biggest differentiator – you, the operator, need to find the system that closest match your needs and presents information in a way you can easily understand.

That is really all a user needs to know about the system. There is obviously a lot more going on, but operators will pick this up as they go along and perversely, will often learn a lot through the odd malfunction, where the explanation will demonstrate how the system does or does not work. A system supplier or manufacturer will provide some basic training, with more advanced training provided later, probably at an on-cost.

Two important pieces of advice on system training here:

- Make sure your management and staff use their training immediately after it takes place, if not, the speed at which telematic training is forgotten is beyond belief. There is something about the technology, which is very easy to understand at the time, but without practice, just as easily forgotten after a few days or weeks.

- It is best not to agree to any further training immediately after the initial basic training (unless included in the purchase package) until your staff have used the system on a daily basis for at least a fortnight, preferably a month or so. At that point they will become more familiar with the basic operation and have a raft of questions on how to use the more complex features.

3) How do you know whether to fit Telematics to your fleet or not?

The starting point is to have a very clear idea of what goals you want to achieve by fitting telematics, other than doing it because everyone else is. My recommendation would be to first ask relevant colleagues on their experiences of telematics, then follow this with a brief research of the market to see the sort of systems on offer and what products they provide. With this information in mind, sit down with whoever is managing your transport and the fleet and decide what are the key pieces of information that you require and more importantly, what information is not essential for your operation.

A word of caution here; some systems offer so many features, there is a danger of being seriously seduced by them, like kids looking into a toy shop window. It is really important to sift through potential features and decide if they are essential to you or not. What is business critical, what is important and what would be just nice to have? Remember every feature comes with a cost, either an increased monthly subscription, training time or management time in sorting out the meaning of the data and taking action.

Actually deciding on whether to go ahead with purchase and fitment is relatively simple. A simple ROI (Return on Investment) calculation of benefits versus costs can be carried out . If you have run a trial, the potential figures should be easy, however, do not forget to reduce the potential savings figures from the trial by around one third, or if being super cautious, one half. This is because the trial will probably have had plenty of management time and interest spent on it, whereas in real life, there will never be as much attention spent on the data, meaning the savings will not be as great. This may be annoying for managers and directors alike, however, that is just how life is.

Although there should be plenty of operational savings arising from fitting telematics, I would strongly recommend to just focus on fuel as the main saving and for simplicity, just use that figure in the calculation. It should be possible to achieve savings, giving relatively short payback periods, using fuel alone, however, this does, of course, depend on how good or bad your current fuel figures are now.

My advice is to ignore most of the usual savings claimed by the vehicle or system manufacturers. They nearly always publish their best savings as an attractive potential figure, conveniently forgetting those customers who hardly save at all. Fleet Technology, our sister organisation, once achieved over 40% fuel savings at one particular recycling depot, but this was mostly due to the vehicles used and a very specific method of operation and I would never claim that as the norm. For HGVs, a sensible saving would be in the 5 to 8% range, fairly easy to achieve on a continuing basis and should result in an ROI of under a year, depending how this is calculated. Vans are more variable, depending on the mileages run, average fuel consumption, average speeds, weights carried and, as ever, how the vehicles were driven before, however, it should be possible to achieve double digit fuel savings.

In the unlikely event that you discover that your favoured telematic system does not justify itself in purely financial terms, it may well still be a worthwhile investment, providing it enhances customer service or it has been demanded by a particular customer or contract. There may also be a case for using telematics simply in order to compete in a particular market or stay safe and legal, especially if required to comply with an operator recognition scheme or meet insurance company requirements in order to reduce premiums.

However, if there are not some clear business reasons to fit telematics, or a clear financial case, I would suggest not going ahead, as unless used sensibly, telematics can be an expensive luxury.

4)   How do you select either a factory fit system or after-market?

Some years ago, perhaps ten or so, many vehicle manufacturers did not quite fully understand how useful telematics could be to the average operator. Instead, they got very excited that they could establish, in real time, such really important things as the gearbox temperature of one of their vehicles going up a hill in Kazakhstan and lost no time in sharing this with any customer that would listen. This information was great for the manufactures, but virtually useless to the vehicle operator as these offerings were mainly geared towards the technical aspects of running a vehicle and not the operational benefits. Thankfully, that situation has now completely changed and manufacturer supplied telematic offerings match what the customer wants and needs.

The history of telematics for UK vehicles and manufacturers is a fascinating and convoluted story, requiring another book to describe fully. It probably dates right back to the Datatrak system developed by Securicor in the 1980s, to provide security for their high value loads. Some manufacturers such as Volvo, Mercedes-Benz and Scania have developed their own individual telematics systems, often with support from other suppliers, whereas other manufacturers such as MAN and DAF chose to partner with a third-party supplier. Both the latter companies are now looking at their own subtly different systems in parallel to the third-party option. Iveco were originally also partnered with a telematic suppliers for some years, now having their own connected vehicle solution.

Van manufacturers now also largely have their own Telematic offerings, very much geared to a different style of operation due, of course, to the fact that most vans are either engaged in customer or business door-to-door deliveries, or used as a tool for the job. So, Mercedes-Benz, Renault Vans, Iveco vans have differing levels and similar options to their Truck divisions, either their own version or with a third-party supplier. Ford vans also offer 3 versions of their telematics from a full platform through to an app aimed at smaller fleets.

It is probably fair to say that all vehicle manufacturers do now fully understand the true operational benefits of telematics to their customers and their offerings reflect this. Most systems can now report on such items as:

- driver performance, in order to manage fuel and safety related issues.
- vehicle location and the load state, in order to manage efficient delivery progress.
- driver's hours remaining before a break or rest, in order to manage driver utilisation.
- proof of delivery & job completion, in order to manage schedules.

From all system suppliers, there is now a trend back towards more technical information, but this time in order to manage the mechanical condition and maintenance of various items of vehicle equipment, such as brakes, tyres and ancillary devices. This is especially important with large equipment such as trailers, which because of their mobility, can sometimes tend to get lost within the maintenance process

So, if, therefore, one can obtain a Telematic product similar to the aftermarket specialist supplied versions from the vehicle manufacturer, fully fitted to the vehicle at birth, with full manufacturers' warranty, all the features you need and at a reasonable price, why would you not do so? The answer is fairly simple; not many operators run a single make fleet and there is a huge advantage in seeing all of your vehicles on just one system screen. In addition, there is quite an advantage in being able to move the system hardware from vehicle to vehicle, perhaps a to different make, at will, when replacing or moving vehicles around.

So, in summary, there is a huge variation in packages offered either by third-party suppliers or from the vehicle manufacture. For the operator, trying to decide which system to use, there is no shortcut to matching a potential systems' features listing against your shortlisted system requirements. A vehicle manufacturer will probably be offering a system that suits their vehicles and their connectivity needs, so maybe slightly limited in functionality. However, if their functionality meets your needs and is provided at the right price; then it often provides the simplest solution. If, however you need a wider selection of report data functions, or you have a fairly mixed fleet, then the solution will most probably be the third-party supplier.

5) *What information do you require from your system?*

To give you an idea of some of the ways basic data is presented by many tracking systems, here are some very typical available readouts:

- Road speed – current, maximum and average.
- Over speeding events, number, location, percentage of driving time.
- Vehicle geographic position, direction, speed and navigational data.
- Distances covered by time, route, day.
- Comparison of actual routes against planned.
- Replay of driving history, with details of "events".
- Fuel consumption, current, by route, by time
- Length of time vehicle stationary, engine idle time, number of events, % driving time.
- Time in engine rpm "green" band; overrevving events, number, location, % driving time.
- Use of cruise control, distance, location, time, % driving time.
- Harsh braking over pre-set limits, numbers, location, % of driving time.
- Harsh cornering over pre-set limits, numbers, location, % of driving time.
- Harsh acceleration over pre-set limits, numbers, location, % of driving time.
- Monitoring pre-set service data; presenting vehicle diagnostics fault codes.

A number of points on the above examples.

Firstly, most telematic suppliers know that the operator will suffer "data overload" at a certain point, so will probably not present all the data, unless requested by the user.

Secondly, when first using telematics, it will feel like you are swimming in data, which all becomes a bit meaningless. After a time, things start to make more sense and each user will develop their own criteria that they will follow and understand.

Thirdly, when all is said and done, it is the driver that is key to all progress and they will have their own favourite criteria that they will respond to. The trick is to remember the number one objective is generally to save money, usually by saving fuel and making efficiencies, with the added bonus of almost automatically improving safety at the same time. Everything else is just smoke and mirrors.

Fourthly, it is essential to tailor the data to whoever is managing it, so, for example, one set for a transport manager, one to Accounts, a synopsis to directors and one for driver feedback.

Lastly, almost all systems now present data at a top level first and then allow the user to "drill down" into the detail to examine, as necessary, individual events. This follows the 'management by exception' principles and makes the data easier to handle.

The latest systems can offer so much more than the examples above. However, as also mentioned before, it is very easy to get overwhelmed by the sheer mass of data available. It is therefore really important to employ the Pareto principle and decide on what really are the key performance data that you need to monitor. The Pareto principle, also called the 80-20 rule, is named after an Italian engineer, who said that 80% of outcomes, (he was referring to economics, but in almost any walk of life), result from 20% of causes. This tends to be true in the vast number of cases, although the figures can vary somewhat, so a 90-10 relationship would still be called the Pareto effect. In other words, work on the few major causes of your issues and you will find that will take care of the bulk of the results.

In order to give you some ideas, it is suggested that the following KPI's (Key Performance Indicators) could become the core of system generated fleet management information, adapted for your fleet needs and reported on a regular basis. As for overall fleet KPI's, less is more, so I suggest keeping the number of KPI's reported across the organisation to a minimum to reduce overload.

1. Fuel economy figures by vehicle measured against aggregated fuel economy of the relevant group of vehicles - this is the basis for the core of the savings available from telematics by highlighting such behaviours overrevving and excessive speeding. Once identified, selected drivers can be trained or

coached to avoid and reduce these behaviours. Make sure you use the base figures for fuel economy, don't be tempted to start using averages of averages, which may be mathematically incorrect.

2. Idling time by vehicle measured against the relevant group of vehicles – this factor can be described as a "quick-win" as it is simply a bad habit, therefore pick up on the few drivers with excessive times, which should virtually stop idling and helping to keep within low limits. Once identified and eradicated, it is a habit that tends not to return, but it helps to keep a constant eye on the figures to prevent idling time increasing again.

3. "Empty" miles run by vehicle – a useful operational measurement to help maximise vehicle utilisation. Unassigned mileage by vehicle is a key fleet statistic and if exceptions exist, they need to be explored and minimised.

4. Asset utilisation – time spent by vehicles, trailers and plant carrying out profitable work, again a useful measure of fleet utilisation. Gaining a clear view of empty miles and how assets are being used on a daily basis will aid fleets in optimising asset utilisation and, in many, many cases, allow companies to reduce the total number of fleet vehicles. This of course has the effect of further reducing all associated running costs such as fuel, maintenance and insurance.

5. Driver safety information, such as speeding occurrences, harsh acceleration, harsh braking and harsh cornering incidents. As item (1) above, correcting poor performance in these areas will also greatly help fuel saving; the two issues are inextricably linked. Ideally, this data should be made available to fleet managers in real time and shared with drivers on a regular basis, either by regular face-to-face reviews or through an app or portal which allows drivers to review their own performance and compare it to that of their peers, something virtually all drivers are very keen to do. Reducing instances of such poor driving behaviour will also reduce wear and tear on vehicles, decreasing maintenance requirements, producing safer driving and hence fewer accidents.

And for those fleets with telematic systems that integrate tachograph information, the following minimum compliance data is important:

6. Critical operational data such as driving hours to the next break, the driving day or week. Van operators should still monitor daily working and driving

times. This data should be available live and used in the traffic office when planning loads and deliveries.

7. Driving Hours infringements – these should be reviewed on a daily, or certainly a weekly basis, reviewed with the driver and recorded and may either indicate planning issues or a driver error, intentional or non-intentional.

8. Missing mileage by vehicle – it is a legal requirement to record and investigate any unaccounted mileage missing from tacho records.

Handy Hint   👍

*   Most organisations who do not already have telematics find that when they install it, they uncover any number of vehicles that are totally under-utilised, such that they can safely get rid of them. In most cases, local managers knew they were not well-used, but kept them "just in case".

---

6) How do you select a system from the large number of telematics suppliers & how do you select the best system for your fleet?

Assuming you have decided you do want to fit telematics and as suggested, you have sat down with your relevant staff to decide what items you want to measure and what is not necessary for your fleet. Then go through the following process -

*   Decide on the few specific goals you want to achieve with your GPS fleet tracking solution, such as;
    o   Improving driver safety
    o   Reducing fuel costs
    o   Improved customer service

*   Along with some targets or goals;
    o   What does improving driver safety mean? - A reduction in accidents of x%;
    o   What fuel savings are we looking for? - A reduction of x,000 litres p.a. or x% of the fuel bill

If you have not already done so, it is useful at this point to seek out some form of benchmarking group within your corner of the industry and have a look at competitors operating in the same field to try to benchmark your operating statistics. This should give you guidance on how you are performing and which areas you may need to focus on. Once you have fitted telematics, the system will tell you more accurately where to focus, but having some targets at the start always aids the process.

Sharing the above information on your objectives with potential suppliers will help them to demonstrate to you how their solution will help you achieve those goals when they present to you. When in discussions with them, querying exactly how that will work in practice will give you a better feeling as to whether their system will work for you or not.

Then decide which features will be most important to your business and staff. Also, determine what features you think you and your staff will interact with most. This is very important as your staff will spend a large proportion of their time working with just a few screens and a few reports. If you determine at the outset what they could be, you can focus on the offerings of each supplier, for example;

- o Will these screens be easy to use?
- o Will these reports give me the information required easily?
- o Would I be happy sat looking at this screen for hours a day?

After some consideration, most customers decide their system requirements will be something along the lines of:

- o An easy to use, quick responding, mapping feature
- o A clear, easy to use, reporting function, with reports geared to your operation and a simple to use interface
- o Simple management of driver & vehicle data, with easy setup of roles and permissions
- o A clear, user-friendly dashboard which can logically display your key fleet criteria
- o A set of clear benchmarking reports, separated by logical vehicle/ driver/ depot groupings
- o Any reports generated must be easy to schedule and export
- o A suitable trend & alert functionality that will help you manage your fleet

It is obviously important to work with a supplier that fully understands your individual challenges and goals — ideally, they should become your partner rather than just a supplier. Your encounters with the various suppliers and their support staff during the buying process will give you a good sense of whether or not you "gel" together and that you are not just a sales target for this month.

Do not forget the vendor will be on their best behaviour during the selling process, so you can legitimately expect 100% attention to your needs during this period. Also remember that as soon as the contract is signed, you will be handed over from that really nice salesperson to an account manager – find out exactly who your account manager or managers will be before the sale and check you are comfortable working with them. At the same time as deciding the system criteria, make a list of ideal supplier qualities before starting the process and use it to narrow down your choices during buying.

Your trawl of likely suppliers will have given you an idea of potential costs – decide what your budget will be on a monthly or annual basis to see which suppliers can match or improve on your price target for a given level of service. Keep going back to your original listing of key criteria you need from the system. Make sure these criteria are fully covered to your satisfaction, any other features will just be nice to have. If some features are not on the original listing, in my experience, they often do not get used, so do not be attracted towards, and definitely do not pay extra, for features that are seem nice, but not essential.

Lastly, be very specific in the negotiating stage about the implementation plan and timing, especially regarding a go-live date. There are almost invariably going to be some hiccups in the fitting stages; some vehicles will not be available as planned or fitting will throw up some technical issues needing resolution. Specify and agree a date or timeframe and agree this with your supplier, however, privately, allow some slack in the project timeframes in case issues arise. As with any subject in this book, if at any stage you are feeling lost in the process of finding a telematic supplier, please contact us on 07771 768080 or dwilson@thedwconsultancy.com and we can assist you in the selection process.

7) *What are the basic costs, pros and cons of the various ways of buying systems?*

Over the last 10 to 15 years, Telematics systems have largely become commoditised, so although system providers try to give you the impression they are unique, in truth they are all fairly similar in terms of what they offer. In fact, it is not so much the features that you should be evaluating, but far more the way data is presented to you, how easy is it to access and how useful it is to you in its standard format. In addition, you should be evaluating the support and service received at every stage during the buying process or any trial as this is the make or break for any system. It is not when everything is going swimmingly that you should judge the supplier, but how quickly any little niggles get resolved as and when they occur.

Telematics are generally provided in one of two ways;

Firstly, by purchasing the hardware and installation up front. This then leaves a relatively small monthly fee for providing the on-going reporting function and service provision.

Secondly and increasingly the more usual option, is leasing the whole package and paying a single monthly charge. Note that this will include some level of interest as it is effectively a finance package.

Buying up front will probably be the cheapest option but does risk leaving you with an unusable asset if the supplier should be unfortunate enough to cease trading. Leasing your equipment largely avoids this risk, although you may still be liable for some on-going fees, however, the latter route will obviously cost more on a monthly basis. Try not to go for really short contract periods, for which the suppliers are likely to charge very high prices.

Contract periods tend to be between two to five years, the most common being three years. Vehicle manufacturer telematic contracts are likely to be linked into whatever vehicle contract has been arranged. Be aware that I come across a significant number of operators who are approaching the last year or so of their telematic contract and are very keen to get out in order to move to a more appropriate supplier, but are usually financially or contractually constrained and have to wait to do so. If you can negotiate more flexible "get-out" arrangements at the start of the contract, it may be worthwhile to do so, even though at the time, you will obviously be hoping to go the full length with the one supplier.

As a guidance, at 2021 prices, vehicle hardware, including installation, will cost somewhere between £250 to £950 per vehicle, leaving an on-going monthly fee of between £10-£30 per vehicle. The lower end of this scale will be for a cheap and cheerful system, giving very basic data, whereas the upper end will be a full can-bus system with all bells and whistles attached.

A monthly leasing style package will typically cost between £15-£45 per vehicle per month, including the data transmission costs, which, incidentally, have reduced considerably in recent years. For international travel, check to see roaming charges in some format are not re-introduced across Europe post Brexit. As for a fully purchased system, the price range depends very much on the specification of the system provided.

This chapter has so far talked about mainstream telematics, designed for vans and trucks that are prime movers. There is a whole section of the industry that is devoted to unpowered vehicles, so largely trailers, but also items like boats. Some operators do not bother tracking the prime mover and are totally concerned with the load, especially if it is sat still for any length of time.

If tracking the trailer and its load is as or more important than the vehicle, then it is worth looking at specific trailer tracking systems that are battery operated, often recharged from the towing vehicle, via the electrical connections. These types of systems specialise in keeping the transmitted data packages small and only poll the unit at extended intervals in order to reduce battery consumption. Recent systems may also fit solar panels on the roof, handily not visible, which often give almost infinite battery life, providing the unit is not hidden indoors. These systems are particularly valuable if your trailers are hauled by contractors or if you need to keep track of standing trailers which are dispersed around the country, or even the globe.

Although trailer tracking systems are useful for keeping track of loads, if you carry high-value items or perhaps use more expensive specialist vehicles, including plant and equipment, then there is another sector of the industry specialising in potential theft. These systems differ in a number of ways from mainstream telematics. Firstly, although regular telematic systems are tucked away to help prevent tampering by unscrupulous drivers, anti-theft tracking devices are usually hidden in some extreme places. The location of the kit is supposed to be known only to the tracking system manufacturers and fitting agents and also keep changing as criminals become more used to where they may be hidden.

Anti-theft tracking systems also carry stand-alone internal battery back-ups, designed to keep going when the criminals may have ripped the standard vehicle electrics out. In addition, many carry alternative means of transmitting, such as VHF radio, in case the standard antennas are compromised. Most of these system suppliers have links to the police as the intention is to find the vehicle before the load has gone too far, or, if it is the vehicle that the criminals are after, before it is dismantled or placed in a container for shipping overseas. For this service, you will probably pay a premium over standard tracking, however the increased security is effectively an alternative insurance policy.

8)   What improvement results would it be realistic to expect for your operation?

As touched on briefly elsewhere in this chapter, the starting point here is to take most predictions given by the system providers with a pinch of salt. Firstly, they tend to only quote the very highest figures taken from a small selection of their customers, not the averages. Secondly, how other organisations utilise telematics may be different to your organisation and depends very much on your operation, how your staff adapt to the process, how good and sustained your management is and of course, how well the system is implemented.

However, the key word in considering results is simply 'visibility'. In all but the very smallest of fleets, where the activity of each vehicle is generally known and monitored closely, it is absolutely astounding what is revealed once all the vehicle data is compiled in a meaningful format. There will often be management disbelief that one part of an organisation will have vehicles stood up in the yard, whilst another part is happily hiring in vehicles on a daily basis. In a fleet of any size, it is almost guaranteed that some vehicles will hardly turn a wheel and should be sold and replaced by hiring or sub-contracting when necessary. Some vehicles, carrying out similar roles in the same locations will return exceptional fuel consumption, whereas others simply drink fuel. Until the stats are in, all this will get lost in the mix, all these potential savings just will not happen.

Because of all the possible variations in how a fleet is managed and operates, it is almost impossible to predict what savings you should be looking for. Perversely, this depends largely on how well you were managing your fleet prior to fitting telematics. The poorer the driving before starting, then the better the potential savings. Also, as with almost everything in life, it is so true that you will get out results in proportion to what you put in. So, against the potential savings must be balanced a certain level of increased management input. Many organisations do not allow for this and believe the sales pitch from suppliers that they will obtain savings and in parallel, management will actually save time.

So, what sort of savings should you be looking for and in what areas? I would suggest you should look to save in at least five areas, which are:

1. **Fuel** – To me, this is the core justification for fitting telematics; it will need some management to obtain results, although without any management action, you should still see savings of at least a few percent, just because the drivers know they may be being monitored.

    - HGVs should look to save between 5 to 7% on fuel costs.
    - Vans are far more variable, but should save at least 5%, possibly up to 15%, with good driver feedback and the right fleet profile.

2. **Insurance** – there is a large body of data to say very considerable savings can be achieved in reducing accidents and hence premiums, to the extent that some insurance companies may even contribute to the initial telematics fitment. It is always worth asking at renewal time if you can strike some form of a deal. You should also benefit from the evidence against false claims. Most fleets have stories to tell in that regard. Allow an absolute minimum of 5% savings; really, with a bit of attention to the drivers and some training, 15%+ should be achievable

3. **Fleet Numbers** – probably this saving is for larger fleets, although smaller fleets still benefit from visibility; I have seen some amazing reduction figures from some medium to large fleets over time. This will need a little time, discussions with other managers and decisive action at replacement time. Allow somewhere between 2 to 5% savings in capital costs, along with associated running cost savings

4. **Maintenance** – You will not see any sensible savings in maintenance costs for probably six to nine months and this assumes your driver behaviour is improved, so you should notice fuel savings and reductions in accidents first. The main savings will be in wear items such as brake linings and tyres; expect around a 5% annual reduction in figures

5. **Mileage** – without any clever technology, just the fact that your staff are tracking and monitoring routes and times will result in a natural improvement in scheduling and performance. Changes should not require much extra management time and should be achieved through day-to-day improvements; expect at the very minimum a 2.5% reduction in mileage and consequent running costs, perhaps considerably more.

9) *How do you get the best out of your Telematic system for the minimum management input?*

Some organisations just use telematics to know where vehicles are and what they are doing at any given moment, but do not use it for much else. They tend to get small efficiency improvements due to the fact that drivers know they could be watched, even if there is no evidence that anyone actually is managing the process. That is fine if that is all you want it for and it is not costing you too much.

From the very start, it always helps to try to take your staff with you on the journey. Emphasise to them the benefits, such as increased safety and security, automated functions that will save them time, such as automating proof of delivery or job completion data entry. Many people use their system to help in the reporting of compliance items, thus saving them considerable time and effort.

Try not to focus on the "Big Brother" aspects of the system, instead emphasise how useful it can be to your drivers, such as countering erroneous complaints received from the public or customers – these tend to reduce when people know you are accurately tracking. You can also legitimately emphasise the wider benefits to the environment and also to the company bottom line, thus helping to make their jobs safer. It also assists acceptance greatly to try to "Gamify" the process (using the modern parlance), so set up a highly visible league table or have a monthly prize or similar, to introduce a level of competition into process, which virtually always works wonders on all your drivers.

However, if you would like to get far more out of your system, then you have to accept that it will not manage itself, so accept that it will absorb at least some of your precious management time. The trick then, is to use the system to automate as many of the things you are doing more manually now, leaving you some spare time to take new forms of management action.

To allow more management time in order to take management action, have the various reports set up and automatically sent to the right persons, at the right time, in the right format, so they are most likely to take action. Set your vehicles up using geofencing to report when they are entering or leaving set zones, but obviously only get notified by exception, when something may be wrong and you may need to take action. If possible, depending on the system you have picked and how you operate, consider sending selected data to your customers to allow them to see where a vehicle is and how their load is progressing – it will reduce your time spent on discussing trivial information and give you more time to have meaningful conversations with your customers.

Finally, when managing drivers, use Pareto's rule and only tackle the low hanging fruit. Select the bottom few performers of your charts in terms of driver behaviour, have a short meeting with each one (no more than a couple of minutes each) and then set them a few simple and clear future targets. Always follow up later with results and set them further targets, if required. Once you are relatively happy with their performance, then move on to the next lowest drivers, rinse and repeat. Doing this for a couple of months will have a huge impact on your average figures and hence reduce costs to improve the bottom line. Although it may seem like an effort to call your drivers for a chat, you are unlikely to find any other use of your time that will match the payback you receive. And do not forget to also praise the good drivers, something that UK transport managers, for some strange reason, are hugely reluctant to do.

10) How can you combine telematic data with your fleet management and other systems to improve data quality and reduce manual input?

For a long time, many Telematic systems have been able to upload vehicle maintenance data and allow you to monitor actual progress against the schedule. Possibly because this process will absorb quite a bit of administration and management time, plus this schedule is usually already in existence elsewhere, up to now I have found a very low take up of this option by operators, which is generally freely available within the standard package and sold as one of the many 'benefits' of telematics.

However, many vehicle manufacturers are moving quite rapidly towards far more use of predictive maintenance, where, in place of a schedule determined by time or distance, service times can now be calculated largely upon actual use. Statutory inspections will, of course, still be required at pre-determined intervals, but servicing can be aligned far more to actual wear and tear, as determined by the telematics and matched against historical aggregated data. At least one major manufacturer will now increase or reduce the on-going contractual maintenance charges based on the driver's telematics driving performance score, as they fully recognise the correlation between the two and are prepared to share the savings (or cost) with the operator. For the transport world, this is a major shift forward in maintenance thinking, which has been talked about for some time. There may be a small charge attached to this service, which should be far outweighed by the efficiency benefits.

These same techniques can be used by an operator conducting maintenance in-house, by linking operational performance into their maintenance systems. Predictive maintenance has been a 'buzz word' in the commercial vehicle industry for more years than I care to remember, but thanks to telematics, this has finally become a reality. Indeed, thanks to the fault code generation on a can-bus driven system, many un-scheduled repairs can now be rapidly scheduled and parts obtained, perhaps delivered to a repair location on-route, thus minimising any potential downtime for the vehicle. This type of semi-automated repair scheduling has been in operating in the aviation industry for many years, driven there mainly by the much higher cost of downtime.

Telematics systems can obviously also interface with most other computer systems, both your own organisation's and especially those of third parties, such as customers.

Comparing the routes and schedules planned by your staff, probably using your route optimisation software, with the actual journey times and progress recorded by your telematics system is now fairly commonplace. The term 'real time' scheduling has been around for a while, but in reality, this has been very difficult to achieve and more often the system actually matches against pre-determined routes and makes adjustments. Improvements in systems coupled with telematics mean real-time scheduling changes are now possible and can take account of traffic disruptions as they occur.

Job allocation software linked to the telematics has been common for managing mobile workers for some time and allows drivers to receive instructions from the firm's job management or order processing software on the move, as well as recording when on-site and when jobs are completed. The use of real-time location data means that a system generated job can take many parameters into account and produce very efficient job allocations based upon such items as time and distance, used extensively, for example, by courier companies to minimise time and distance, thus increasing efficiency.

These systems can obviously be used to log staff on or off jobs or work for the day, meaning much better accuracy for billing or payroll systems and a high level of traceability and auditability of historical data. This automation also helps to remove a number of links in the data chain, minimising the opportunities for potential errors and speeding up the process. It is also fair to say that if data required from a driver is also linked to their pay, that means that any previous problems associated with obtaining the data tend to disappear!

Delivery confirmation software, such as that used by parcels delivery, is often linked to the telematic system and we are now all used to the series of automated emails telling us where your parcel is, who might be carrying it, which van it is in, followed by the confirmation text or email on your phone received almost at the same time as the item is received. Sometimes you get a picture of a parcel being delivered before you have opened the front door!

The fact that mobile phone technology is integral within telematics systems means they can also provide, if desired, both voice and text communications between the driver and base, allowing drivers to communicate with their manager, or any other desired parties and send digitally captured signatures confirming delivery and other essential data back to base. This will normally require some form of ancillary equipment such as an in-cab terminal to be fitted and they are now virtually all configured so as not to disturb the driver whilst in motion, saving any messages for the next stop.

All the above is technically possible and in use today. However, if starting from scratch, it is suggested that operators start with just a simple vehicle tracking package and then gradually add more sophistication as time goes on, allowing any hiccups in the systems to be ironed out, plus user training and acceptance to take place, before moving on to the next stage. This does mean that your initial sift of what products and suppliers are available on the market should take account of potential future developments and the ability to expand and interface with other computerised systems, but this should not be the main criteria in your buying decision.

Top Tips for Telematics ✔

- Driver training undertaken without telematics feedback tends to get forgotten far too quickly; using telematics dramatically improves your ROI on training budgets spend by helping to retain good habits.

- Alternatively fuelled vehicles benefit just as much from the use of telematics to improve driver behaviour as conventional engines; electric vehicles especially benefit by extending their range.

- Before incorporating telematics in your fleet, accept that it will take up considerable amounts of management time, however, the benefits accrued will far outweigh the time spent.

- As with any IT system, ensure you establish ownership, or at least rights, to all your data before implementing the system.

- Ensure all the usual GDPR protocols are applied to any personal data held on the system.

- Decide early on in the process what the KPI's are that you wish to measure; telematics can provide so much data that it is better just to focus on a few key parameters that are useful to your operation and not get side-tracked by the rest.

- Customer service in telematics is far more important than features; most suppliers offer very similar packages but their service provision varies considerably.

David's Don'ts ✖

- Don't overlook how intrusive telematics is for drivers; they will need careful handling to persuade them of the benefits of the technology right through the implementation phase.

- Don't take as gospel telematics companies' claims of savings and either run trials yourself or gather evidence from similar operations using the same system. Remember savings in real life will be roughly 30% lower than a trial.

- Don't forget you will not be dealing with the sales manager after purchase – establish who your contract manager and support team will be and try to establish a rapport before purchase.

The Ultimate Guide to Commercial Vehicle Fleet Management

Chapter 9 – Fleet Management Systems

1) *What is a Fleet Management System – in what way is it different to the information that telematics gives me?*
2) *Why do you need a fleet management system?*
3) *How do you select a system supplier from the wide variety available for your particular operation?*
4) *What differences do you need to consider if you run either an internal or use an external workshop?*
5) *What other important factors should you take into account when selecting fleet management software?*
6) *Why is calculating whole life costs so important?*
7) *How do you use lifetime vehicle costs for true cost comparisons?*
8) *How do you best manage your FM system for maximum advantage?*
9) *What parts of your FM system should you consider integrating with your organisation's other IT platforms?*

1) *What is a Fleet Management System – in what way is it different to the information that telematics gives me?*

There is endless debate about the origins of the phrase "what gets measured gets managed" or even "gets done". Most people attribute it to the management guru Peter Drucker in his 1954 book, "The Practice of Management". Other historians say it dates way back to the 16th century. Whoever said it matters little, the important thing is, it is both accurate and true, or more particularly, the opposite is so very true when managing vehicles. If you do not carefully measure the important metrics of a fleet of commercial vehicles, you stand absolutely no chance of managing it effectively or efficiently.

If you google "Fleet Management (FM) Systems", most of what you see today will be related to telematic systems. True, in recent years telematic systems are getting much better at providing more of the pure "fleet management" information you need; however, they are still far more geared towards the physical day-to-day management of the fleet. This relates to issues such as where the vehicle is, how many miles it has travelled, how fast, and of course, a huge amount of data on how the vehicle is being driven. Now that's great and as the previous chapter explains, has a very important place in managing your fleet, but they are still nowhere near as good at holding the basic management data of running the vehicles themselves, or holding the core data on the vehicles. Most importantly, they are not yet as good at keeping track of all the associated vehicle running costs for budgetary purposes.

The way I like to view it is that a true core fleet management system will give you all the information you need to make the longer-term decisions on your fleet that we discuss in some detail throughout this book. Such things as which vehicles to replace and when, maintenance and running cost trends, together with all the administration and legislation details you need to manage each vehicle. In contrast, telematic systems provide you with dynamic, real time, proactive data to enable you to manage the day-to-day running and efficiency of the fleet so as to produce, hopefully, fairly immediate running cost savings.

This gives rise to another issue. In Chapter 8 we discuss choosing telematics systems and mention their ROI (Return on Investment). For telematics, it is relatively easy, especially if you run a trial to see how much you can save, mainly on fuel. You can simply adjust the figures for day to day running in place of a trial and extrapolate savings for the whole fleet. The ROI is generally under a year for a purchased system, which should make it an easy decision. This is not so simple for purchasing or replacing a fleet management system. What I can clearly say is that if you utilise it fully you will definitely save. If it just sits in the corner and gets interrogated every now and then, you probably will not.

However, the simple fact is, without it, you will not be able to manage the fleet efficiently, so it is kind of a given that if you wish to manage your fleet effectively, you must have an FM system in some format. If you are trying to justify the expenditure of investment in a system, you can go through all the potential information gains and estimate small savings here and there, then total them up, but apart from potential administrative savings, you will not really know what you can save until after the event. Instead, I suggest biting the bullet and going for it, with or without an ROI, but of course, as ever, keep costs under control and only buy the systems and modules that you really need.

Telematic providers are getting closer to providing more of the information you will need to run a fleet, but at the moment, you will be better off ensuring that your fleet management system is your central database, containing all the core fleet data and then introducing the on-going data, such as mileage from telematics or tachograph feedback to update the main system at appropriate intervals.

At its core, a fleet management system should handle all the basic fleet administration, with modules that include:

- recording full asset details for financial, legal and management purposes.
- a full maintenance history, internal or external, including monitoring the maintenance and statutory inspection schedules.
- managing any internal workshop activity, including times, labour and parts.
- tracking any warranty activity.
- recording and monitoring all compliance activity.
- recording and monitoring all external equipment inspections, such as lifting equipment.
- recording and monitoring vehicle utilisation and availability data.
- recording and handling accident data & records, personnel and assets.
- recording all driver associated data.
- recording each and every piece of expenditure on a vehicle.
- recording all fuel use, internal or external.
- providing data to support vehicle replacement.
- recording all the financial information associated with these vehicle records.

A telematic asset tracking system, however, may provide some associated data, such as predictive maintenance or error alerts. But its prime functions will be:

- real-time tracking of the asset.
- providing mileage, speed and location data.
- possibly handle delivery proof data or job allocation.
- assisting in routing optimisation, and most importantly -
- all the data associated with driver behaviour and optimising productivity.

Much of this telematic data, or at least, a summary of it, can usually be incorporated into the main fleet management data records in order to provide a fuller picture of a vehicle's history.

In the last five years or so, there has also been another class of fleet management system gaining prominence; that of FM systems monitoring compliance. The main focus of these systems is the recording and acting on driver's daily checks and then recording and monitoring the wide range of issues required by primary and secondary legislation for vehicle operators to evidence, such as driver's hours and licence checks. These systems are great at what they do, however, the focus is very obviously compliance and they are not so good at monitoring and reporting on fleet costs and efficiency. My view, again, is that you are better off with a good fleet management system which has added suitable compliance modules and can easily accept relevant telematic data to give you a complete and all-round picture of your fleet.

For completeness, it is worth noting at this point that there is yet another class of fleet management system that again has been around for many years, but improved a lot of late, that of the workshop management system. These systems used to only really be good for managing vehicle workshops and focussed on doing just that, either for internal workshops, i.e., carrying out maintenance on your fleet, or external workshops, where the work may be for third parties. Once again, these systems were good for their primary purpose of controlling and measuring workshop throughput, but obviously not designed to handle the core fleet functions, so unable to provide you with comprehensive data to help make strategic fleet decisions. However, these systems have also moved on in recent years and have got much better at dealing with the non-workshop related data. Once again, I would say a good fleet management system with the appropriate workshop management modules attached is the better choice, but there is certainly no longer so much of a gap between these two types of systems.

A last cautionary financial note before we move on. FM systems used within the private sector are normally quite good at integrating their data with the company's other systems, especially finance. This is really important for two main reasons. Firstly, you want to reduce any manual input or intervention of data entry to an absolute minimum, so if data only has to be entered once, then can be shared or posted, there is an immediate admin saving. Secondly, you really want all information within the company to tally; if one system says we have spent £X this year on maintenance, you want all other systems to say exactly the same.

Unfortunately, this is not always the case with FM systems used in the public sector. For a variety of reasons, public sector finance systems are usually fairy inflexible and do not cope with sharing data with other systems at all well. For this reason, public sector fleet departments often have to operate their fleet finances in parallel, and as a duplication to the finance department, which is additional work and can lead, in certain circumstances, to significant differences in the figures. The important thing for public sector fleet managers to do is to record just enough data to be able to measure their actual fleet spend against their budgetary spend on at least a month-by-month basis. Often public sector organisations do not know their final spend until after the year end; waiting until the end of the year is just not good enough, it is too late to take any management action by then.

2) Why do you need a fleet management system?

A good fleet management system should become like a fleet manager's right hand. It should contain all the base records of the vehicle, so details of all the suppliers involved, core registration data such as chassis numbers, costs associated with buying and then all the lifetime costs associated with that vehicle, especially, of course, all the relevant maintenance costs. More importantly, the system should allow interrogation to reveal the answers to the thousand questions that will arise in the course of managing the fleet. A good FM system should also be able to hold, in electronic format, all the relevant information sufficient to comply with O licence requirements, something that although not a legal requirement for vans (yet!) is increasingly being required by operator recognition schemes in order to demonstrate you are a high-quality vehicle operator.

If you have only a handful of vehicles, say up to a dozen, you can manage perfectly adequately with a spreadsheet and almost all fleets of that size do just that. I have also seen fleets that have expanded from a handful up to 50 or even 100 vehicles still carrying out their fleet management using a spreadsheet. The problem for the fleet manager then is threefold. Firstly, there is a limit to what spreadsheet functions can do for you, especially if you want to share information with other departments in your organisation. The second is, that just like dealing with project management software, when there are large amounts of data held on a spreadsheet, managing it becomes quite a problem and if you are not careful, more and more of your time will be spent on housekeeping, rather than the prime objective of managing the fleet.

The third issue is probably the most important. A spreadsheet is just that, a way of handling and manipulating data. However, a fleet management system is a data base, specifically designed to hold fleet information in a logical and specific format, but also having functions designed to aid the interrogation and manipulation of the data in easily accessible and readable formats and produce helpful reports of all descriptions. It can also perform a multitude of administrative functions such as reminders for events like MoTs or vehicle servicing, or flags for dates or mileages limits that have been exceeded. Yes, spreadsheets can be made to perform those functions, but it takes considerable time to set up, they get very "clunky" as they get bigger and only the originator usually knows how they function fully. Once the basics are in hand, you will want to undertake a wide variety of searches on the data to carry out research on items such as your defect records to spot trends over time, very useful in understanding how effective your core maintenance is being carried out.

That is why you often get managers with quite large fleets still on spreadsheets. The spreadsheet owner knows just how much time and effort is involved in the migration and cleansing of moving all that data over into a fleet management system. There will also be time and effort involved in getting used to the new system and training anyone else involved in the process. The fleet manager therefore puts off the evil day to a time that will be more convenient, which of course, never arrives. There is no good time. So, my clear advice is; if you are at all considering employing a Fleet Management system (and you should be), do it sooner rather than later whilst less vehicles and less data is involved.

A good fleet management system should be flexible enough to adapt to your ways of working. There is a huge caveat which needs to be mentioned here. Changing systems obviously takes quite a bit of time and effort on all sides. It is an ideal time to look at exactly what operations you are carrying out and seeing if there are any obsolete steps that you can do away with. Invariably, whenever I visit a fleet department and review the actions they are routinely carrying out, there will be some that are being done that way because they have always been done that way, or they are being done due to the intricacies of the current fleet system. Hence why I strongly suggest a clean sheet of paper and some blue sky thinking about the new system which will perhaps generate some better and more efficient ways of doing things.

A good Fleet Management System is core to managing your vehicles

Lastly, one of the key benefits with a FM system is that any alerts, flags and reminders can be set up in priority order, usually colour coded. This saves considerable time and effort so you and your staff can see exactly what is overdue or about to become overdue and take more urgent action to rectify these issues. If you have a dashboard system that has been carefully set up to bring up your fleet status in priority order, it saves considerable thinking time and enables you to generally take immediate action. If you then have to return your previous system for any reason you will be amazed how much work and time a good dashboard saves. The dashboard function is one part of the system worth spending some time going through with your supplier before purchase to understand what it will look like and how it performs.

Handy Hint   ♨

- When looking at a new Fleet Management system, allow some time to spend with whoever will be the main users of the system to get their dashboards exactly how they want to see them. This will uncover the KPI's they need to be watching on a regular basis. Get advice from your supplier, who should be able to advise on the easiest way to set them up – time spent early will pay dividends later and also encourage users to use the system more often.

---

3) *How do you select a system supplier from the wide variety available for your particular operation?*

The first step in selecting a supplier, in keeping with most purchasing exercises to do with fleet, is not to start looking at systems and think "that one looks good to me". Instead, start with a clear desk, a pad of paper and a pen (or electronic device if you so desire) and perhaps a cup of coffee or whatever tipple takes your fancy and jot down all the key objectives you require for your operation from this system. That is not as easy as it sounds, but it helps to start with all your problem areas, such as;

- What issues are you currently struggling with where you could really do with clearer or more accurate data?
- What issues have cropped up in recent months or years where you feel things are not being managed as well as they could have been and you would like closer control?
- What fleet related information do Directors or senior managers ask for that you have been struggling to obtain?
- Ask some of your colleagues and employees what information would they like to see to help them control the efficiency and costs of your fleet?

You can then edit all these thoughts, together with other fleet information issues you are aware of to arrive at a clear list of objectives you require from your system. A word of warning here: if you already have an FM system that is old hat or creaking at the seams, please don't start the criteria list by identifying what it can do and then adding and subtracting a few things. Completely ignore the old system and start with a blank sheet of paper, really think through what you now require. Strangely, as a management consultant, I do not spend much of my time advising organisations to seek external advice, I like to see them resolve their own problems. However, in this case, when looking at a new fleet management system, it might be the right time to bring in external help to bring experience and an impartial view, and of course we would be delighted to help you in the process, so if you need support, please contact us on info@thedwconsultancy.com or telephone 07771 768080.

I will give you a big clue here; your first and most important core criteria should be for any FM system to be able, simply and accurately, to regularly provide you with the key KPI's you decided were essential to running your fleet back in chapter 3. That is an absolute must, so please ditch any system that cannot provide this data in an easily readable format, such that everyone in the organisation can understand them.

The next step is then to simply match your core criteria to a shopping list of likely suppliers. List out your criteria and match them against a checklist of each supplier's key benefits; a simple tick or cross will do at this stage to evaluate them. You should then select the top three or so providers to investigate further. System suppliers tend to specialise in particular fields, so you are very likely to find the same short list of suppliers cropping up in your competitor's fleets. If they have optimised their platform for your field, you should already have a head start.

The next stage with suppliers will require some time. Although you are effectively buying an "off the shelf" system rather than bespoke, there will probably be some minor "fettling" required to get closer to your needs. Listen carefully to the replies to your questions and challenge how much time and effort any adjustments will take and especially if there is any programming time involved; who Is paying for that and how much? Be a little cautious about bespoking the standard system. Generally, this will have a cost or time implication further down the line. The more standard you can keep the system, just using all the built-in adjustable features, the less problems you are likely to incur at a later date.

Ask a lot of questions about the initial transfer and uploading of data. Nearly all suppliers will say this is really easy and we can accept multiple formats, but go into it in a little more depth, as in order to preserve any historical records you have, this can be a time-consuming task and may involve some data cleansing to get it into a useable state on the new system. It often helps to have someone who handles your IT to assist you in this discussion in case it starts getting too technical. It is also good to have a more independent view on how much effort the process might take.

I have also mentioned above it is quite difficult to estimate the ROI on a fleet management system, in comparison, say, to a telematic system. However, one issue may make that process easier. When comparing FM systems, one particular system may be able to automate more of the data input that you need more than the others. If that is true, and you can conduct a few simple calculations on the input time involved, it may just be that you can save enough time to reduce the number of administration staff required, even if it is only half of a person's time. If that is the case, you can clearly include this figure in the financial justification. What you then do with those freed up members of staff becomes another issue. Obviously, any other really clear, obvious savings can also be included in the ROI.

Talking of IT, an amazing number of IT departments have a blind spot concerning fleet management systems. I have come across many operators where IT take the view that fleet bought the system, so they can look after it. Of course, you can contract out the system maintenance, at a price, but issues often arise whenever transferring data from the fleet management system to other IT systems such as finance and payroll; you can really do with on-going IT support at that point. Involving IT at the early stage of system selection helps to get buy in later on. You really want your fleet management system to be a part of the organisations' overall IT systems, used by as many people and departments as possible, supported by IT, not that "funny system" that only fleet use.

One word of warning here. It is really important to spend some time on producing that core criteria list, and then stick to it. What tends to happen is that the salesperson gives you a demonstration of the system and you suddenly start thinking "that would be good" about a particular function. I am embarrassed to admit that I did that a number of times in my early days and what invariably happens is the price goes up and many years down the track, you discover that you did not really need that extra feature after all. Use the Pareto rule here; if the new system gives you 90% of what you think you need, that is great and it will do the job. Do not double the price to get the last 10%. Imagine this is your money and your company and stick to that core criteria list.

4) *What differences do you need to consider if you run either an internal or use an external workshop?*

Good fleet management systems will handle both internal or external maintenance or both. This is fairly obviously an important feature to provide as many operators have decided to keep maintenance in house, because they have the facilities and the staff and like the control it gives them, but still externalise some maintenance. This could be for geographic reasons as the vehicles are too far away to be looked after, or contractual reasons, perhaps some vehicles are cheaper in their earlier years with dealer maintenance. Or it could be warranty or diagnostic reasons which cannot be catered for in house. Whatever the reason, both types of maintenance records are likely to be required.

The issues that a FM system for internal workshops will need to cover will naturally vary according to your operation. Once again, try not to be tempted by every option, thinking "that would be good", but just make sure that every function you currently use will be provided for in the future. The sort of functions you are likely to require include:

- The ability to access detailed historic maintenance and vehicle records.
- A fleet maintenance and inspection longer term planner.
- Some form of service booking diary and workshop loading planner.
- A means to convert the planner into vehicle job cards, electronic or paper.
- An ability to estimate costs for each job.
- Record and access a vehicle's job history.
- Send out service, inspection and MoT reminders from the planner to operators by a variety of means at suitable intervals.
- Provide a system of handling defects from a defect system and allow monitoring and sign off of repairs using an auditable process.
- Allocate time spent on jobs to technicians' time sheets to calculate individual, departmental and workshop efficiency and utilisation figures.
- Provide all necessary timesheet data for technician payment.
- Ability to order, hold and dispense vehicle parts stocks.
- Ability to handle parts going direct to the shop floor & kits of parts.
- Ability to record and process all warranty claims.
- Handle parts order purchasing and payment of invoicing.
- Ability to issue and monitor invoicing.
- Ability to store and send data to other departments, such as finance.
- A complete workshop reports suite which is very easy to operate.

An FM system that is required to cater for external suppliers will still contain some of the core functionality necessary to manage the fleet, as shown above, such as:

- The ability to access detailed historic maintenance and vehicle records.
- A fleet maintenance and inspection longer term planner.
- Record and access a vehicle's job history (probably to a lower level of detail).
- Send out service inspection and MoT reminders from the planner to operators.
- Provide a system of handling defects from a defect system and allow monitoring and sign off repairs using an auditable system.
- Ability to record and process all warranty claims.
- An increased ability to issue orders and monitor invoicing.
- Ability to store and send data to other departments such as finance.

The main difference in using the FM system to manage and control external suppliers, as against an internal workshop, will be the level of detail required and a much greater emphasis in controlling contractual requests and finance. If your fleet, or part of your fleet, is operated under a contractual maintenance package, to some extent you are not too interested in the detailed costs of the operation. However, for compliance reasons you will need to know the type of work undertaken, who completed it and the date it was carried out, with the necessary inspection sheets signed off by the relevant technician, supervisor, or manager.

Your routine maintenance will normally be paid for through a fixed monthly sum, so you can argue that the actual time taken is not absolutely crucial to log, but the operation undertaken is important, so that you are fully aware of the vehicle's history. What becomes really critical, however, is all the additional work undertaken outside of the contract which can make the difference between external maintenance being a cost-effective undertaking or an extremely expensive luxury. The efficient recording, monitoring and handling of external maintenance by your FM system can be hugely critical to managing the whole process.

5) *What other important factors should you take into account when selecting fleet management software?*

- **Customer Support** - Probably the most important factor of all is that of after-sales or customer support. However good the product, you will need help, possibly sooner rather than later. You and your staff could spend at least the next five years talking to your supplier, often at points of stress, so it is well worth the effort now to check out their customer support. Find out everything you can about how they provide support, the size of the department, opening hours, availability after hours, what kind of support do they provide? As mentioned elsewhere, find out who you will be dealing with and have a discussion with them – how quickly do they respond, do they sound like someone who knows what they are doing and will help solve a problem or even assist in a crisis? When you talk to referrals, check what levels of support they are receiving and their response times. Talking of referrals, the supplier will almost certainly offer up some of their best clients to talk to. When they previously go through the list of organisations they are supplying, (they almost always will at some stage), note down any that you know and if they are not in the list they give you, or you just want more evidence, ask for their contact details. You are likely to get a much more realistic response that way and hopefully it will be from someone you know and trust.

- **Security & Access** – you should be able to specify who has access to the system and at what level. This sounds a simple operation, but can actually be quite complex, so allow some time to think through who will be working with which parts of the system and seek advice on how best to set it up. Whatever permissions you start with may well need adjusting over time, so do not consider it as set in stone. You will almost certainly need some other departments to access certain data, so, for example, HR will need to look at, or even be able to update, driver records. You need to make sure that specific departments will be able to access the data they require and no more. It will probably pay to have your helpful IT person on hand here to ask pertinent questions. The issue is that certain people, such as the fleet manager or the workshop manager, may want to be on the system at multiple times during the day, so logins need to be relatively straightforward. However, the system still needs to be as secure as possible from any outside interference, so there is a compromise between the two – you, or your IT expert, will need to judge if the system is sufficiently secure but still accessible to those who need it.

- **Training** - Spend some time discussing initial and on-going training. A small amount of training may be included in the set-up package, but you will almost certainly need more and of course, you will have to pay, unless you can incorporate further training in your purchase agreement. Check arrangements and particularly costs – measure this per person to get a true comparison. Much more training is now virtual, with a consequent cost reduction – training multiple users can obviously reduce costs further and still be effective. As with most software systems, it helps to have training (after the initial set-up) after your users have tried the system for themselves for a while – they are then primed with questions, rather than just having information thrown at them. One key point here; both telematics and fleet management systems, in my experience, often suffer from huge underutilisation – in other words, they can do far, far more things than most operators ever get to utilise. Obviously, it is not a good plan to over burden the end user, but there may be many features available within easy reach that can reduce the time to carry out tasks. That is why regular training updates can often be really beneficial. As ever, you may be able to strike a good deal for on-going training and coaching in the negotiation stages.

- **Speed of Processing** - Always insist on a full demonstration of your chosen shortlist; try to have them use your internet connection. If there are any delays on loading data, they will invariably offer a feasible sounding excuse. You will have to determine if you think the excuse is valid and compare it with their competitors. What you are looking for is speed of response – if you have to enter considerable amounts of data, the last thing you need are delays in processing, especially if storage is in the cloud. If possible, arrange for a trial of the base software to experience speed and useability for yourself. Have all your potential system users attempt to enter and retrieve the data that they will need to use and get feedback on how easy the system is to use from their point of view. Check what the supplier's recent downtime records have been and check this quoted performance with your referrals.

- **Scalability** – how your fleet has expanded in the last five years is a good indication of how it will behave in the next five. Unless your organisation has plans to grow by acquisition, if it has stayed relatively static in terms of numbers, it is unlikely to suddenly grow, so scaling up is probably not an issue. However, do allow something in your plans in terms of potential system growth so you are not caught unawares. If you have been steadily growing in size, check scaling up will not cause any problems. For example, make sure you know if there are step changes in the cost of adding users for example, or no issues with the hosting if the volume of data really increases.

- **Future-proofing** – This is where you may have to dig a little deeper. Most fleet management systems evolved from just one or two original offerings long ago; now there are so many versions on the market which have improved, expanded and developed over time. You do not want your system to be changing too often, but you do want to be sure you are keeping pace with the industry, so check your supplier has a plan for updating and find out exactly what that is. Find out what their R&D department is working on – if it is simply de-bugging operating problems, be very wary, but hopefully there is a development plan in place to outline what can be future improvements are expected and by when. This is another question to ask referrals in order to check how the supplier has performed against their development plan in the past.

Some operators get stuck on a previous version of the system as it would be too much trouble to change and that is OK, providing that system is also being updated regularly to take account of recent features. For example, in the last five years or so, compliance has been the big thing, so all sorts of features have been added to record your compliance related data. Similarly, over time, there has been a general move to enter data automatically, for example mileages coming from telematics – anything to save tedious and time-consuming manual data entry.

You obviously want to make sure you can capture these sort of advances in the future. Lastly, and this may seem a bit crackers, but autonomous vehicles are almost here with us now, but not yet fully in operation. Has your system supplier at least got a plan for how to deal with the mass of information that a fully connected vehicle and the Internet of Things (IoT) will provide; then a little later a fully automated vehicle?

- **End User Buy-in** – everywhere in this book, you will see that I extol the virtues of talking to the people doing the job, because I know from bitter experience, it is the one thing that most managers involved in fleet do not do enough of. So many FM systems are installed with little or no reference to the poor person doing the task. By all means come up with your initial criteria list as a thought starter, but I then strongly suggest you have a meeting with all the people who will be involved with a new system and get their thoughts. Really listen to their ideas and incorporate all the sensible ones in your plans, letting them know you have done just that. If not, as ever, you are likely to get resistance to any new system you try to install, however good you think it will be.

- **Data** – There are a number of issues to think about here. Firstly, do not forget that the quality of the reports and output of your system depends largely on the quality of data going in. What procedures does the system use to guarantee the quality of data input? Secondly, especially if you are going to be providing or sharing data, check, in writing, who owns it, especially if it is stored in the cloud. Most people think it must belong to them, but that is not always the case. Make sure if you change provider you will still retain full rights to historical data. There will be a significant amount of personal data on the system, especially relating to drivers, so pay special attention to all the potential GDPR issues, making sure any system you purchase can comply with your own organisational and legal guidelines. If you are going down the earned recognition route, or similar, check how easy it is to provide the right data in the right format to external organisations. For the same reason, also check how easy it is to anonymise any data you may have to provide.

- **Paperwork & Devices** - You could probably write a full book on this subject alone. Suffice to say, if you are still handling large amounts of paperwork, then a new FM system is the ideal time to find out how much can be digitised. Certainly, you are now unlikely to want any new system to be using paper defect sheets, so how daily checks can be undertaken on mobile devices will be a key issue for you. Having drivers undertake daily checks fully and properly is a perennial issue for all transport operators, so the checks and balances required by the system can help in the process. Check the useability of each system, as some are much easier to use than others. There are some clever ideas out there to try to make sure daily checks are carried out properly, but don't get too clever; a random request for photos can be quite useful and photos of the defect itself help greatly, just be aware of the need for management reviewing time and storage space.

In the workshop, touchscreen will probably be a time saver, but it all depends on your processes. Barcoding is still very popular, especially for parts management due to its simplicity and widespread adoption. Voice transmission of data is now making an appearance and looks set to save time for those who can master the technology. Digital information has also revolutionised mobile technician working. Before, once the mobile workshop van had left the depot, you were reliant on calls to keep you updated on progress. Now you can know where they are, what they are working on and what other work can be scheduled into their work programme.

The most important factor of all to remember is that paperwork sits somewhere on a desk or in a file; digital information can be made available instantly anywhere in your organisation or externally, so efficiency improvements are almost guaranteed. Just be aware that the swop from paper to digital will take quite a bit of effort, so allow plenty of time for the background work and try to go one step at a time to make the change process more manageable.

- **Dashboards** – Long gone are the days when fleet information was only available in a set format. One of the ways in which suppliers try to differentiate themselves is in how they present key fleet information to the user. These are always customisable to some extent, so users can choose to see certain information first or not see it at all. Similarly, the graphics of the various presentations have got better and better in recent years, information is generally now very clear to read. However, as ever, there are limits and some systems are not as customisable as others, so do check the particular configuration you desire is achievable. Ask as many of your end users as possible how they like the graphics of each system and how they like it customised. Check the majority of these requests can be accommodated by each supplier and check that information that is key to you, from any modules you are using, can be incorporated into your dashboards.

- **User Groups** – As a generalisation, system suppliers who run regular user groups have a higher level of confidence in their product than their competitors who do not. User groups normally function by customers getting together to discuss their current issues and problems, share information and discuss potential future improvements. Ask if you can see the minutes from a recent meeting, although you may be prevented by confidentiality restrictions. Never-the-less, the existence of a user group is a very good sign and if one exists, I would recommend joining as soon as purchase is made, as other users can be very helpful in getting you up to speed as quickly as possible.

- **Compliance** – Whatever else the system does, you will want it to record, store and be able to interrogate and monitor all the legal documentation required to meet DVLA or operator recognition requirements, not least to meet the conditions of your O licence, if you are operating at the heavy end of the spectrum. It helps to be able to view all the upcoming inspections and services due quickly and easily and be able to automatically send reminders, by whatever means your organisation uses, at appropriate intervals to the operators. You will obviously need to be able to store all the required legal documents associated with your fleet and have access to a full audit trail of maintenance documentation. If you operate under O licence rules, even if you are not thinking of joining the DVSA earned recognition scheme, it would make good sense to use a system that could cope with it and present all the necessary information in an easy-to-use dashboard, ready to send to the DVSA on your behalf.

To explain to those not familiar with the DVSA fleet compliance scheme, it focuses on areas such as risk and safety management, along with vehicle maintenance & driver behaviour. It is a continuous process that allows the DVSA to interrogate your Fleet Management system and reports to ensure you are meeting the standards they set out. To be part of the scheme you are therefore required to use a DVSA-validated IT system which automatically uploads vehicle maintenance records and drivers' hour data every four weeks. The data you provide is then monitored against a set of KPIs and if figures are below par, you will get contacted by the DVSA in order to agree an action plan to get back on track.

The benefits of the scheme, in theory, include being able to demonstrate that you are an exemplary operator to clients and customers, access to the DVSA team for assistance and a reduced likelihood of your vehicles being stopped for roadside checks or an ad-hoc inspection of your premises and records. I say in theory, as at the time of writing, there are still some operators involved in the scheme who do not think the work involved in belonging to it is currently outweighed by the benefits. However, these are still early days, the scheme is still being improved and must be a good way forward for operators keen to demonstrate their compliance.

6)   Why is calculating whole life costs so important?

Part of the benefit of operating a good fleet management system is the ability to operate true whole life costs on all your vehicles. Many fleets take a short-sighted route of concentrating on specific cost factors rather than the true cost of ownership, which takes all expenditure into account. The only drawback in this method is that by the time you have the full lifetime costs of operating a particular vehicle, the next model will probably be out, with differing depreciation, maintenance and fuel costs, so some intelligent extrapolation and estimation will be required.

When you are making any strategic decisions concerning your fleet, you must be doing so based upon the whole life cost of your vehicles. This means taking into account not only the capital cost less the residual cost, so effectively vehicle depreciation, but all the other operating costs that you will incur over the lifetime of the vehicle. Any cost that your organisation incurs as a direct result of owning and operating a vehicle can be considered part of the whole life cost. A good fleet management system will be able to give you whole life costs of a vehicle on an ongoing basis, providing you have accurately recorded all the necessary data. Obviously, during the life of the vehicle you will have to estimate or calculate some things such as the residual value in order to get a usable figure.

The important step then is to measure this total figure against one or two suitable operating metrics – pence per kilometre (p.p.k.) or pence per mile (p.p.m.) is common, pence per pallet delivered could be another or cost per delivery; whatever makes logical sense for your operation and organisation. This last step is important as the total cost of ownership for one vehicle may look high, but if it happens to be on a route that is productive, the p.p.k. or cost per delivery could be considerably lower than similar vehicles in the fleet. If you do not calculate the true whole life costs for your vehicle, not all comparisons will be truthful.

When buying new commercial vehicles, for comparison purposes with other models and comparison with your existing vehicles, I suggest keeping the process really straightforward and simply look at depreciation, fuel and repairs. These figures will be available from your FM system for your existing vehicles and can be obtained, with a fair degree of accuracy and a bit of extrapolation, for new vehicles. It is also useful to look at generalised whole life vehicle costs produced from time to time in trade publications such as 'Transport Engineer' (the IRTE magazine), 'Motor Transport', Commercial Motor' or figures produced by trade associations such as the RHA (Road Haulage Association) or Logistics UK (formerly the FTA). All these will be average figures for a particular weight of vehicle, but they are useful to measure your statistics against or where you do not run a particular weight of vehicle as yet.

7) How do you use lifetime vehicle costs for true cost comparisons?

What puts many operators off the process is the thought that it must be complex and trying to predict lifetime costs on new vehicles for which you have no statistics. The answer to this problem is straightforward – keep the process simple and do not over complicate matters. You can read much written about whole life costing in trade papers, most of it, however, is written for cars. When looking at cars, calculations usually include such items as insurance, employee allowances, taxation and mileage allowances, many things that we do not really need to worry about for commercial vehicles.

For the exercise of comparing current vehicles with potential new vehicles, running costs such as driver costs and VED (Vehicle Excise Duty) can usually be taken out of the equation, as they should be fairly similar for each vehicle within a similar group. Obviously, if there is a big difference, such as looking at an electric vehicle, factor these costs in, otherwise, try to keep it as simple as possible.

HGV and Van fuel figures can be obtained for comparative purposes from the Vehicle Certification Agency. Useful fuel figures can also be obtained from regularly published cost tables in trade magazines, such as the ones mentioned above. Better still, obtain some test or trial demonstrator vehicles from the dealer or manufacturer for as long a period as possible and utilise them in your actual operation to monitor real-life fuel consumption.

Similarly, do not try and over-complicate calculating depreciation. Simply take your quoted final purchase price and subtract any expected residual value, over the period you expect to be operating the vehicle. Use straight line depreciation to calculate monthly figures unless your finance department requires something more elaborate. Just be aware that if you do have to get rid of the vehicle early, it may not realise your predicted book value.

Forecast residual values are available from organisations such as Glass's guide or CAP, allowing some factoring to account for your specific vehicle specification and operation.

For forecasting servicing, almost all dealers and manufacturers will be keen to supply the vehicle complete with a Repair & Maintenance package for varying length of life. If you do not have your own maintenance costs for a particular vehicle, getting manufacturer rates for varying length of ownership can be a useful guide to costs. Keep in mind this will only cover the routine servicing items, almost everything else will be an additional cost. For those with internal workshops, have your workshop manager review maintenance schedules and have them predict likely R&M costs; they will probably have to undertake some research on spare prices using the "basket of spares" approach.

So now you have the true cost of the vehicle over its life, plus the likely servicing costs and often the highest running cost of fuel. You may possibly find the cheapest vehicle to purchase will be the most expensive to run over its life, but that is not always the case, which is why it is so important to carry out this exercise, armed with the facts about your current fleet.

8)   How do you best manage your FM system for maximum advantage?

In this section there will probably be quite a lot of stating the blindingly obvious. Unfortunately, I feel it is probably a good idea to do so, as many operators fail to carry out the basics when setting up their software, so the system operates sub-optimally for most of its life.

Firstly, most fleet managers are generally meticulous persons; that is, they like getting involved in the detailed parts of fleet management. This tends to make them people that like to be in control and therefore reluctant to relinquish the organisation of their fleet management system. You are invariably going to be too busy in your day-to-day role to also manage this system. It is therefore a good idea, right at the start, to make someone responsible for the administration and upkeep of the system for your organisation.

If your fleet is large enough it could represent almost a whole-time job, or for a smaller fleet it will most likely become a part of someone's role. This person will also become your conduit to the software supplier and of course their main contact within your organisation. One other tip here is to make the core objectives of installing this system part of this person's role objectives. Of course, this is big picture stuff, but it helps keep your system administrator on track, rather than getting involved in the small stuff.

Secondly, and I cannot emphasise how important this is, you need to start a central listing of all the terms and descriptions that you are going to use on the system. Only let people enter data using exactly those descriptions. Just remember the average age of both trucks and vans in the UK is around 7½ years, (unfortunately getting older at the moment due to a lack of new vehicles), so some of your vehicles may be with you for up to 15 years, especially trailers and some specialist vehicles, which may be with you even longer.

This means it is crucial to use the very best possible description for a vehicle, part of a vehicle or item of equipment, that will be recognised by the greatest number of people in your organisation, for some time to come. Just because you regularly call something by a particular name does not mean everybody else will recognise it. When I visit organisations, I wish I had a pound for every time I have to ask, "what's this item?", on a vehicle listing and the description is nothing like the vehicle; it perhaps made sense at one time, but maybe only to the person entering the data. Beware of using temporary staff for data entry (very common), who often enter the most interesting, but completely unrecognisable descriptions!

Spending some time on this core listing will save you an awful lot of effort down the track. Once you have established it, the system will probably prompt you to enter descriptions at the appropriate point which then usually later appear as drop-down selection lists for the operators to enter. Even when you have carried out this work to the best of your ability, you will not believe how many members of staff try to overwrite that description with their own one, sometimes succeeding. Check when purchasing the system if those selection lists are lockable. Conversely, if you want a group of vehicles or equipment to appear separately, for example, with a higher-powered engine, then incorporate something in the title to indicate the change, which again, is as obvious to as many people as possible. Yes, this is incredibly basic, but so many operators get this bit wrong, which then makes every calculation from then on, much more difficult.

Organise your system training from the outset, otherwise it has a tendency to get forgotten with all the other issues that the fleet Department will be handling. As mentioned previously, do allow time between training sessions so that staff can utilise what they have already learnt, and start building a list of questions to ask at the next session. The speed at which you achieve this training will depend largely on your staff's capabilities, but also on their desire to learn, which is why involving them at the outset is so critical.

When transferring data, it is worth spending as much time as feasibly possible to cleanse that data and remove everything that you know to be incorrect, or even that which you suspect to be incorrect. Otherwise, it is exactly like moving house and taking the contents of the attic with you, because you have not had time to sort through it, but you know much of the attic's contents should have been thrown out years ago. You will probably be keen to install fleet software as soon as possible, once a decision has been made, but I suggest allowing, say, at least a week or more in the installation project plans for cleansing and organising your existing data - time well spent.

Once the system is up and running, some training has taken place and staff are starting to become acclimatised to the new system, it makes great sense to keep the ongoing management of the system as a regular item on the agenda of your routine management meetings. This ensures that any hiccups emerging in how the system is being used are aired, discussed and a solution can be agreed and implemented as soon as possible. This helps keep the system running smoothly, rather than letting idiosyncrasies build up until they become a real problem.

9) What parts of your FM system should you consider integrating with your organisation's other IT platforms?

Most of the points at which you should consider the integration of information with other IT systems in your organisation have been mentioned above, so to summarise:

Finance – there will be a myriad of information that finance will require from you which can be provided by your FM system. There is the obvious information on capital expenditure - this is more likely to be dealt with directly, but requires recording accurately on your system. If insurance is dealt with by finance, a considerable amount of data will need to be exchanged for instance to record accidents, although this may go directly to your accident management company or through your insurance broker. Whatever the route, the target will always be to enter data only once. The faster data about an incident can be recorded and sent to the insurance company for action, the more the claim can be reduced.

Accounts – accounts payable will want to know all the fuel, parts and consumable expenditure on an ongoing basis and how this is dealt with by your organisation depends on how flexible your systems are, but the overall objective again must be to handle each piece of documentation or information only once. If possible, as mentioned elsewhere, at the end of each suitable period, but the longest should be one month, you need to see your outgoing expenditure against your declared budgetary expenditure – this is crucial for knowing if you are operating at a profit or loss, even on a notional basis for the public sector.

HR – you are going to want to exchange a large amount of personnel data on your drivers and technicians, obviously observing all your GDPR guidelines. Make sure you keep accurate records especially for things like obtaining an individual's consent to hold their records. The target must be to have just one database of these details, such as education records, driver license checks, training certificates and training records

Payroll – detailed information for the hours of work necessary to pay your technicians should all come neatly packaged from your FM system, saving unnecessary administration time.

External organisations – most FM systems will integrate sensibly with data coming from your fuel card supplier and any internal fuel tank monitoring systems you may possess. You will probably want to be integrating with both the DVLA and the HMRC depending on your fleet profile. You may also wish to link directly with your maintenance supplier in order to make work requests and receive service and inspection reports seam.

Top Tips for Fleet Management Systems ✔

- Whatever systems you end up using to manage your fleet, try as much as possible to consolidate or integrate the systems for simplicity and most importantly, aim for data entry just once – reduce and eliminate existing or potential double entries wherever possible.

- When determining the core requirements from a new system, always start with a blank sheet of paper, not from your previous system/s. First on the list must be providing your most important KPI's in a simple, accurate and timely fashion.

- Spend as much time as you can checking out your potential supplier's customer support – find the actual people you will be speaking to and establish if they are helpful and understandable.

- Find referrals other than the first ones given to you by the supplier and question them in detail about their relationship.

- Maximise your chances of getting buy-in from the end users of the system; involve all the users when deciding what outputs you require from the system.

- Spend some time setting up dashboards and reports for end users to suit their particular needs.

- When selecting which vehicles to replace, always use true whole-life costs to give realistic comparisons between makes, models and operations.

- Organise system training at the time of purchase and make sure it happens at the appointed times, else it will probably get forgotten due to operating pressures. Allow sufficient time between sessions for staff to absorb and use fresh features they have learnt.

David's Don'ts ✖

- Don't forget to involve your IT department in the selection of a new system at an early stage to obtain their agreement and ensure they will give you all the internal support you will require.

- Don't be tempted by any bells and whistles on a new system; just stick to your core requirements and do not start purchasing add-ons because they look "useful", unless there is a clear, justifiable and demonstrable need for that option.

- Don't assume you will own all the data you generate – establish in writing, before purchase, exactly who owns the data and that you will have access to it should something happen in the future, such as a move of supplier.

- Don't transfer out-of-date or incorrect data to the new system – use the transfer as an opportunity to cleanse your records.

The Ultimate Guide to Commercial Vehicle Fleet Management

Chapter 10 – Vehicle Repair & Maintenance

1) *What do I need to know about commercial vehicle maintenance?*
2) *What should I do to keep maintenance and repair costs to a minimum?*
3) *What are the pros & cons of internal and external workshops?*
4) *What facilities do I require to operate an internal workshop?*
5) *What are the key issues involved in managing an efficient internal workshop?*
6) *What factors do I need to consider when contracting out maintenance?*
7) *How do I manage external maintenance contractors?*
8) *How do I effectively handle vehicle defects?*
9) *How do I manage parts supply and quality?*
10) *How do I manage breakdowns?*

1) *What do I need to know about commercial vehicle maintenance?*

This is one of the most important parts of managing vehicles and is quite complex, possibly mysterious, to some people. It is probably easiest to start at the heavy end of the spectrum as they are the vehicles that have the most legislation regarding their maintenance management. Effectively, most people operating vehicles over 3.5 Tonnes will be running under their O licence obligations, which has very clear regulations about how to maintain your vehicles and what records to keep. For most commercial operations, a senior member of your organisation will have signed a legal document declaring that you will ensure your vehicles are fully maintained in a safe and effective manner. The definitive text here is the DVSA's 'Guide to maintaining Roadworthiness', freely available on the internet: https://www.gov.uk/government/publications/guide-to-maintaining-roadworthiness and usefully updated in Dec 2020. It is very wise to double check that you have incorporated all the latest revisions to that document into your fleet processes.

The DVSA guide is pretty clear in most matters, although annoyingly, it is still a little vague in some areas, like brake testing. For this it recommends best practice, but does not legally enforce it, although, as ever, if you do not follow the guidelines and are unlucky enough to have a visit from the DVSA, the Traffic Commissioner may take a dim view of your practices. The important thing is to have regular, fully documented safety inspections undertaken at the declared intervals. Servicing is up to you, but you will want to stick with the manufacturers' recommendations, not least to keep warranty valid, unless you have very good reasons to use an alternative. You will need a forward service and inspection maintenance planner of some sort, clearly showing progress to date. Your maintenance records, either paper or electronic, must be held for the regulatory time as evidence of your good repute.

At the lighter end, in theory, van operators get away lightly with less legal control about what to do and when. However, in recent years a little thing called corporate responsibility and even corporate manslaughter has changed the way van fleets operate. So much so, that most good van operators use a maintenance system and records which are not that far away from those used for HGVs. One big problem is that as vehicles have got more reliable and many are now using fully synthetic oils with extended mileages between servicing, often at self-diagnosed periods, it is not unheard of for vehicles not to see a workshop for at least two years. In theory this is perfectly legal. In practice, I would strongly recommend that every vehicle in your fleet has a safety check at least once a year, better at six-monthly intervals. Even if your van drivers are undertaking religious daily checks on all your vehicles, you cannot rely on all of them to spot all possible defects, so you need the assurance of a technician giving your vehicle a clean bill of health at regular intervals.

The guide to maintaining road worthiness has improved immeasurably over the years and is now a comprehensive document for all operators running their fleet, or part of it, under O licence obligations. As it is comprehensive, I don't want to repeat it all here, but it really is worth summarising the key points of a good maintenance system, as for all the best of reasons, some parts of the required system often tend to get forgotten:

1. Everything starts with the vehicle driver (or nominated responsible person) undertaking a daily walkaround check of any owned, leased, hired or borrowed vehicle, preferably just before being used, especially if has not been used for some time. Although commonly referred to as the daily check, really it should take place for each and every shift.

2. The person carrying out the checks must be competent to assess the significance of potential defects, so should be either qualified or trained and given clear written instructions about their responsibilities. Assistance should be available as support of the process.

3. You then need a clear system to promptly report and record any defects or symptoms that could adversely affect the safe operation of vehicles. Serious repairs must be carried out before the vehicle goes out on the road; less serious defects that do not affect roadworthiness may wait for the next appropriate

point to repair. Records must also show the details of any rectification work done and be kept for 15 months (including vehicles removed from the O licence). The system needs to be monitored, especially in the early stages for effectiveness.

4. It is important when reviewing your system to recognise that too many defects found on service can indicate that the inspection intervals are too long or daily inspections are possibly not being carried out properly by your drivers; zero or few defects could potentially indicate meticulous or over-servicing or that your inspection intervals could possibly be extended. If there are few defects being found on daily inspection, but those same missing defects are then found at the time of routine safety inspection, this indicates your drivers are not undertaking their inspections properly and probably require further guidance on the subject. You will have to look deeper into each defect found by your service agent to determine whether or not it should have been found on daily inspection. Having said that, of course, zero defects is your ultimate target.

5. Safety inspections, including any intermediate inspections, should be pre-planned, preferably using a time-based programme following DVSA guidelines and you must ensure they are carried out at the stated frequency. The inspection should include items covered in the annual test and records must show the:

   - name of the owner or operator
   - date of inspection
   - vehicle identity (registration or trailer number)
   - make and model
   - odometer reading
   - a list of all the manual items to be inspected
   - details of any defects
   - name of inspector
   - full details of any repair work and who carried it out
   - a signed declaration that any defects have been repaired satisfactorily
   and the vehicle is now in a safe roadworthy condition.

6. The DVSA still like operators to have a wall chart planner (despite the latest technology, they are probably still the best method for managing your inspections) to identify inspection dates at least six months in advance, but will, of course, also accept a dynamic electronic planning system. Whatever system you use needs to be regularly monitored for effectiveness; in practice, that means you make sure you are not missing any inspection dates.

7. It is crucial to have a robust system to ensure that a responsible person removes unroadworthy vehicles from service and takes them off the road, again, this part can easily be missed.

8. If you undertake your own inspections, you must obviously have the correct tools and facilities for the size and type of vehicle fleet operated, including a

means of measuring brake efficiency and setting headlamp aim. When vehicles show signs of visible exhaust smoke, a smoke meter must be available

9. Most importantly of all, even if you contract out your maintenance and inspection, you still retain full responsibility for the condition of your vehicles and that all agents, contractors or hire companies are correctly carrying out the inspection and repair work. You will therefore require evidence, written or electronic, that the work is being undertaken to the required standard. You need to also retain the records for at least 15 months and have a means of regularly monitoring the quality of work produced by them. This last part is probably the most often missed or forgotten – there is an assumption by many operators that if the contractor is being paid, they must be doing the job properly, sadly, that is not always the case.

10. Any changes by operators to the above arrangements for safety inspections must be updated on the Vehicle Operator Licensing system (VOL).

All of the above very clearly applies to all O licence operators, in essence, most vehicles operating above 3.5 tonnes. However, there are now around four million vans on the UK's roads, who in theory, do not all have to comply with the above legislation.

Some of the increase in the number of vans on our roads is due to an increase in home deliveries, some is also due to an increase in self-employed tradespersons or mobile servicing vehicles and some due to companies downsizing to avoid the costs that come with HGV vehicles. This means that a van is often a means to an end, just a tool to get the job done, so van drivers are not always vocational, sometimes lacking an understanding for the vehicle they are driving.

I say above, in theory operators do not have to comply with the legislation, but of course, roadworthiness and driver regulations still apply. Although HGVs require an annual test from year one, vans do not have their first MoT test until year three. Back in 2017, a FOI (Freedom of Information) request revealed first time MoT failure rates as high as 45% for some vans, not a good sign of a high-quality maintenance regime taking place. An MoT failure for HGV operators (less than 20% fail on test) will result in a poor service record as it shows against your OCRS (Operator Compliance Risk Score), so an HGV operator tends to work hard to avoid failures. The suspicion is that many van operators use the MoT test as a diagnostic tool, that is, they put the vehicle through the test to find out what is wrong – not what is intended, nor good practice.

As mentioned above, despite the lack of legislation (currently) for van operators, corporate responsibility and corporate manslaughter legislation, coupled to existing HSE legislation means that most good van operators use a maintenance system and records which are similar to those used for HGVs in order to protect themselves.

There has also been an expansion of operators wanting to demonstrate their compliance to higher standards, signing up to operator recognition schemes. For obvious reasons, these schemes all want operators to work to a higher standard than the basic minimum.

So, what does the van equivalent to the guide to vehicle maintenance look like, using advice for van operators taken directly from the gov.uk website: https://www.gov.uk/government/publications/running-a-fleet-of-vans/running-a-fleet-of-vans

- You will need to carry out daily walkaround checks on your vehicle before using your vans and record any defects, exactly as 1 & 2 above.

- You then need a system to repair any major defects before sending your vans out on the road, exactly as 3 & 7 above.

- You also need to keep records of your van repairs, as 2,4 & 5 above.

- You must service your vehicles to at least the minimum standard, in line with the manufacturer's guidelines. This is where vans start to depart from HGVs, as there is no legal requirement for safety inspections, although a plan as in 6 above is obviously very sensible.

- However, the guidelines also state you should have qualified personnel frequently check safety critical components, such as brakes, if your vans are subject to demanding work. As mentioned elsewhere, I would strongly suggest every vehicle in your fleet gets a full safety inspection conducted by technically qualified personnel at least annually, as an absolute minimum.

- You must, of course, make sure your vans are always insured, taxed and MoT'd and document this process, as for HGVs. Keep records for 15 months minimum.

Once again, some of these processes are not legal requirements, but given that they are declared government guidelines, in view of corporate responsibility to your employees, you would have to be a pretty poor operator not to follow their guidance. Also, any fleet operator that has unfortunately suffered any kind of serious vehicle incident, perhaps involving a fatality, knows the huge time, cost and trauma involved. You may have your vehicle impounded for a long period of time, not to mention the bad publicity caused plus potential legal and insurance fees. It can also have severe and sometimes lasting psychological effects on the drivers and sometimes managers involved, which I have unfortunately witnessed over time. I would strongly counsel doing everything possible to avoid such an incident, not least for your own and your staff's peace of mind and consider the time involved in a comprehensive maintenance regime as good corporate practice and as an insurance policy.

Without wishing to frighten senior managers and directors, if a vehicle incident is thought to involve corporate responsibility, it may be dealt with under criminal law and is investigated as a crime. This could mean your records being impounded and key members of staff involved in giving evidence, tying up considerable amounts of their time, not to mention the legal costs involved. Just to avoid this one factor alone means it becomes complete sense to make absolutely sure you can demonstrate that you have robust systems and processes in place to show all the correct management procedures for your fleet are being carried out on a regular basis. Please do not wait until something untoward happens before taking action. Refer to this Crown Prosecution Service website to establish the latest legal position on your responsibilities: https://www.cps.gov.uk/legal-guidance/corporate-manslaughter

As a light van operator, you obviously do not have to inform the O licence system of changes, but it still makes good sense to have a written contract with any external suppliers. All the other guidelines, such as having sufficient equipment and facilities are just common sense. You can therefore see that virtually all of points 1 to 9 above apply equally to vans as much as they do HGVs, albeit the service and inspection intervals are generally much further apart. Perhaps unsurprisingly, many van operators that I see find the daily inspection one of their biggest challenges, given that problems also exist in conducting regular checks, to some extent, on HGVs. The issue seems to be that cars do not often receive a daily check (although, or course, they really should), so why do vans, especially car derived vans? The answer is that they are very different vehicles, used in a different way for commercial purposes, sometimes by multiple drivers and the daily check is the only practical way to avoid your staff driving a potentially unroadworthy vehicle.

Handy Hint	👍
• Defects found on service or inspection can be really good indicators; too many may mean daily checks are not being carried out properly, or previous maintenance was not carried out properly, or inspection intervals are too long. Very few is usually a good sign, (as long as items are not missed) but may mean service intervals can be extended.	

2) What should I do to keep maintenance and repair costs to a minimum?

- Firstly, it must be said that in the last ten years or so, vehicles are getting increasingly reliable and therefore suffer reduced downtime. This is due, in the main, to improved manufacturing quality, increased service intervals, not least due to improved oils, and reduced component replacement times. This is good news for fleet operators as generally, where maintenance is concerned, time equals money. It is probably also fair to say that when a vehicle does require an unscheduled repair when out of warranty, they can get quite expensive as the technology being used and the complexity of parts and systems increases. So, one of the most important factors for fleet managers to measure is what is increasingly being called "uptime", (obviously the converse of "downtime") or when a vehicle is available to operations. We need to think holistically about maintenance as it is not just the direct cost of a repair, but also the opportunity cost to operations of the vehicle not being available and the potential cost of a replacement vehicle.

- For an HGV operator, after making sure your inspections intervals are set at the optimum period, your servicing agent is working as efficiently as possible, the most important thing you can do is ensure your drivers conduct their daily checks diligently and repairs are carried out as soon as efficiently possible. I know it has been said before, but it is critical to reducing costs and many fleets just do not conduct their daily checks properly. For evidence, just look at the DVSA statistics whenever they hold roadside checks, the statistics for defects found are truly frightening.

- For van operators, it starts with measurement. According to Logistics UK (formerly the FTA), nearly half of van operators do not know what their downtime (vehicles off the road for maintenance) statistics are. Logistics UK also report that vans are off the road longer for unplanned repairs than for their scheduled maintenance, in fact unplanned time is almost double planned. The way to tackle this problem is to measure downtime accurately, then make sure planned servicing and inspection is carried out exactly as described in (1) above and that daily driver checks are carried out and rectified exactly as for HGVs. Once you know your downtime, set a target and take action to improve your figures. If you need impetus to do this, just calculate the true daily cost of one of your vans and then add the average cost of a replacement vehicle and potential business disruption – but be prepared to be shocked.

- Correct vehicle specification is crucial in keeping maintenance costs down. When correctly chosen, the right vehicle will carry out its role with ease; an incorrect vehicle will always be a struggle to operate, suffer more breakdowns and require more repairs. It is obviously important not to over-spec the vehicle, especially the power unit, in order to save fuel, but equally, do not be tempted to skimp on engine size, making the vehicle strain when loaded, just to keep up with traffic.

- Make full use of extended opening hours from your service agent, including weekends (providing the hourly rates still stack up) to keep vehicle downtime to a minimum. If you are operating your own workshop, look at flexing your current working times to suit the operations and maximise the use of your assets, again to reduce downtime. If you are not doing this, you can bet your life more of your competitors will be, meaning, if you take no action, your costs will become uncompetitive.

- Whether using internal or external maintenance, prioritise the repairs according to the financial effect on the operation, not according to how it effects the workshop. Like many words of wisdom in this book, this seems glaringly obvious, but not all workshop managers are consistently fully sensitive to the needs of the operation.

- Elsewhere in this chapter, I suggest that a lack of defects found on daily inspection could possibly be seen as a symptom of over-maintenance. At this point, I would like to make a counter-observation, that operationally and usually financially, it is so much better to be repairing vehicles during scheduled downtime rather than as an unplanned repair. An unplanned repair will usually involve extra expense of some sort, even if just the necessity to obtain a part from somewhere and generally result in some form of compromise for operations. Therefore, maximising repairs during scheduled downtime should always result in the lowest lifetime costs for the vehicle and the operation.

- By the same token, the current lack of fully skilled technicians, the rapid increase in van use and a lack of DVSA staff for HGV testing means that booking maintenance and MoT appointments well in advance has now become a critical process within fleet management. Do not let late booking or the unavailability of slots, resulting in a "distressed purchase", give rise to an increase in your R&M costs. As mentioned elsewhere, early pre-booking also gives your service agent a real chance to get all the parts in that they may require.

Handy Hint   👍

- Most repair agents now offer extended opening times, some even work 24 hours a day. Utilising out-of-hours servicing can remove a considerable number of 'spare' vehicles from the fleet.

3) What are the pros & cons of internal and external workshops?

For a long time in the transport industry, the split of operators carrying out their own maintenance against those contracting out was around the 50/50 mark. Then manufacturers decided this was an area they really needed to capture, resulting in a harder sell and more attractive terms when operators were buying the vehicle. Now the number of operators running their own workshops has shrunk to a little over one-third, with main dealers also capturing a little over one third and one quarter going to the independents. I do not see that many new operators, or operators moving to new premises, investing in maintenance facilities, presumably they see it as an unnecessary expense and do not see it as a core activity. However, there is still a committed group of existing operators with workshops that do believe it is a core part of the business. They tend to look at it as an attractive additional revenue stream, possibly adding an ATF (Authorised Testing Facility for HGVs – when allowed) or MoT (Ministry of Transport Test) facility and definitely trying to attract income from external clients, so the ratio may not decline too much further, although the overall trend has definitely been moving towards externalisation for some years.

If you are trying to decide whether or not to use external maintenance, or deciding whether to add R&M to your vehicle purchase, then what are the pros and cons?

What are the benefits of running your own workshops?

- Number one in my book must be control. You may be affected by outside influences, such as parts price rises or new legislation, but almost everything else remains under your control. Providing you establish a willing and flexible workforce, how you operate is in your hands and you can set the workshop up to suit the operation. When emergencies of any form arise, you can flex your working to suit and respond, not always so easy with a contractual arrangement, where you have to share with other customers. You can prioritise your work at any time to suit the operation.

- In the current climate of a shortage of well qualified technicians, the quality and standards of repairs and maintenance is fully in your hands. You can set those quality standards up to specifically suit your fleet. Although it takes time and effort, building up a well-qualified workforce, with the right range of skills for your vehicles means a high quality of work can be maintained and quality control is also in your remit. This is especially important for HGV operators due to O licence obligations.

- In theory, providing you operate reasonably efficiently, even allowing for overheads and training, running your own show should be cheaper than external maintenance, especially if you are offsetting overheads by carrying out third party work. The prime reason for being cheaper is simply that the profit element for the contractor is removed.

- As mentioned elsewhere in this book, a fairly standardised fleet will benefit an internal workshop and reduce running costs of both the fleet and workshops, an option not really available to dealerships or independents, who have to cater for a multitude of models or makes.

- Invariably, the workshop/s will be situated on, or at least close to, one of your sites, probably the main operating location. This reduces travel time and cost, also meaning running repairs should keep your vehicles in a slightly better condition than contractual vehicles, which may have to wait for the next visit before repair.

- Providing your drivers know and trust your technicians, which is the case for most operators with workshops, there is a tangible psychological benefit to maintaining your own vehicles; it gives the drivers a feeling of confidence if they can discuss and resolve potential vehicle issues with their own members of staff.

- Third party work can be seen as a very profitable revenue earning stream for the organisation and a great way to offset the overheads, thus further reducing maintenance costs for the core fleet. Providing, that is, it can be undertaken without affecting your core fleet work and is carefully monitored by someone in the organisation with a real understanding of finance and profit & loss, preferably remote from the workshop operation. If opening hours are extended and staff flexible, third-party work can be undertaken at slack times for the main fleet. This means you should be looking for clients that have the right pattern of working to dovetail into your schedules.

- I should just mention the elephant in the room when you conduct third party work; there is always the thorny problem of whose vehicles take priority, especially for urgent defect work. In theory the organisation's vehicles should always have priority; in practice both the workshop and the customer feel that as they are paying (and no cash changes hands for the organisation's fleet) they should have priority. It is a perennial problem with no right or wrong answer, you must work out your own set of operational rules, but remember who invested in the workshop in the first place.

- In addition to third party work, many own account workshops have also chosen to set up MoT testing centres or ATFs. This not only attracts additional work but has a great advantage for the core fleet by reducing travel & waiting times (not inconsiderable for HGVs at the current time) and making the scheduling of tests much easier. You will have to do some very diligent market research on your locality before investing in the facilities and gaining authorisation according to the stricter criteria recently introduced, but look beyond the current vehicle parc and surrounding test facilities. Make use of all your networking contacts to try to find out who else intends to open additional local ATF or MoT facilities and take these into account in your estimated throughput. To be safe, deduct around 30% of your expected throughput when doing the calculations.

- Even when the figures do not stack up, some operators choose to go ahead for the convenience factor alone. Unfortunately, there has effectively been a "moratorium" on opening new ATFs for the last three years or so, which is hopefully about to be lifted, but this means there may be a rise in the number of applications in the near future. The availability of DVSA testers, a real problem before and during the pandemic, I would like to have hoped would be resolved in the relatively near future, although the DVSA show no real signs of changing their processes and appear to be dragging their feet on the possible privatisation of testers. Some simple changes to procedures in this area would make these options more attractive and more efficient for many operators.

What are the disbenefits of running your own workshops?

- There is the obvious issue of having to invest (even if renting or leasing) in premises and equipment, for what is generally thought of as a non-core business. Workshops today generally need to be much cleaner and built to a higher standard than of old, due to the requirement to be energy efficient and to be able to deal with modern technology and electrical systems. This investment is also on-going; technology continues to improve at a rapid rate, so facilities need to keep pace. The minimum cost of investment will make the own workshop option less viable for smaller operators.

- One of the biggest problems for internal maintenance facilities and independent workshops is keeping pace with vehicle related IT and diagnostics. EU legislation means that manufacturers are obliged to share servicing data with outside agents, however, they do not allow interaction with safety critical systems. Manufacturers have always been reluctant to fully share diagnostic facilities with independents and the development of improved systems with greater connectivity between vehicles and their systems means it is often difficult for non-franchised operations have full access to data. This can mean further investment in third party diagnostic systems, taking more time to conduct diagnostics or sometimes resulting in an additional trip to a dealer to conduct a more in-depth investigation using manufacturer's resources. Certainly, vehicle systems have become incredibly complex in recent years. This factor is, of course, offset by a large amount of inspection and repair still being a straightforward mechanical operation.

- The changes and improvements to vehicle systems mentioned above, also give rise to an increased need for technician training. Already a considerable running cost of an internal workshop, the requirement has only increased in recent years, meaning slightly decreased utilisation due to additional training. This has resulted in two further issues for the internal workshop. Firstly, it is not possible for every technician to be familiar with all the necessary technology on your vehicles, so each technician will generally have to specialise in particular areas, which means schedules then become more difficult to organise. Secondly, when one of those technicians leaves for any reason, you are then left trying to fill that position with a person with skills in that particular area, difficult in the current climate. Having said all of that, dealerships will suffer the self-same problems, albeit they probably have greater resources to call upon.

- Currently, especially on HGVs, where inspections are required by legislation, maintenance is largely undertaken at specific time intervals, also governed by mileage. Predictive maintenance technology is increasingly dictating when items should be repaired and this information is not always available to non-franchised agents.

- There is, of course, an on-cost of the management of the workshop, which is not possible to offset, other than by third party work being carried out.

What are the benefits of externalising your maintenance and repair?

- Obviously, there is no capital outlay on the facilities required or the on-going costs of staff and training, thus freeing cash for use elsewhere in the business

- Rates and times can be agreed at the start of the contract and kept for the life of the contract, or more likely, have an RPI (Retail Price Index), or similar inflation index clause, built in - so costs are relatively fixed and known

- Depending on your contractual arrangement, you only pay when the service is required, so there is no expensive outlay required when vehicles are not being repaired. Alternatively, a fixed monthly payment covers all the routine work arising, so costs are fairly fixed and more predictable

- In theory, dealerships should be utilising best industry practices with fully skilled and up-to-date technicians, although it has to be said, with the current skills shortage, of late, that does not always seem to be the case. They will, however, be using the latest equipment and certainly the latest software and diagnostic updates. Independents may lag behind slightly in these regards and may need some contractual management and encouragement from you to keep their skill, equipment and IT fully up to date.

- There is an opportunity for cross-fertilisation of ideas from management of the external contractor by gaining their knowledge of what other fleets are doing. Unless your own workshop undertakes substantial third-party work, this is not really viable in-house. This can sometimes be useful in resolving fleet problems, although there are other ways to obtain this knowledge, such as joining user-groups.

- Due to the ability to only use the service when needed and the lack of investment required, it is the go-to option for smaller fleets

What are the disbenefits of externalising your maintenance and repair?

- There are always risks involved in relying on an external contractor to provide your maintenance and repair, such as incurring additional or excessive downtime, as you are not the only customer relying on that contractor. There are also risks involved with seemingly reputable agents such as incurring unnecessary repairs. Often an internal workshop would keep an eye on a particular item and replace only when it becomes necessary. An external supplier may take the view that they will not see a vehicle for another eight weeks or more, so replace anyway to be on the safe side, thus marginally increasing costs. There are further risks such as potentially slow response times at periods of high demand. All these risks can be mitigated, to some extent, by suitable clauses in the contract.

- You have no control over a contractor's staff. So due to a high turnover of staff, or indeed if they have a large number of staff, there may be unfamiliarity with your vehicles, your company and your operation, leading to possible misunderstandings over what is required.

- If you have no engineering expertise in-house, in order to ensure that your vehicles are being maintained to the correct standard, you will probably need to employ a third party, such as one of the trade associations or independent consultants to inspect, from time to time, a sample of your vehicles to audit the contractor's quality and standards.

- Although most work will be contained within the declared contractual terms, unfair wear and tear and damage will not be and will be charged as an extra. Sometimes, this is where the supplier makes their money, so labour times and parts costs need careful scrutiny. Items such as tyres and glass are very likely to be additional to the contract.

- You will not have so much control over the recording of information on the servicing of your vehicles. If you require specific items recorded, this can obviously be done, however, if it is not standard to the supplier, it may get missed and you will often expend more time getting information to the standard and level you require.

- Unless the contractor is local to you or just happens to be next door on a trading estate, there will be time and money involved in collection & return of vehicles, necessitating moving drivers about to collect and deliver. Even if you fully sub-contract this part of the operation, you will still have to pay for the supplier's time in some shape or form. If the workshop is more than a short distance away, there may be considerable fleet time, mileage and fuel costs to allow for.

- There are obviously no opportunities for attracting third party maintenance work to your organisation, however, recognise that this would be a non-core revenue stream.

- A very mixed fleet will probably restrict your choice of workshop to an independent. Franchised dealers are likely to want to repair at least the majority of their own make. This may mean having to split the contract with a number of suppliers if your chosen supplier will not cater for certain types of vehicle on your fleet. Similarly, some workshops will not handle trailers; or if you operate certain bodies such as petrol tankers, the workshop may not be accredited to the appropriate regulations.

- Hopefully, the contract will be set up with regular named contacts for both parties. However, there will be times when the regular contacts are not available and others step in. There is huge opportunity for errors in communication to creep in at this point. In theory, you can set matters up to avoid these errors, in practice, there are always some gremlins that appear. Be aware that it will generally take longer to manage communication with an external facility. There are, of course, further options available, such as retaining ownership of the building, but outsource the running and management of the staff to a third party, even to a franchised dealer. The benefit of this set-up is being able to specify certain standards for the work being carried out, whilst avoiding all the hassles of training and management of staff. This will probably involve a TUPE transfer (Transfer of Undertakings [Protection of Employment] Regulations) or similar, so is not something to be undertaken lightly, however, it does offer a route back should you ever want to bring maintenance back in house. Many operators use a hybrid system where work is mixed depending on in-house facilities and the quality of suppliers based at specific parts of the country. If you require advice when deciding whether to keep things in-house or externalise, please don't hesitate to contact us on 07771 768080 or info@thedwconsultancy.com .

Typical Fixed Lift Arrangement in a modern Vehicle Workshop

4) What facilities do I require to operate an internal workshop?

Well, there is definitely another book to be written on this one topic alone. There are also many varying views on what works best. For as long as I can remember, there have been heated debates amongst engineers as to whether pits or hoists are best to enable the most efficient work on their vehicles. In essence, a workshop in its smallest form is simply an enlarged garage, capable of housing one, or maybe two vehicles, at a time. I have seen many such workshops, most operating very successfully, in my career. Remember that around 80% of commercial vehicle operators run a fleet of 10 vehicles or less. At its largest, a workshop is simply a warehouse type construction, perhaps with additional doors to allow vehicle access, preferably both in and out. Then add heat, lighting and power, throw in compressed air, lubrication, a parts stores and an office and you are in business.

Once you have the outer skin, what items of equipment do you need to consider? To keep this very simple, I am offering just a few words of guidance about the main items you may wish to consider.

Probably the best starting point to consider is the minimum equipment required in order to run an ATF, therefore this gives a level of guidance to HGV operators. In addition to a full-length pit facility, in no particular order, the minimum equipment is:

- A Roller Brake Tester
- A Headlamp Tester & Standing area
- A Load Simulator
- A Hoist and/or Lift Jacking Equipment
- An Exhaust Gas Analyser
- Wheel Play Detectors
- A Diesel Smoke Meter

In terms of the age-old argument of pits versus hoists, it says a lot that an ATF demands a pit, however, that is, of course, for fast turn-round inspection work. If you are attempting to work out what is the minimum equipment your workshop can run with, this list also is a huge starter for ten, although you will very quickly decide you need more than one of some items and there is a lot of other useful equipment, like fluid drain containers and dispensers, wheel handling equipment, working lights, lifting devices, presses – the list of items you are also going to need will keep extending. A brake tester will cost you around £30k and the full ATF works will probably not leave change from £125k (2021 prices), so any workshop is not a minor investment. You can use second-hand kit to save money, but for an ATF, you will need to pass inspection, so anything second-hand must be of high quality and in good condition. Note that an increasing amount of your equipment will be required to be "connectable" in order to record test data directly,

Van workshop bays do not tend to mix that well with HGV workshop bays, so for more guidance at the lighter end we could look at the specification for an MoT facility, to cope with vehicles from Class 1 to 7. The minimum requirements are slightly more prescriptive than for an ATF and are as follow:

The DVSA prescribe that you will need to have a computer of some format, with an internet connection and printer that meets their minimum standard; that's kind of a given for any operation.

You will then need their minimum approved testing equipment, which varies slightly according to the class of vehicle you are testing. It goes without saying that all equipment must be kept in good working order and calibrated properly. The equipment includes:

- brake pedal application devices
- diesel smoke meters & oil temperature measurement
- exhaust gas analysers for both catalyst and non-catalyst vehicles
- headlamp aim testers
- plate brake testers
- roller brake testers
- tow bar socket testers
- tyre tread depth gauges

- wheel play detectors
- decelerometers for each class of vehicle you test

In addition, there are minimum bay sizes and workshop dimensions for each of the vehicle classes you will be testing, including designated parking spaces.

There really is not time or space here to review all the equipment you will want in your workshop, but let us look at some of the key items.

- As mentioned elsewhere, it is becoming increasingly difficult to operate without a basic level of diagnostic equipment, even for something as simple as renewing brake pads. If you are linked to the manufacturer in any way, for example, authorise to carry out warranty repairs, you will probably have to use OEM (Original Equipment Manufacturer) software. This tends to be expensive but comes with the benefit of constant updates and the very latest software, along with potential links to manufacturer parts and service information. If your fleet is largely one make, you may also want to go down the OEM route and purchase manufacturer diagnostics and training.

- If you have a more mixed fleet, many operators go for the all-makes diagnostic systems. They tend not to carry out quite all the functions that OEM kit can do, hence possibly requiring the odd trip to a dealer when all else has failed, and they are probably not quite as up to date as the manufacturer, but they can usually give you most of the functions you will require. Allow for additional connecting cable bills (unless wireless) and once more, regular technician training, which is become increasingly necessary due to rapid technology advances. Remember also, not everything requires diagnostics. I find there is a growing tendency for technicians to nearly always plug in their laptop and expect an instant diagnosis, but surprisingly often, issues need a little human thought and a return to the basics.

- The pits versus hoist debate will continue for a long time to come. I think for vans, the argument has been won for some time in favour of lifts or hoists, you simply have to specify the type, of which there are many, and the weight capacity. They are also safer for petrol engine vehicles. Generally, it makes sense to go for up to a 25% or more uplift in capacity as vehicles keep getting heavier and the lift will generally last longer, with less operating faults, if operating under capacity. Modern lifts will have electronic controls and considerable integrated safety features, such as hose burst valves. Do allow for the height of the vehicle, body and hoist when considering roof space height (you would be amazed how many people forget this!). The benefits of hoists and lifts only really work when you can raise fully and comfortably stand under the vehicle. Column lifts are a very flexible and space-efficient solution, but allow some time in the schedule for manoeuvring and setting up. Although if you can afford it, modern lifts with radio control and battery power (thus cable free) have reduced that time somewhat. To counter the increased cost, the cables for lifts always seem to get damaged at some point, so running costs should be cheaper plus the power supply can be standard 240v AC rather than 3 phase, recharged overnight.

- If you are using a pit, make use of all the latest safety features to minimise the risk of falls. This includes non-slip tread all around the pit, clear marking around all the edges and moveable barriers for when not in use. The latest lighting (which needs to be dust, waterproof and flameproof) can make it as bright as day underneath the vehicle. When I first started, being under the vehicle in a pit could be truly like going down a very dark mine – definitely not the case now. Restrict access around the pits, with one main point of entry and exit. Generally, pits are now made of prefabricated steel to prescribed regulations which are virtually maintenance free and have a long-life expectancy. Do not forget you will need planning permission and if renting, the landlord will have to agree to installation and may require a flat floor back after you leave. Also remember gases or vapours often sink to the bottom of the pit so devise work routines to avoid releasing vapours over or near the pit and use venting or ventilation where necessary. If the pit is not being used fairly constantly, consider a retractable cover, however, if it is not being used regularly, do you really need it?

- One item of equipment often gets a bad press and tends to get overlooked by many workshops. Depending on your fleet mix and location, running one or more mobile workshop vans can be a real money saver. It requires a little more thought; you will have to work through the "lone worker" issues if the technician is on their own and their productivity, by default, will be lower than a normal workshop technician due to time spent travelling to and from locations. However, it negates the need for the vehicle to visit the workshop with consequent lost time to operations and personnel transport issues. As for the van and equipment, these have come on leaps and bounds in recent years and there is precious little that cannot be accommodated in the back of the van, limited only by weight limits and your budget. They are obviously brilliant for more remote defect work and maintenance on trailers and the like.

- Two quick tips here; using one of the proprietary van installation firms often looks expensive at first sight, but most of the equipment they supply is first class and long-lasting, so can often be moved into a replacement van later on. It also means every layout can be standardised, helpful for efficiency. They also look so much better and the layout generally keeps the back of the van neat and tidy and a safer place to work, rather than a general tip where the operator has to hunt for every item. Secondly, please go for a sufficiently high-roof van; I have lost count of the number of tall technicians I have seen with permanent cricked necks because the roof is too low! Talking of technicians, they tend to divide into two classes; those who love mobile working, enjoying the challenge of organising their day and solving issues on their own. Then there are those who really like the comradeship of the main workshop. Do make sure you choose the right person/s for the mobile role or you are heading for personnel issues and poor productivity.

5) What are the key issues involved in managing an efficient internal workshop?

There are obviously quite a few factors that you need to measure in order to ensure your workshop is running as it should be. As with KPI's for measuring fleet performance, I would suggest keeping the number of metrics you measure as low as practically possible, so that they get used and looked at by all involved. That last part is very important. Often, when I am on the shop floor of a workshop and I ask a technician how they are performing on a particular KPI, I often get the answer "don't know, you'll have to ask Jim", Jim being the foreman or manager. If you are running an efficient workshop, you will be holding regular staff meetings and all the staff will be aware of how they and the workshop is performing.

Most good fleet management or workshop management systems will collect all the data you will ever need. However, I'll let you into a really big secret that not everyone in the industry appears to fully realise. There are just two KPI's that stand head and shoulders above all others when it comes to workshop performance. They are, quite simply, measuring workshop efficiency and workshop utilisation. If you get these two right and keep quality standards high, that is almost all you need to concentrate on, although many other issues will, of course, try to get in the way.

Efficiency is simply measuring the time taken to do each job against a "standard" time allowed, generally originating from the manufacturer. Then, depending on your fleet age and mix, you will probably have to make some time allowances for issues such as a complex installation or an older vehicle (meaning some items may be corroded in place) or similar. Also, the number of times a technician carries out a particular operation has a big impact on repair times, hence why vehicle specification standardisation helps in this regard.

There are still a number of workshop managers who come up with many reasons as to why they should not measure efficiency; personally, I cannot see how you can possibly do without it. Public sector workshops are generally the ones most likely not to look at efficiency; those that do sometimes keep figures that do not quite record efficiency fully. However, it has to be remembered that the public sector work to differing objectives, constraints, guidelines and rules, so they cannot be fully compared to the private sector. Manufacturers will set times which private sector workshops will often improve on, thus having efficiency figures over 100%, as their primary objective is revenue earning, not something that the public sector generally has to worry about. Whichever sector you operate in, if you run a workshop, you really must measure efficiency. Have I said that enough?

Utilisation then takes the actual number of productive hours (or "sold" hours when working for a customer) and measures it against the number of available hours. Available hours are what is left when you start with the technician's paid hours and then deduct training time, meal and rest breaks, then an allowance for sickness, welfare and holidays. Depending how you measure it, your available hours will be around 75 to 80% of the paid time. Anyone not employed directly on the shop floor undertaking work is, I'm afraid, unproductive, which includes cleaners, drivers, parts persons and, of course, management. However, the role of all unproductive persons is simply to support the productive technicians so they can book as many hours as physically possible to the job. You should therefore be measuring the net utilisation of each and all the technicians and the gross utilisation of the whole workshop, two different but very important figures.

Efficiency is largely in the hands (literally) of the technicians, however, it can be greatly supported and improved by things like targeted training, good quality equipment and tools, good systems and recording, a good workshop layout, replacement fluids locally delivered and parts readily available; so good management planning will always help efficiency.

Utilisation is largely in the hands of management – the trick is to keep the workshop loading at just the right level to maximise throughput. Unfortunately, you will always have to allow some slack for unplanned jobs, or conversely, vehicles that just do not turn up, neither of which ever happen at a fixed rate. (You may well consider imposing some form of a "penalty" charge for customers who do not turn up for an appointment, to reduce their occurrence).

There can be a little confusion in the minds of some workshop personnel between the two measures of efficiency and utilisation. The two are interlinked, but they are separate measures and both are important. In effect, utilisation measures productivity and highlights the rate at which results are being achieved by the workforce within the workshop – perhaps also described as the quantity of work; whilst efficiency focuses instead on the resources invested, the speed of carrying out a task and the level of any waste involved, perhaps also described as the quality of the work.

So, it should be clear that if you monitor and constantly improve these two KPI's through management tweaks, the workshop will be operating at its maximum efficiency. There is little else to really worry about, apart from a few important topics like Health & Safety and quality management. If you ever end up managing a workshop, never let anyone distract you from these two crucial KPI's.

There is one other factor, not mentioned elsewhere, that is really important in the running of an efficient and effective workshop: that of providing parts. At its simplest, for a really small operation, parts can be provided directly by manufacturers or a parts factor. Sooner or later, however, you will want your own stores operation and that is when the fun begins. Ideally, you want to carry stock of all the fast-moving regularly used parts. You will then require a rapid system for obtaining other parts when needed and replacing stock items, not an easy task. As soon as you hold a sensible level of stock, you will require at least a part-time stores person; for a larger workshop perhaps a number of them. Not forgetting, a good stores-person is worth their weight in gold, but they are, of course, all non-productive, thus affecting your overall productivity figures. Key to managing parts is your fleet management workshop system – when trialling your system, you need to include parts stockholding and parts ordering to see if it meets your organisations requirements. Test to see whether you can order parts and handle invoices and payment with only one input of data each time.

Some years ago, imprest stock was favoured by many. This meant parts were on your shelves, but not paid for until drawn from stock by your technicians and used. Your parts supplier then visited at regular intervals and topped up the used stock and billed you for the parts used. This meant someone else was replenishing the stock and it significantly decreased the cash involved in your stockholding, which could be quite considerable for a larger workshop. It needed a little extra recording and handling to avoid debates about who used what, but when it works well, it is an excellent system. From my perspective, imprest stock holdings usually seemed to be better managed than a workshop's own stock.

For a number of reasons, this route has fallen out of favour in recent years, in part due to the extra effort involved by the parts supplier. The industry, like many others has moved away from carrying expensive stock and towards JIT (Just in Time) deliveries. It is quite common for suppliers to provide at least 4 or 5 deliveries per day, which on a standard shift is effectively under two hours apart. By the time a vehicle has been disassembled, the part will often have arrived. Generally, suppliers guarantee that a very large and agreed proportion of parts will delivered on the next visit to the workshop, with a small percentage of more specialist parts delivered in the next 24 hours, sometimes shipped by air. Recent events have upset the supply chain somewhat, so it remains to be seen if imprest sees a comeback. When setting up a parts supply deal, make sure to agree that unused parts can be returned, that way you can order parts that may be needed, safe in the knowledge that they can go back if not required.

Whatever method you use to supply, if you possess a stockholding, you need to be measuring your usage. A good fleet management or workshop management system will allow you to monitor supply and usage to quite fine detail. The key figure to manage is the number of stock days per unit held. Pareto's rule should once again apply here and the vast majority of your stock should be in and out very quickly. Parts from a Tier 1 supplier (see section 9 of this chapter) should be available within 24 hours, so ask yourself the question, do you really need to hold this item?

Once a part has been in stock for over 6 months, you need to have a serious think about whether it should be on the shelf or not and anything over 12 months has to have a very serious reason for being there, or be declared obsolete. Rather than assuming that some specific parts have to be held due to potential delays in supply, check out if there are faster routes to use instead, or if you can get agreement for the manufacturer of the part to make sure they can hold the stock on your behalf instead. This kind of action, taken gradually over time, can have a really beneficial effect by reducing your average length of time on the shelf and increase your stock turn figure.

I mentioned Health & Safety above, as it is a subject that has massively increased over the years, and quite rightly so. The basic principle behind workshop Health & Safety is that anyone going to work in the morning should have a reasonable expectation that he or she will return home in the evening in roughly the same physical condition as when they started. A not unreasonable concept in my humble view. There is, therefore, a raft of Health & Safety legislation that affect workshops, commencing with the original 1974 act, updated in 1999, along with LOLER (Lifting Operations and Lifting Equipment Regulations) in 1998, PUWER (Provision and Use of Work Equipment Regulations) also in 1998 and COSHH (Control of Substances Hazardous to Health) in 2002. There are others, but these are the key ones to keep up to date. Yes, of course it can be a pain to keep up with the latest legislation, partly because they are worded so badly, but remember two things; firstly, as with RTC's (Road Traffic Collisions), any incident is hugely expensive in terms of time and money. Secondly, it is all part and parcel of being a good employer and being a nice place to work. With the current shortage of skilled technicians, anything you can do to make your staff feel more valued and well looked after, and hence to help retain them, must be beneficial for you, your organisation and the staff.

In essence, all this H&S legislation means that you need good up-to-date workshop operating procedures that encourage good housekeeping and a tidy workshop, with all spillages cleaned up, especially oil. Guards and rails should all be in place (especially pits) at appropriate times and all equipment used calibrated and safety checked regularly according to regulations, not forgetting items like ladders. Nowadays, you must try to minimise any working at height, but if technicians have to for any reason, a fall restraint harness will almost certainly be required. You need regular, updated risk assessments on all your operations and work processes along with regular training of staff and a comprehensive induction on H&S at the start of employment.

Do not forget visitors, who should be steered away from any high-risk areas and also inducted with the essential site basics when they first visit. If you have any doubts at all as to whether your procedures are comprehensive or not, it pays to invest in a third-party audit or inspection by a workshop H&S expert. An observant third party should be able to spot issues that you see every day but take as part of the scenery. To protect yourself, always get signatures from staff and visitors to state all the training has taken place and has been understood – you may sadly need to prove it at a later stage.

6) What factors do I need to consider when contracting out maintenance?

- Manufacturers tend to like shorter life maintenance contracts, generally three to five years, primarily because the shorter the contract, the easier it is to predict their own costs. When pushed, they will extend that to seven or eight years or so. If you therefore want to keep a vehicle beyond that, you will need another option, such as moving to 'pay as you go' for the vehicles' final years or maintain it yourself if you have the facilities. Note that extending a contract at the end of life will seem expensive compared with the initial cost, part of the reason for that is obviously picking up the much-increased risk of additional repairs.

- At the same time as deciding exactly what work you require your contractor to carry out (see item 7 below) you will also need to conduct a brief risk assessment on whether your organisation may need to change some of these parameters over time. This may require involving other personnel from your organisation to contribute to a little blue-sky thinking. Ask yourselves questions along the lines of:

  o Could the business grow faster than expected and result in much higher mileages, a change of operation, or area, covered by some or most vehicles?

  o Could we lose one or more of the organisations' contracts which may reduce mileages or eliminate the need for some vehicles?

  o Could there be upcoming legislation changes which may affect our operation?

  o Could there be previously unforeseen market changes, similar to Brexit or Covid, around the corner, that may affect our operation?

Once you have established what could possibly happen, estimate the risk of it happening, then work towards mitigating the risk in the contract. If there are penalties for a particular change, try to move it to an area that is less likely to happen to your organisation, or negotiate more acceptable terms for making changes during the term of the contract. There can be huge variations between contractors in these excess charges, so it is well worth checking and comparing at the outset. Also check if you can withdraw from the contract, either in part or in total and what the consequences would be at various points in the contract. Factor this into your overall risk evaluation.

- For the larger ancillaries, such as fridge motors, chassis mounted cranes or tail lifts, you may like to source repair and maintenance of these items from specialist companies, who may be able to undertake this activity at a lower cost and may have better specialist knowledge than your contractor. Alternatively, if your contractor can cater for them, there is a definite benefit in having all your maintenance undertaken under one roof.

- Before starting negotiations on a contract, you need to have decided in your own mind what level of maintenance cover you will require. Most truck manufacturers will have a basic service contract which covers just routine inspections and scheduled servicing. There are then a series of levels, depending on their service offerings, which take you up to the full R&M (Repair & Maintenance) contract covering all wearing tear items and should include unexpected parts replacements, often including breakdown assistance. Most comprehensive R&M packages include cover for the annual test, but do check this includes everything including steam cleaning preparation, presentation, fees and a retest should that unfortunately ever be required. Be aware most contracts will include a clause linking charges to inflation, which will increase each year. It is possible to arrange for rates to be fixed for the whole contract, making them dearer in the early stages. This latter route has been less popular since low inflation became the norm.

- If you are leasing a vehicle, check carefully that the required conditions of return synchronise with your R&M contract so that there will not be too many cost surprises at the end of the lease. Similarly, there may be some potential expenses that can be avoided at the end of the lease, if not necessary under the leasing agreement. If the method of leasing includes maintenance, this will naturally run concurrently. The level of contract should reflect your attitude to risk; if you are risk averse, you will probably move towards all inclusive; if you do not mind some risk, you may go for the basic level and pay for other issues as they arise. Do allow a budget for these extra costs, many operators just budget for the R&M contract and are sometimes surprised by the level of additional costs that arise.

- You will also need to decide whether or not you require on-site technical assistance, most useful during the winter months at the start of a shift, and of course decide on both out-of-hours servicing and collection and delivery. The need for on-site assistance is linked to the age of the fleet and very much depends upon your history of requiring support in the past. All of these services obviously come at extra cost, so you have to do the sums and decide if it is worth building into the contract or pay as you go. With or without on-site support, you will need to arrange a supply of top-up fluids in case these are low on the daily checks. Decide and agree how common replacement items like mirrors, bulbs and issues such as flat batteries are going to be dealt with.

- Similarly, some contracts provide a replacement vehicle should one of yours be off the road over a specific amount of time. Providing the cost of this addition is low enough, this is a useful technique for increasing the odds of your vehicles being repaired in good time, as the contractor will naturally do everything to avoid having to supply you with another vehicle. Replacement vehicles tend to be offered when the majority of your vehicles are of similar specification; also check the terms and conditions applied to the replacement vehicle, do not assume these at the outset, as there may be something like a mileage limit hidden in the small print.

7) *How do I manage external maintenance contractors*?

If you have decided running your own workshop is not for you, probably due to a lack of time or resources, you still need to invest some time and effort into managing external contractors if you are to run a well-maintained fleet.

Managing external contractors starts before you have your first meeting with them to see if you can work with them. The first step is obviously to provide them with the dimensions of your fleet or just the specific vehicles you want them to maintain; so the number and full specification of the vehicles you are seeking to maintain with mileages and inspection intervals. Then it is thinking time again, you will have to sit down with a blank sheet of paper and decide exactly what you require from this agent, but be prepared to negotiate, as a long list of desires will probably put the price up.

For example, many commercial vehicle workshops now open extended working hours, from early in the morning to around 10 pm at night. If your working day ends at 3 or 4 pm in the afternoon, and the vehicles are single shifted, there is ample scope to have your vehicles serviced and returned ready for the next working day, so incurring zero downtime. If, however, you do not finish until sometime after 8 pm, the workshop either has to operate a night shift, probably at extra cost, or you suffer a day's downtime.

At some stage you need to meet and tour the premises of your potential contractor. As you walk round, keep imagining what the place would look like with your vehicles in their workshop – would you be happy to see them in there? There are a lot of important operational questions to be asking yourself, such as:

- Do they have enough facilities, enough bays (with hoists) or pits?

- Is the place clean, brightly lit and well laid out, looking efficiently run?

- Do they have enough tools and equipment, is there a roller brake tester?

- Are staff wandering about aimlessly, or does everyone seem to be working with a purpose? With experience, you can tell if a workshop is being efficiently managed or not within ten minutes of entry, simply by observing the staff and noting their behaviour.

- How large is their stores facility, is it well laid out & what arrangements do they have for procuring spares, how fast are their lead times – is the stock they are holding large enough for their throughput?

- Check their annual test performance; it is getting more common to motivate your contractor by including a clause in the contract that either rewards a good first-time pass rate or even one that penalises poor performance. This is obviously important as for O licence holders it can directly affect your OCRS (Operator Compliance Risk Score). When checking their pass rate, also check the average age of the vehicles they are presenting; franchised dealers in particular, often have a very young average repair fleet profile which can skew the figures in their favour.

- Check out their systems and particularly their inspection and service sheets – how up to date are they, are they DVSA compatible and will you be able to access them as soon as complete? Will you get notification of jobs complete?

- What diagnostic facilities do they have and what IT links to the manufacturers and service functions?

- If they run an ATF or MoT facility, check on the volumes of work and how it functions alongside the workshop, so how are the technicians organised? – you want the use of the facility but not at the expense of losing a quick turn-around for your vehicles on a day-to-day basis.

- Check how many of the technicians are irtec qualified (an independent industry qualification) and to what level, and if the workshop has been IRTE (Institute of Road Transport Engineers) audited (also check the certification is up to date). Ask to see the latest workshop report which also covers the premises, tools and equipment, staff, management, clerical staff, documentation, parts and quality, so should confirm your own observations.

- Check out all other training, accreditations and insurances.

Assuming the results from above are largely positive and you have successfully negotiated all the commercial and financial aspects of an agreement, how do you now set up the contract and manage your supplier? The most important part, without a doubt, is to set the arrangement up properly in the first place. Time spent at this point will be repaid many fold during the life of the contract. If you are an HGV operator, make sure that whatever is agreed, you cover off all your DVSA or TC (Traffic Commissioner) requirements.

Many Workshops maintain a mixed Fleet Profile

- First step, before signing, is to agree the minimum service standards; so items like collection and delivery, lead times, servicing times, on-site or mobile fitter, replacement vehicle and so on. This should be in the form of a service level agreement, but try to steer clear of a long document with lots of legal speak – no one will read it or use it until there are serious problems. Attempt to end up with a short very clear document which everyone involved can understand. Agree, as far as possible, future financial arrangements, so things like your current parts discounts need to continue, or be improved, in the future.

- When setting up the contract, make it very clear that you expect a high level of proactivity from your contractor, so you want them to be identifying to you on a regular basis any trends relating to the fleet, important financial implications, parts implications coming up and any technical or legislation changes they are aware of. Also make it clear you want honesty, integrity and transparency in the relationship; by the same token, if your organisation messes up, own up immediately, apologise and put things right as best you can and as soon as you can. If there are stipulated times for you to present vehicles, make absolutely sure your organisation adheres to them. To get the best out of them, you want to become an easy customer for them to work with.

- Set up regular and routine contract monitoring meetings, at least once a month, but make sure there are daily routes of communication kept open. Most importantly, make sure the contractor gets advance and comprehensive warning of defect repairs so they can ensure parts and labour will be available before the vehicle arrives.

- Also include in the contract a brief description of what happens if there are disputes, hopefully it will not be needed again, but it is important to have it documented.

- The results of all routine events such as inspection, service and test should be notified to you instantly, but as a routine report of fairly low priority.

- However, unusual or adverse events require a priority communication and agreement from both sides as to the action required.

- Absolutely critical is to set up and keep a log, within your organisation, to record all calls, notices and instructions to and from the contractor. You must set up the protocols for who can issue instructions and then everyone who does so, must record the transaction, including any incoming calls and information. So many operators fail to do this successfully and then end up with the "he said; you said" syndrome. Modern technology should mean everyone involved can enter information in the log from wherever they are at any time.

- Keep all contract correspondence in one file location – paper or electronic - any important instructions or information should always be recorded in writing.

- Make sure you keep a very regular track of contract parameters, especially the core one of mileage. Generally, contract mileages are checked and agreed at specific intervals, often annually. If you are able to spot early on that certain vehicles are clocking up excess mileages, you may be able to swop vehicles or make some other change to the operation to avoid incurring charges. Alternatively, include a mileage pooling arrangement in the contract. If there are changes in your operation, let the contractor know as soon as possible in the interests of honesty and transparency; you may well be able to absorb changes within your contract terms, but it helps future relations to be open about what they may be.

- Attempt to future-proof your contract and contractor, so set out the level of irtec trained staff you expect them to employ in the future, hopefully at or above their current level. Agree and specify future performance levels and targets, including the level of test passes, again, hopefully, at or above their current level. Broadly agree and specify a level of investment in their facilities, without it, future improvements or refurbishment may not happen and as your supplier, you want them to keep pace with, or be in advance of, the industry as a whole. The same also applies to their systems and IT development.

- If, despite your best endeavours, using all the advice on running the contract spelt out above, your contractor is still not performing and you have given them sufficient chances to improve, do not feel bad about walking away as their poor performance will ultimately reflect on your good repute. This is even more important for O licence holders, but is still significant for any other vehicle operator.

8) How do I effectively handle vehicle defects?

There has been so much publicity and writing in the commercial vehicle press about daily vehicle checks and defect reporting over recent years that I do not want to repeat it all here. However, as it is such an important component in the maintenance regime, and it still does not always seem to get carried out properly, it is worth noting the important basics.

Daily walk-round checks

There are some well-used infographics produced by DVSA for both vans and trucks showing what items to check on the daily walk-round, which are worth looking up on the GOV/DVSA site and giving copies in some format to your drivers.

https://www.gov.uk/government/publications/van-drivers-daily-walkaround-check

https://assets.publishing.service.gov.uk/government/uploads/system/uploads/attachment_data/file/833166/heavy-goods-vehicle-walkaround-check-diagram.pdf

The driver is obviously the one in closest contact with a vehicle and therefore the most likely to be first aware of any fault that may develop. You need to give them regular training in terms of what is expected of them, what to check and how to check; they will also need guidance on how to determine what aspects or components of the vehicle may be faulty, or in need of repair or replacement. They do not necessarily need to know exactly what is wrong, or what action is required, but they should be able to identify clearly when some aspect of the vehicle is not performing as it should. If done correctly, the routine daily vehicle check should give both drivers and managers confidence that their vehicle is roadworthy and fit for purpose.

If you are currently using paper defect reporting successfully and are happy with it, I am not going to suggest you change. However, be aware the world is going paperless and there are so many apps and other systems and devices out there which make this process easier. If you do not already use digital driver defect reports, I would suggest putting evaluation of a suitable system on your "to do" list. Every fleet manager I talk to who utilises such a system says the administration is just so much easier, plus most fleet managers say that because of the built-in checks in most apps, it has increased compliance, i.e., more drivers are carrying out their checks fully. They can also often come with incident recording apps at the same time, a useful additional feature.

Digital Daily walk-round check Apps

Any digital drivers' walk-round check app is effectively an electronic version of the manual inspection process, normally used on a smart phone or tablet device, helping to alleviate the inefficiencies associated with paper inspections. All the systems I have seen so far are easier to use both for drivers and managers or supervisors, than paper systems, with added benefits. The system needs to record the current mileage at the start of each safety check and check it against previous inputs – it should display some form of alert if the mileage is less than, or out of kilter, with previously records. The system should record the time of the check and the time taken to carry out the safety check. Some systems may use the device's GPS to location stamp the activity.

There should be a standard library of DVSA style standard checklists for all types of vehicles and trailers, along with non-HGV checklists, if applicable, for van operators. You will almost certainly want a system that allows you to easily customise the check fields to suit your fleet. Where defects are discovered - the driver selects the defect description from a list; indicates whether or not the vehicle is safe to operate, notes the defect, may take a picture to both record the defect and aid remote diagnosis, plus using a free text field for additional comments. One useful addition used by some systems is to place Quick Reference (QR) or bar codes on the vehicle at key inspection points. The driver then scans the code at each check point around the vehicle and the system displays the appropriate checks to be completed at that inspection point. The process itself can also be made auditable, acting as an additional check that the inspection took place.

Defects should be reportable immediately in real time through a secure accessible database to the responsible supervisor or manager via email, text message or similar. Selected workshops can normally be alerted manually or automatically of the need for any repair, along with any details recorded. A sensible amount (probably a week's worth) of safety checks should be storable for reference on the device, dependant on the device capacity. If the device temporarily has no internet connection, the data should be held until a signal returns and the data can be downloaded. A complete history of actions taken should be able to be kept on file for the life of the vehicle, including photographs of defects.

The history of the vehicle needs to be un-editable and therefore auditable. The two really important parts of any defect system to check for before purchase are the ease of data entry by the drivers and the ease of later manipulation of the data for monitoring or reporting of defect checks and repairs. For O licence users, the system must obviously meet DVSA defect reporting requirements and if applicable, the system also needs to be compatible with Earned Recognition reporting procedures.

When considering a digital system, you need to review if you want regular checks on other issues such as any HSE regulation checks, ADR equipment checks, LOLER & PUWER equipment checks and for international travel, any additional checks for Border Force. You may also wish to capture road incidents or near misses at the same time. If you were conducting these checks before by paper, you may wish to transfer them to a digital system and therefore require that it is able to handle these additional checks.

Daily Check Contents

Whichever system you are using, there are basic items that your drivers always need to be looking at. They vary slightly according to who publishes the listing, but in essence, and in no particular order, they are:

Wheels & Tyres – a visual review of tyre pressure (even if TPMS is fitted), tread depth across all tyres, no cuts or damage, wheel security, all wheel nuts and any tell-tale devices fitted, no damage, corrosion or missing items.

Vehicle fluids – levels all adequate, no leakage; includes coolant, brake fluid, AdBlue, windscreen wash, fuel & oil.

Glass & vision – wipers in good condition & functioning, windscreen & glass all clean, not cracked, washers functioning & topped-up, cameras all functioning correctly, sensors & alarms (if fitted) functioning correctly, mirrors correctly adjusted.

Diagnostics – check all dashboard indicators light, self-check and extinguish.

Electrics & lights - all electrical components verified for proper function, including brake lights, running lights, headlights, indicators, side lights, marker and warning lights, no visible loose wiring, or loose connectors.

Brakes & air – check parking brakes & main brakes (when rolling before setting out) for function & no pull, air pressure system leak free, functioning alarm (if pressure dropped) air pressure rises promptly to normal setting, air suspension no leaks and correct ride height set.

Bodywork & load – check all secure, no loose fixings, doors closed and flush, load secure & correctly restrained, no loose items.

Artic or Drawbar only – check trailer coupling secure and locked, legs raised.

Ancillary equipment – any ancillary equipment securely stowed and restrained, no loose equipment, extinguisher/s present, first aid kit present.

Obviously, the above guide covers all vehicles, so items such as air suspension and couplings will not apply to all vehicles – this listing is just a guide that needs refining for each operation and is obviously not supposed to be a comprehensive listing.

DVSA staff, quite rightly, take a really dim view of items that have obviously been failed for some time and should clearly have been spotted on the daily walk around. It is exactly those sort of items that the daily check should focus on and attempt to eliminate as far as possible. Of course, the driver is equally responsible for defects occurring whilst the vehicle is being driven, so should always be on the look-out for any warning signs of potential failure as they progress. It helps to remind drivers that it is not just the organisation that is at risk when driving, they are legally responsible for their vehicle when out on the road and could incur a fixed penalty notice, even a prosecution, with potential fines and licence penalty points.

One point worth noting is that of daily checks on tyres. The emphasis of the check should focus on condition, in terms of no damage and sufficient tread, not forgetting wheel security. The problem is how to ensure tyre pressures are correct. Years ago, drivers were advised to regularly check tyre pressures and top up whenever necessary. A little research by the tyre industry revealed that this was often causing more problems than it resolved, either because drivers were not checking or inflating tyres properly (even with training), or because continuously operating the tyre valve had the potential to introduce dirt, sometimes resulting in slow air leaks. Obviously TPMS is the way forward for the future, but until all vehicles are so equipped, what should a good operator advise?

The general consensus is that the answer is to have regular fleet tyre checks carried out by a professional tyre technician, which include pressure checks. You can see that these really need to be undertaken at weekly intervals, as monthly is useful, but would most likely result in a tyre being damaged beyond repair if it had started to deflate in that time. The other key component is for the driver to keep a visual watch on the tyres during the daily checks, as deflation can be noted by the shape of the tyre, making allowance for the load being carried.

The Driver's Daily Walk-round Inspection is a key part of any Maintenance Regime

Drivers' defect report action

You must ensure that operations are keeping written or electronic records of their daily checks; easier said than done. Records should include the vehicle registration mark, the date, the details of the defects or symptoms and the reporter's name. You must ensure that a suitable person (i.e. someone with technical skills or with suitable training) within the organisation is checking the records and repairs are being completed on a regular basis. Defects must be rectified promptly and therefore there must be a robust system in place to ensure drivers know who to report to if a defect is found, including drivers away from base. This is where an electronic system makes it easy to see what has been completed and flag up any outstanding issues. Of course, "Nil Defect" reports require keeping along with other reports. There is no requirement for the length of time these should be kept, generally until the next safety inspection is sufficient. Reports containing a defect and repair should be kept for the full 15-month period. There is no reason for van operators not to follow the same procedures and it is highly recommended you do so.

Monitoring systems

One other commitment on the O licence is that the operator should continually review and monitor the quality of the systems in place. In practice, this means that you need to be confident and able to demonstrate that all defects are being reported and rectified promptly and that inspections are done on time. You also need to be confident and able to demonstrate that drivers and those involved in maintenance inspections have been trained sufficiently and are competent. So, keep accurate and comprehensive training records (or ensure someone in the organisation does) on driver training relating to inspections.

Any incidents such as prohibition notices, failures at annual test or convictions need to be investigated and recorded. Most importantly, note any action taken to help prevent such an occurrence again. When you are looking at your filing system, paper or electronic, simply imagine a DVSA official is at your elbow – would the records be sufficient evidence that you are doing everything that is required of you? If you have any concerns, it may be wise to seek the services of a consultant or trade association to assist in improving and maintaining your systems to prevent any issues arising in the future. As ever, we would be delighted to assist you if you contact us on 07771 768080 or email info@thedwconsultancy.com. Although not a legal requirement, it makes complete sense for van operators to undertake a similar review at suitable intervals.

9) How do I manage parts supply and quality?

I have very briefly mentioned managing your own parts stockholding in the section on managing in-house workshops above. I also mentioned that part supply could be yet another book all on its own, so for that reason, I just offer a few helpful hints here.

If your vehicle is purchased with a manufacturer's inclusive R&M contract, and up to 75% of HGVs are, then you should expect genuine manufacturer parts to be fitted. A core reason for that is that the parts will come with full warranty, as will the labour and any other component downstream of the repair. So, if an engine blows due to a faulty filter, you are covered. In addition, manufacturers obviously want to control and maximise the use of their own parts network.

However, what parts should you be using in-house and what parts should you expect an independent workshop to be using?

This brings up the thorny question of pattern parts. These are parts made by a third party other than the OEM (Original Equipment Manufacturer) or their direct suppliers. Production of these parts is largely governed by EU "Block Exemption" rules, which states that pattern parts must be of "matching quality". In order to be considered as being of matching quality, pattern parts must be of a sufficiently high quality that their use does not, according to the EU Commission, "endanger the reputation of the authorised repair network". However, the burden to prove that a part does not fulfil this requirement falls upon the vehicle manufacturer who must bring evidence to that effect, if it wants to discourage authorised repairers from using such parts. You can see that the last part of that sentence effectively discourages the manufacturers from taking issue with the majority of pattern parts suppliers.

Manufacturers and their suppliers can spend years and many millions of pounds developing the components fitted to their vehicles. As I started my career with a major vehicle manufacturer, I can warrant that the level of component detail to which a manufacturer or supplier can go to in developing components has to be seen to be believed. In contrast, non-OEM suppliers can produce products that look similar, but are of widely varying quality, such that some just do not fit when offered up to the vehicle. The problem is, I cannot categorically say do not fit pattern parts; they sometimes have a role to play in repairing your fleet and some are of acceptable quality. What I would say is, please consider value rather than price. If a pattern part fails early, which they may not, but often do, there is the downtime to operations to consider, plus the additional unnecessary repair time. Whenever I have seen studies by my colleagues on the true cost of pattern parts, OEM parts win out almost every time.

By the way, for those unfamiliar with the automotive industry, I think I need to offer a word of explanation here. When vehicle manufacturers (OEM's) first started all those years ago, they generally manufactured all their own parts for their own vehicles. Very quickly, supply chains set up to provide component parts to the manufacturers. When I first started with Ford, we still had our own foundry for engines, gearboxes and the like, along with giant presses for most body parts, but many other parts arrived as sub-assemblies. Nowadays, most vehicle manufacturers are effectively giant marketing organisations who also assemble virtually a kit of parts from their suppliers. This is a huge simplification as it ignores the design, research, development and testing that may take place, but I am sure you get the general idea.

The suppliers themselves are now organised in levels, Tier 1 being the major component manufacturers, working directly for the vehicle manufacturers, who often carry out much of the research and development on their own components, such as suspension and brake suppliers; Tier 2 who mostly supply components to Tier 1, and then Tier 3, who supply to both Tiers 1 & 2 and may not be exclusively engaged in the motor trade. So "true" OEM parts are now a deceivingly small part of the vehicle parts supply chain, which are more likely to be manufactured on the OEM's behalf by a Tier 1,2 or 3 supplier. Although this muddies the waters, these parts should still be branded with the vehicle manufacturer's brand.

Most fleet operators, even the ones fitting pattern parts, take the stance that for "life & limb" items such as steering and brakes, they will only use OEM parts. This would seem to be a sensible place to start. Most then also use OEM parts for routine servicing as manufacturers tend to keep prices on fast moving items relatively low and make their profit in this sector by the volumes sold. It makes financial and practical sense to go for OEM on such parts. My advice would then be, for all other parts, go for OEM unless you are extremely confident of the quality of the part or supplier you are fitting. A general statement from the supplier that their parts are of 'OE quality' does not cut the mustard for me and beware of "bargains", as with most things in life, you tend to get what you pay for.

There are then three issues that arise from this OEM only stance. Firstly, for external maintenance, if you have specified OEM parts only, you will need to keep an eye on your service agent to make sure that is what they are using and pattern parts do not creep in by mistake or, perhaps, dare I say it, to make more profit. One obvious key symptom to watch out for here, is repeated failures or repairs on specific items. Secondly, for your own workshop, as well as the manufacturers or dealers, you will probably be getting your supplies from a number of parts factors. Some provide OEM only, which are easier to monitor, however, some provide both OEM and "OEM quality", the latter sometimes meaning pattern parts. You need to be careful that pattern parts do not slip into the supply chain, which is easy to do and can be difficult to monitor. Lastly, there is the thorny issue of your insurance company.

For a long time now, the insurance industry has been governed largely by price, due largely to domestic and business customers all hunting for, and being driven by, the cheapest quote. What that means in effect is that the insurance companies are gradually taking more and more out of their offerings. The policy small print continually and increasingly contains more clauses that are not good news for the insured, including that of parts. Many policies are now worded such that pattern parts are the norm and when repairs take place, you have a real battle on your hands to get repaired using OEM parts. It is one thing to be replacing mechanical parts with sub-standard items – at worst you have a stranded vehicle at the side of the road and a potentially disappointed customer. If you now replace manufacturers' body or suspension parts with pattern parts, you may be risking life and limb due to the structural integrity of the vehicle. My suggestion would be to attempt to include a clause in your insurance policy that only OEM parts will be used on repair, which may well increase your premium, or be prepared argue each and every case at the time of repair.

Lastly, it is worth noting that quite a number of the main manufacturers, and even some dealers, have set up their own all-marks parts operations, branded under another trade name. Naturally, most, but not all these organisations, largely deal in fast moving parts, so mainstream servicing items. Given that manufacturers now assemble parts from 2nd and 3rd tier suppliers, who also supply most of the other manufactures, this means these part organisations are supplying original equipment specification parts, albeit in a different box, but generally at a cheaper price.

10) How do I manage breakdowns?

Thankfully, as mentioned elsewhere in this chapter, vehicles are becoming more reliable and breakdowns are becoming less common. You can witness that by not seeing so many vehicles littering the hard shoulder (if the road still has one). Having said that, when breakdowns occur, it is always at the most inconvenient time and definitely at the most inconvenient location. Step one must therefore be to build in some form of breakdown cover into your maintenance contract, so that your maintenance supplier takes care of any eventuality and you may also have been able to build in a replacement vehicle, albeit usually at extra cost.

For those with their own workshop, or those without breakdown built into their maintenance contracts, you need to determine how you will handle breakdown scenarios. Some organisations with their own workshop, operating locally, have their own breakdown service and their own breakdown vehicle or vehicles. However, this becomes less and less feasible as vehicles travel further afield and the disruption one single breakdown has on normal maintenance services, especially for a small workshop, means that this form of working is not really feasible for most operations.

Alternatively, you can simply pay for services as and when you require them, which obviously works, but lacks coordination for anything but a very small fleet. One step up from this method it to use a "pay-as-you-go" system, but utilising the breakdown services of someone like the RHA or Logistics UK. This gives you a centralised call point and usually slightly reduced fees, depending on your usage. The big benefit in such a scheme is coordinated invoices and a single call centre for drivers to use, the downside is there is normally an administration fee involved.

If you are using a vehicle purchase method that includes maintenance, generally they will include breakdown cover within the annual or monthly fees, which makes so much sense. The cost should range from nothing (i.e., inclusive within the maintenance) to a fee that should be sensibly less than buying breakdown cover separately. Apart from anything else it puts the financial onus on the supplier to maintain the vehicles well, therefore helping to reduce the number of breakdowns to an absolute minimum. Similarly, if you are using external maintenance providers in whatever form, it also makes sense to include at least a basic level of breakdown cover. Manufacturer provided comprehensive maintenance arrangements should include it as a matter of course.

Then, of course, comes the alternative of full separate external breakdown cover. The idea of such cover is to obviously minimise business disruption and delays by getting your vehicle back on the road in the fastest way possible. The cost of cover puts many businesses off, but can often be worthwhile if you consider the potential business impact of a vehicle being off the road for any significant length of time, both financially and in terms of performance or reputation. Depending on the number of times you use the service, it will usually work out cheaper and faster than paying one-off fees for roadside services, towing and repair. Administration should also be substantially reduced and never underestimate the monetary value in reduced time spent on administration.

Before seeking cover, it is worth taking stock and deciding exactly what services you are looking for. As with vehicle insurance, this is a very cut-throat market with customers increasingly seeking reduced costs each year. So suppliers have responded by continuously taking out little parts of the service or increasing excess charges – you tend not to notice this at renewal time, but certainly do when the final bill arrives and you are left wondering how that particular breakdown cost your organisation quite so much. Also, don't forget that if you are running Electric or other alternatively fuelled vehicles, you will need to check that the breakdown provider has given their staff sufficient training in the different techniques that will be required and that enough vehicles carry any additional equipment that may be necessary – don't assume this has taken place as the preparation in this area varies widely by supplier.

No breakdown cover contract will be the same, even if the declared level of cover provision is identical, so unfortunately, yet again, there is no substitute for requesting the terms and conditions and patiently sitting down to compare like with like. My advice here is please do not assume a particular detail of cover is included in the provision – if you cannot see what you require in writing, then speak to the supplier, otherwise assume it is not included and will be at an additional cost. For example, different providers might have differing restrictions on the amount of time that a mechanic can work on your vehicle at the roadside before additional charges may be levied. It is almost certain that there will be increased charges as the size and weight of the vehicle increases, these need comparing carefully, especially if your fleet operates a variety of weight ranges.

Top Tips for Repair & Maintenance ✔

- Vans under 3.5T are not yet so heavily controlled or regulated as HGVs, however, corporate responsibility and operator recognition schemes means many van operators now utilise similar maintenance regimes to HGVs.

- A daily walk-round check (before each shift) for both vans and HGVs is the cornerstone to a good maintenance regime.

- Defects found on service or inspection are good indicators; too many could mean daily checks and previous maintenance were not carried out properly. Very few defects are usually good news, so long as inspection items were not missed, but may possibly mean service intervals could be extended.

- If you already run your own workshop undertaking some 3rd part work, carefully examine the figures for opening an MoT or ATF facility (when allowed) – as well as core inspection work, it can also generate 3rd party work; ensure the throughput is expected to continue before investing.

- Running your own workshop eliminates fleet service travel time and costs, which can be considerable for anything other than a local agent.

- The two most important KPI's by far for managing your own workshop are Efficiency (how long technicians take against standard times) and Utilisation (how many available technician hours are filled with productive work).

- A well-run parts operation is crucial for running an efficient workshop with well-developed networks to quality parts suppliers.

- If not already doing so, van operators must be measuring both their planned and unplanned maintenance time by vehicle.

- When contracting out maintenance, thoroughly inspect your contractors' premises and spend time specifying and agreeing the contract details to ensure a smooth-running operation.

- Log every single call or instruction to your maintenance contractor and record all actions and events. Hold regular meetings to discuss and improve performance and iron out any issues quickly.

- Consider utilising your supplier's extended hours (if available and cost-effective) for servicing in order to reduce downtime and perhaps, spare vehicles. Consider extending opening hours for an in-house workshop to better suit the needs of the business.

- If you are still using a paper daily defect reporting system, it is probably time to review the many digital systems available for the advantages they bring in terms of compliance recording.

- When taking out breakdown cover, once again, decide exactly what you require in advance and spend time comparing the small print from your short-list of suppliers – contractors have extended the number of items that are charged as extras in recent years.

- Take care with the quality of parts from independent workshops and especially for insurance repairs – specify up front if you require OEM parts and constantly monitor repair quality.

David's Don'ts ✖

- Don't think that contracting out maintenance absolves you from any of your O licence responsibilities; you must keep records and ensure full maintenance is being undertaken at the correct time – the same guidance applies equally to lighter vehicle operators.

- During periods of high demand, don't forget to book MoTs well in advance, especially for HGVs, so as to achieve the time slot you need.

- Don't forget to agree with your contractor exactly who is responsible for preparation and presentation for MoT.

The Ultimate Guide to Commercial Vehicle Fleet Management

Chapter 11 – Fuel, Oil & AdBlue Management

1) *Why is fuel management so important to the success of the operation?*
2) *When and why should I operate with bulk fuel on site?*
3) *How do I set up a bulk fuel operation, what's involved? How do I manage my suppliers? How do I manage my systems?*
4) *When should I use fuel cards?*
5) *What type of fuel card should I use & how should I select a supplier? How should I operate my fuel cards?*
6) *What Questions Should I ask my Fuel Card Supplier? (Checklist)*
7) *What alternatives are there to diesel; how should I manage them?*
8) *How do I go about saving fuel for my fleet?*
9) *What do I need to know about Oil?*
10) *What do I need to know about AdBlue?*

1) *Why is fuel management so important to the success of the operation?*

There are an astounding number of operators I have met over the years who take the view that fuel is a necessary operating cost and therefore it has to be paid for, so there is nothing they can do to minimise the expense. With that mindset, they are correct, in that they will never save any money.

Recent shortages of fuel are often claimed by the press as "panic buying" but are, in reality, more due to the JIT supply chain, a shortage of tanker drivers and the Brexit/Covid effect. This very public situation just emphasises the need to take all the sensible measures that you possibly can, in order to help guarantee future fuel supplies for your operation. It has also introduced the lesson of supply shortages due to JIT delivery to a whole new generation, who perhaps thought unconstrained fuel supply was a fact of life.

A better mindset, I would suggest, is that fuel is a scarce global resource and we all need to save every drop, so anything and everything that can be done to minimise expenditure and put cash on the bottom line, should be happening. That also misses out the increasingly important factor of trying to reduce climate changing emissions.

Even though fuel costs and duties until very recently have stayed relatively low for a number of years, for many operators of heavy vehicles, fuel will still be their first or second biggest operating expense, so time spent on reducing fuel costs just has to be worthwhile.

Even for van operators, where fuel is a lower percentage of your total operating costs, that percentage is much more variable, depending, amongst other things, on the weight carried, the speed of travel, the distance covered, the amount of urban driving and, of course, your drivers. That means for van operators, the amount that can be saved is a lower percentage of the total, but the variation can be far greater than for a heavy vehicle. Therefore, it can have a huge effect on your profitability, compared to a competitor, with tighter cost controls.

Good Fuel Management reduces trips to the Pumps

There is also the fact that fuel is relatively easy to go missing. The tighter your controls, the less likely this is to happen. I worked for one operator who spent considerable time and administration effort keeping a close track of their fuel, but they did not close all links in the chain. It was only the sharp eyes of a neighbour to a member of staff, who was concerned about the number of jerry cans disappearing into their neighbour's garage, that alerted anyone to a problem.

I am amazed that people will put their whole career on the line for a few litres of fuel, but sadly, it happens all too often. I was also slightly saddened in the early days of telematics that many operators were fitting it purely to try to counter fuel theft, without gaining the benefit of the other functions; they just wanted the greater visibility of fuel. So, the message has to be, the tighter your controls, the less temptations there will be and the less likelihood any potential light-fingered members of staff are to take liberties.

2) When and why should I operate with bulk fuel on site?

Fuel strikes and protests that have taken place over the last twenty years have emphasised the fragility of the fuel supply chain network, which effectively operates on a just-in-time basis. Protests in the year 2000 and to a lesser extent, later in 2005 and 2007, restricted supplies drastically for a while, leading to priority schemes for the emergency services and queues, or even fights, at fuel stations. Fuel delivery drivers also took action in 2011 and 2012 which had a similar effect, although the government had learnt somewhat from the previous shortages and had a more robust back-up plan at that point. What it did emphasise is that operators without their own fuel supplies could have their operations severely curtailed within days, or even hours in some cases. Bulk tank suppliers in intervening years have reported increased sales for that very reason. Most operators with tanks look at holding at least a two-week supply; probably four weeks or longer makes better sense.

In addition to the logistics of supply, having your own fuel is generally the cheapest way of providing it to your organisation so it makes good financial sense, saving a couple of pence per litre over that purchased at the forecourt, even with the most generous fuel card. Depending on the size of your fleet, the mileage run and average consumption, that could result in a payback period of one to two years for a basic installation. However, there is obviously more to it than providing just the basic tank, so you need to think through the implications. In addition, the style of operation of the fleet is important; if all vehicles return to base each night, it becomes a 'no-brainer'. If the majority of the fleet is on the road and only returns occasionally, the calculation becomes far less certain and more complex.

The fuel supply market is one of the most volatile in the transport world, so having bulk tanks means you can take advantage of price fluctuations and buy when prices are low. These reductions in bulk prices can sometimes take a long time to feed through to forecourt pump prices, if it reduces at all. Some operators enjoy this side of the business and often haggle with local or national suppliers in order to get the very best price, also trying to time their purchase in line with low prices. Others view this as non-core to the business and utilise buying co-operatives or use the services of trade organisations who offer a fuel price information service to aid operators buying fuel.

3) *How do I set up a bulk fuel operation, what is involved? How do I manage my suppliers? How do I manage my systems?*

Fuel tanks are essentially very simple pieces of kit, however, the process of deciding on the size and position of bulk fuel tanks, along with all the peripheral equipment to manage them sensibly means there are many things to think about. The following is a suggestion of the main items to consider, however, this is definitively not a complete guide and expert advice should be sought from fuel and tank providers and the relevant government agencies. Compliance with government regulations is important to ensure safety to staff, the public and the environment, but also to reduce the risk that you may fall foul of the law.

If a fuel oil leaks or spill occurs, it can be hazardous to the surrounding environment, posing risks to people in the area as well as wildlife and vegetation. Tanks must therefore be regularly inspected and maintained to ensure they remain in good condition and in compliance with regulations. It is suggested this maintenance is diarised and fully recorded, probably takes place annually, perhaps in line with other vehicle or workshop safety inspections.

The most important item to service is to ensure the pump/s are running correctly, which should include cleaning the filters, checking the drive belts, examining for any leaks, and checking the meter calibration. The inspection should also include checks on the whole fuel installation including the bund, gauges and ensuring the alarms work. With increasing biofuel content in fuels, it is really important that the water content and any contamination in the fuel is assessed.

Providing the annual inspection takes place regularly and any items found are attended to, I would suggest the only other maintenance necessary for above-ground tanks would be a mid-life re-paint (for steel tanks) after 10 to 15 years or so. It would also be advisable to repair any damage found to the external coating to avoid further corrosion, which could be done on annual inspection. If a build-up of water, bacteria or corrosion within the tank is found or evidenced in the filters, there are specialist suppliers available for cleansing fuel tanks and refurbishing the condition of your fuel stocks, well worth doing to avoid poor fuel getting to your vehicle tanks.

Regulations and Guidance

Regulations for Fuel tanks in Wales & England were published by the Environment Agency (EA) and Department for Environment, Food & Rural Affairs (DEFRA) in May 2015 and updated from time to time, with corresponding regulations for other parts of the UK. https://www.gov.uk/guidance/storing-oil-at-a-home-or-business .

One of the most important part of the regulations states that for commercial premises, storage containers with a capacity of 200 litres or more must effectively be stored in a bunded tank, bowser or other container, such as a drum or Intermediate Bulk Container (IBC), with a secondary containment of no less than 110% of the maximum contents. The extra 10% is to take account of any other fluids, such as rainwater, that might gather in the bund. Ensuring the bund remains secure is the most important thing you can do to avoid spillages.

The EA and DEFRA also publishes guidelines on preventing pollution and specifying and managing bulk fuel installations. Find them at https://www.gov.uk/guidance/pollution-prevention-for-businesses. Strangely, they are not all legally enforceable, however, in the event of a serious fuel spillage, if you cannot show that you have followed the guidelines, prosecution may follow with potentially expensive clean-up costs. Most operator's yards should already have interceptors or separators built into their existing drainage systems, however, if installing a new bulk fuel tank, you will need to check that the existing separator is sufficient for a new installation.

Bulk Tanks

Most modern fuel tanks fortunately come ready bunded and often just need craning onto a suitable base and connecting to supplies. Plastic tanks are slightly cheaper and lighter than steel and are more common for sizes up to around 20,000 litres; above this you will need to go for a steel tank. The rules assume a tank life span of at least 20 years, with some maintenance assumed to take place over time when above ground, obviously with less maintenance when underground, due to accessibility. Underground installations are obviously neater, take less space but are more expensive and complex to install, with differing component specifications and maintenance requirements.

It is suggested that once you start thinking of tanks above 50,000 litres, they are either individual tanks, which are easier to move around, or a single larger tank, but compartmentalised. This means if any one tank gets compromised by, say, bacteria, other fluids, or corrosion, fuel can still be drawn from the accompanying tanks whilst the problem is remedied. Also, a full artic delivery load, the most cost-effective size, will be around 36,000 litres, making this a suitable top-up delivery without running an individual tank dry. Deliveries below full loads (whatever the size of the delivering vehicle) will attract a premium, so always try to negotiate the most cost-effective delivery with your supplier, suitable for your operation, tanks and usage. However, do avoid the tank getting near to dry just to get a cheaper load – it is all too easy to do, but instead, it is worth paying a small load premium to avoid nearly running out or disturbing sediment in the base of the tank.

To give you an idea of current prices (2021), allow a capital budget of around £20,000 for a basic tank and up to £40,000 for a typical rectangular, bunded 50,000-litre steel tank, with integral filling cabinet, pump, gauge, alarms and delivery to site. Due to current supply shortages, prices are likely to exceed these values temporarily, but hopefully return to more sensible values in the longer term. There will be a wide variety of costs for nearly all the components connected with on-site refuelling. I would strongly suggest not going for the cheapest equipment as they tend to result in operational issues later down the line. A high-quality pump, an electronic gauge and a good fuel management system, regularly maintained, should result in a fairly trouble-free operation for many years.

Once you have decided on your tank size, location and supplier, you will need to source the other key components for the installation, namely the pump/s, fuel-island, monitoring and controllers and fuel management software. You may also need some civil engineering work when constructing a concrete base for the tank or a fuel island to protect the pumps. It is possible to source all these items for yourself, or arrange for one supplier to take the lead by organising the supply of all the items.

Alternatively, you could use one of the consultancy firms available who will design, source and arrange installation for the whole project. The latter may look the dearer option; however, they will project manage the build and most likely be able to obtain additional discount from the suppliers, which should offset their charges. In addition, the consultant's experience should be able to iron out any potential problems during the project.

Remember that diesel and petrol supplies now include increasing amounts of blended biofuel, which carries an increased risk of absorbing water and producing bacteria which in turn can cause corrosion or block lines and filters. Most tank manufacturers have come up with ways, some novel, of reducing the potential problem, at extra cost, but it would make sense to consider such a design feature now in order to future-proof your installation.

Pumps

Your dispensing pump obviously has the most moving parts of the installation, will get used the most and will also be vulnerable to abuse from drivers in a hurry or may suffer potential accident damage. As mentioned above, it is worth paying for the best possible pump you can afford; many buyers assume this means the fastest possible, that is not always the case – your core objective should be reliability.

Establish out who will be doing your pump maintenance and ask them which models get the most call outs and if they recommend a particular pump that requires the least maintenance over time. Vans and car derived vans will probably not accept delivery rates beyond 70 litres/min, due mainly to their filler constraints and designs. In order to reduce filling time to manageable proportions, trucks will require a heavier duty pump for continuous operation, probably best at around 110-120 litres/min. They can go much higher, but frothing in the vehicle tank and breathing or venting issues may cause problems and actually end up slower than a lower rated pump. Seek advice from your suppliers on that score. Do not forget if you are intending to sell or provide fuel on to other operators, you will need a high accuracy pump and you will probably need to check on regulations with HMRC, Weights and Measures or Trading Standards; their response may depend somewhat on your contractual arrangement with the other operator/s.

You will find that many ready-made tank solutions have the pump sited in a cabinet contained at the end of the tank, which is neat and compact, reduces space requirements and is very suitable for low to medium use operations. However, for higher traffic, it is probably better to have the pump/s mounted on a central island which is accessible from both sides. If that is going to be the case, ensure the hoses are retractable or mounted on a high-level arm to reduce potential snagging and damage. Even if traffic is not high enough to justify a two-pump installation, still consider a second back-up pump for when demand is high or in case of damage or fault to your main pump. This could be a cheaper, lower rated version to give short-term continuity and will also be useful whenever there is a rush on the pumps.

Gauges

As mentioned earlier, in order to keep control of fuel, you have to close the links in the monitoring chain. This means constantly comparing fuel in with fuel out, at least once a week, best on a daily basis to avoid any losses going unnoticed. In the past, this was nearly always achieved using a dipstick, which is not without its accuracy problems and relies on someone getting physical on or around the tank. More common now will be a simple, fairly cheap gauge, however, again, not always highly accurate and will still rely on someone on hand to read it correctly. At a cost, the latest electronic gauges have distinct advantages. For multiple depots, on cold wet dark nights, you can remotely check all your tanks from a comfortable office without anyone else being involved. You can also check delivery invoices match the amount received (not always the case) and some versions are accurate enough to detect very small amounts of pilfering or small leaks. The latter type of gauge may seem expensive at purchasing time, but it is one of those investments that pays off in the long term.

That raises an important point on fuel buying. Sometimes, if fuel is delivered directly out of the refinery, rather than your supplier's own tanks, it can be very warm when loaded. As it travels in a tanker, or within your own tank, it cools – and shrinks! So your predicted 25,000 litres can end up a lot less. The invoice may contain the words "rack rate", so you are being billed for the volume out of the refinery, not when delivered. Therefore, delivery terms and conditions become important and you are better off with standard delivery volumes rather than bulk terms. It is just something to be aware of and a good gauge will help check this for you. If you start to have more than very minor variations of volume on delivery, check the delivery temperature. If there is a problem, obviously discuss it with your supplier. Generally it can work both ways where the volume might be slightly more or less than ordered, but continuous losses will need further investigation and negotiation.

Fuel Management System

This is the core of managing fuel supplies. The fuel island will require some form of control to allow fuel to be drawn. It is at this point I would suggest getting your wallet out. Many operators allow manual entry of odometer readings, on the basis that it is all that is required on a fuel card, which is fatal. I can guarantee there will be multiple wrong entries so your administration will spend a lot of time trying to sort out the mistakes and you will always be wondering which entry is the correct one, so never have complete confidence in your fuel figures.

Instead consider one of the many systems that will automatically transfer the vehicle mileage, using a variety of techniques at varying cost, at the same time capturing fuel use. The cost for a large fleet can be considerable over manual input, but thankfully, some versions are now reducing in cost. It is an investment that once again, will pay back over time and allow a much more accurate reconciliation of stocks versus usage. Ensure before purchase that your fuel and mileage data can be integrated with your fleet management software and any telematic data that can be usefully incorporated. You may also be able to utilise your telematic mileage for capture against fuel drawings.

4)   When should I use fuel cards?

There are many reasons why fleets use cards rather than bulk fuels. If you have a small fleet or do not want the hassle of organising your own storage facility, cards are a very flexible route. Even if you have your own supplies, should your fleet travel away from their home base, you may need top-up supplies at some point. Cash or credit cards are the obvious answer, but these do not give you the control that fuel cards can bring, which are more secure and should reduce administration time.

Fuel stations in the UK reduced from around 40,000 in the 1950's, to just 13,100 in the year 2000, due to consolidation by the oil companies and tougher regulations for forecourts. However, today, (2021) there are just under 8,400 left but there is a renewed focus for remaining stations on all sorts of subsidiary activities: coffee, fast food and shopping being the main offerings alongside fuel. What this means for fleets is that the choice of fuel card is all important to avoid vehicles having to travel out of their way to find a suitable station or the cheapest fuel. There is a huge choice of cards out there, so once again, start by listing your priorities – what does your organisation want and need from your card supplier?

Reduced Fuel Stations make Brand Selection more Critical

5) What type of fuel card should I use & how should I select a supplier? How should I operate my fuel cards?

One of the first decisions to make is whether you want to pay pump prices or a set price, fixed every week based on refinery pricing at the time. Another basic decision you need to make is if you select a specific branded card, possibly with some links to other fuel companies to extend their coverage, or one of the multi-branded cards, some of which have coverages of around 90% of the UK fuel stations. Branded cards will normally offer the maximum discount and better deals, whereas the multi-brand cards reduce the need to find the right station, however, some do offer significant discounts, normally on diesel, especially for high volume users.

If you do purchase high volumes of fuel and want the maximum discount prices, then consider bunker fuel cards that offer fuel at wholesale prices. However, maximum discounts can only be given at the relevant bunker fuel sites, of which there are naturally less than regular stations. They are also geared towards HGVs so tend to have taller canopies and easier access to be more accessible to larger vehicles and are situated on main trunk routes. There are also dealers within the network who sell on behalf of the larger fuel companies, but when comparing dealer prices, make sure you get the net price of fuel as the network will add a charge for acting as "banker" for your fuel.

Pump price fuel cards

For this option, as the name suggests, you are charged the price displayed at the pump. Depending on your fuel card provider agreement or the total volumes drawn, you may be able to access a slight discount, or in certain circumstances, even pay a small surcharge on the forecourt pump price. You will be aware that pump prices vary day-by-day and quite dramatically by area, so rural areas tend to be more expensive, the logic being it is dearer to deliver to these outlying locations. The benefit of a pump price related fuel card, especially for smaller fleets, is a better network coverage, with more service stations accepting these cards so drivers are less likely to have to make unnecessary detours. In general, they are suitable for all fleet, industry and business types.

Fixed price fuel cards

For the fixed price card option your fuel rate is set weekly and determined by diesel wholesale prices, it will not change in that period, no matter how retail rates move.

This gives you a small, but useful, level of control over your fuel budget. Being aware of any rises in rates a few days beforehand means you can plan ahead and refuel earlier at a lower rate. Most fixed price card providers give a small discount on the retail pump price.

This type of card suits hauliers, large fleets and high-volume users. With a slightly smaller network than pump price cards, fixed price sites are generally placed along most strategic major transport routes. Despite advice, many drivers will still occasionally fill up at motorway service stations, which are hugely expensive; a fixed rate fuel card will allow access to most motorway sites without the inflated prices

Choice of fuel cards

There are a vast and bewildering range of options and suppliers for both types of cards. It is a case of doing the leg work and negotiating the best deal for your organisation. My advice would be to shortlist suppliers based on the headline numbers, then pay very close attention to the level of service provided. If you have specific requirements on, say, the day of the week or the month you wish to be billed, rule out those suppliers who are too fixed in their systems to comply.

Most importantly, explain what details of usage and expenditure you wish to have presented with the invoice and ask for samples to check which submissions are easiest to read and understand and match your systems. Check on the downloadability of the data provided, so it can be easily incorporated into your fleet management and accounting systems with the minimum manual intervention.

Also look for a fuel card provider offering comprehensive and robust online management tools and service station locators. Depending on your drivers, it is helpful to have an option available to download an application to smartphones or similar internet enabled device, helping drivers to find the closest, most suitable service point en route.

6) What Questions Should I ask my Fuel Card Supplier?

Here is a checklist of some sensible questions to ask each supplier during the buying process and some advice on how to question them to avoid discovering expensive unseen costs further down the track:

1. Check the exact cost of each fuel card – factor in any annual fees and allow for any replacement fee for lost cards (it's amazing how many cards go missing or are used for example, for scraping ice off the windscreen and no longer useable).

2. Exactly how much will they charge for each litre of fuel either by fixed price or by pump and exactly what are their discount rates? Are there conditions on the discounts (certain fuel stations only for example)? Watch out for any minimum usage charges, factor these into your calculations, if necessary.

3. Check the logistics of how many sites are available in their total network and if they are usefully located close to your premises, customers and usual routes. In other words, are they useful to your organisation; it is great to have a large coverage, but no good if they are not suitable for your operation.

4. Be absolutely clear on any potential 'hidden' charges, for example itemised invoices, specialised reports, failed payment fees, paper invoices, card protection, technical help, or online management assistance. Be aware that many card companies have a phenomenal range of reports that will present the figures in a huge range of potentially useful formats, but are often shy in sharing these with the customers and sometimes charge for them, I suspect, in order to

put customers off using them as they like to keep things standard. Discuss all the possibilities during the buying process and attempt to ensure any specific reports you desire, in the format to suit you, are provided free of charge as part of the overall package.

5. Check you can access your account on-line and ask to see sample real-time data – ask for a full demonstration and check the level of data available – can you understand it easily? Some account data is definitely written for the benefit of the fuel card company, not the customer. Also check out what level of account management is accessible from this portal – can you cancel a lost card, for example?

6. Check on the opening hours of their customer services and technical help. Ring them a couple of times to check their average waiting time (this may seem like a lot of effort, but better now than being disgruntled a few years later)

7. Check who will be your account manager and their accessibility. Ensure you have a conversation or two with the actual person to check you feel you can work with them – ask some of the same questions as you ask the sales personnel and check the answers match

8. Check they provide chip and PIN security for drivers – I strongly suggest discounting those who do not provide adequate security. Unless you have a strong reason for retaining some flexibility with your fuel cards, I would advise embossing the vehicle registration and, it applicable, the driver for added security.

9. Decide if you wish other products to be bought using the cards. Personally, I would advise either fuel only, or fuel plus essentials such as oil or AdBlue, to keep the account clear and simple. However, some operators allow other purchases on the card, such as tolls and overnight parking, but be very clear what is available at negotiating time, what the costs are and how it will be reported. Please do not be tempted to let sundries cloud a fuel account, so ensure the reporting is very clear and fuel is separate from any other expenditure. I would also suggest avoiding cards offering gifts or reward points – they can skew employee choice of fuelling.

It pays to keep a Firm Control of your Fuel Card Spend

To summarise then, these are the benefits of fuel cards and the reasons why most commercial vehicle operators use them:

- Removes the need for cash; chip & PIN (or next generation security) makes payment safer and more secure.

- Reduces the amount of admin for your organisation, generally handled through one account with detailed invoicing and usage information.

- You are able to specify exactly what can and cannot be bought using them; you also decide on the level of information required at each transaction.

- Allows fuel purchase at wholesale costs or at least discounted prices from the forecourt pump price, giving savings.

- Flexibility of forecourts; you choose the networks you wish to use and decide how the logistics works with your organisation.

- Choice – there is a large variety of cards to choose from, designed with different fleets in mind, so there should be one to suit your commercial vehicles.

- Reports – can be as detailed as you like and offer significant control over your vehicles from one report. Although the fuel card company will probably push for monthly reporting, weekly reports allow you to control trends much more effectively.

- Employee benefits – with tight controls in place, it helps removes the ability for any wrong-doing and reduces the amount of paperwork.

- Multifuel card benefits – may reduce the potential discounts but increases the availability of outlets and hence reduces time drivers spend hunting forecourts.

7) What alternatives are there to diesel; how should I manage them?

Installing a bulk fuel facility for an alternative fuel source is generally a major investment and currently a bit of a leap of faith. The ROI will need careful consideration and will often depend on the security of duty reductions into the future and what capital grants are available. In addition, the issue of refuelling en-route will remain paramount for some years to come.

For example, at the time of writing, according to UK H2 mobility, there are currently less than 20 hydrogen refuelling stations in the UK and less than 200 across Europe. In 2016, Hydrogen London predicted they would have 35 stations in place by 2020, of which, just a handful currently exist. The same is broadly true of other fuels with a similarly low number of CNG (Compressed Natural Gas) and LNG (Liquified Natural Gas) stations available for users in the UK. It currently only makes sense therefore, to use such fuels for vehicles that will return to base until wider coverage is in place. LPG (Liquified Petroleum Gas) remains the outsider in that it has been an established gas alternative for many years and there are currently 1400 refuelling sites in the UK.

Possibly the most widely adopted alternative fuel to date has been electricity. However, they also suffer from lack of infrastructure. At the time of writing (2021) according to the charger mapping website 'Zap-Stats' (https://www.zap-map.com/statistics/#points) there are estimated to be over 17,000 publicly available charging locations in the UK, but of varying specification. Assuming a vehicle will be stationary at a base location for long enough, the current costs of providing a charging point are not insubstantial and need to be factored into any purchasing decision.

As a guide, Energy Saving Trust figures (Aug 2017) suggest a cost, without any additional installation, of around £1000 for a 7kW charger, taking up to eight hours to recharge, £3k for a 22kW charger, taking up to four hours and up to £40k for a 50kW charger, taking up to 40 minutes for an 80% charge. Find the full guidance here: https://energysavingtrust.org.uk/sites/default/files/reports/6390%20EST%20A4%20Chargepoints%20guide_v10b.pdf

From these figures it can be seen that rapid chargers require significant investment, not least into the power provision up to the charging point itself. As mentioned elsewhere, it is vital to consider the cost of providing charging points and any additional supply infrastructure from your DNO (Distribution Network Operator) before expanding your EV fleet.

Unlike ICE vehicles, the way vehicles are currently being used and your estimation of how they will be used in the future has a big impact on what charging facilities you will require and how they will best be utilised. Vans used in an urban environment during the day would probably be suited to being charged overnight, either at the depot or on an employees' driveway, the latter with suitable compensation for business electricity use. Domestic electricity is still relatively cheap, especially if used off-peak, however electricity from public charging points will attract roughly a 50% to 300% uplift in cost, depending on the rate of charge, so you need to factor this into your equations.

Vehicles with only on-street overnight parking will need to arrive at other bespoke charging arrangements, such as using any available public charging point. Many operators currently report problems with compatibility with so many differing charge operators on the scene. An overnight arrangement should be suitable for most vehicles, except those with larger batteries and heavy usage, which may require some form of topping up during the day, either out and about or back at base. A home wall box installation for your employees will allow faster charging than a standard domestic socket and may be eligible for a grant to install. Don't forget that the rate of charge depends on both the maximum the vehicle will accept and the maximum the socket will provide, whichever is the lower will prevail, and time taken is in inverse proportion to the rate of charge.

Most smaller EV's will be utilising a 'type 2' connectors and the maximum available from a domestic supply charger will be 7.2kW, charging an average sized van in around 6 hours. Higher charge rates for more rapid charging or HGVs will require 3 phase supply, converted to DC (Direct Current) and utilise a variety of plug types. Currently 50kW is the largest charger in common use, but manufacturers are looking at 150kW or even higher. This will give very rapid charging rates, but a consequent high drain on power consumption, so may require upgrades to your site supply. As a gross generalisation, when planning multiple installations, it is assumed that slower, low-rate chargers may be in use for longer periods of time, whereas high-rate chargers will be swopping vehicles around once a vehicle has reached a sufficient state of charge. For multiple charge locations, there will probably be an element of charge balancing between chargers to ensure site capacities are not exceeded, so vehicles may not always receive the charge that was expected.

Fuel cards are gradually getting in on the alternative act. At least one major multi-brand supplier has a specific electric charging card which also allows purchase of other fuels. Many of the larger suppliers already provide cards for a wider range of fuels such as diesel, petrol, liquefied petroleum gas (LPG), gas oil and additives such as AdBlue. The administration benefits of such cards still remain as the individual fuels and usage are still separately and clearly displayed on one invoice.

Smaller fleets also face another problem in moving to alternative fuels as they do not want to lose the discounts they currently receive on fuel prices by using cards to buy diesel. Therefore, the take-up of alternative fuels in the near future is more likely to be greater among larger firms that can make the capital expenditure to keep fuel on-site.

There is possibly more progress being made towards adding alternative fuels to cards used widely across Europe. These can also, in the main, be used in the UK, however, the network is still restricted. One card provider claims electric vehicles can use its 75,000 public charge points across Europe using its roaming network which includes some Shell forecourts.

In case I have made the scenario looks too bleak, there is one thing I should point out here. Although politicians, annoyingly, make grand statements about the rapid rise of alternatively fuelled vehicles, often without any sound factual backing, in the last twelve months, I have seen more progress on alternatively fuelled vehicles and infrastructure than in at least the last three years. That does not mean that there are not major obstacles still to overcome, merely that there appears to be a major head of steam building to support the transition from Internal Combustion Engines. That factor needs to be taken into account when making decisions on future fuel provision.

8) How do I go about saving fuel for my fleet?

There are a massive number of websites, brochures, blogs and information available to you on how to save fuel that you can look at. Most of the advice they contain is true, however, some tips are much more important than others and therefore likely to save more fuel. All the advice, if undertaken by your drivers, will generally save your organisation fuel, the trick is knowing which tips will work for you and which ones are most likely to be used by your drivers. We have had many years of experience in saving clients considerable sums off their fuel bills, so please contact us on 07771 768080 or info@thedwconsultancy.com for a free initial consultation or advice.

There has been no end of advice a few years ago for commercial vehicles on how to use higher gears and keep engine revolutions low – now that most HGVs have automated gearboxes, that advice is not quite so useful, although it can still apply very much to van drivers. So, here are my top tips, in priority order, for saving fuel that come from years of experience and are backed up by analysis and statistics;

only you can work out if it should apply to your fleet and your operation and how you should apply them.

Tip 1. Cut Idling – turn the engine off when stationary

This one is what I call a "quick win". When you go into any fleet, especially when using telematics for the first time, invariably, there will be a proportion of the drivers who tend to often leave their engine running, out of habit, for sometimes very protracted periods when stationary. Half-an-hour's ticking over when doing vehicle checks and paperwork is not uncommon. When you challenge those drivers, they invariably deny all responsibility, until you show them the data of where and when it happened. They then suddenly remember they were "talking to Bill" for 15 minutes, or whatever. It is simply a lifetime habit that most have never thought about and once you challenge them, they generally stop doing it. Telematics is invariably the best way to monitor how often your vehicles are idling.

Modern engines do not use an excess of fuel restarting and the components are now built to take multiple starts. The latest vehicles often include programmable automated engine turn off when stationary, eliminating the need for driver intervention. The simple rule should be, if a driver thinks they will be stationary for more than half a minute, then turn the engine off. If you do not think reducing idling will save your fleet much money (and save the surrounding environment), just measure it and think again. However, once all drivers have got into the habit of switching off, you need to monitor the situation occasionally, but you also need to look elsewhere for savings.

Tip 2. Anticipation and Defensive Driving

This is the least attractive piece of advice you can give a driver or a fleet operator, but crucially, the most important. Unfortunately, it tends to be received by a shrug of the shoulders and a "what can you do about it" attitude, both by drivers and especially managers. In the modern urban environment with tight delivery schedules, today's commercial vehicle driver is nearly always hard on the brakes or hard on the accelerator. In any driving, greater anticipation to avoid unnecessary acceleration and braking is probably the single most important technique a driver can employ to save fuel.

Unfortunately, maintaining momentum is best taught by a sympathetic instructor until the driver starts to understand how much fuel is used by constant speed changes, especially in a heavy vehicle. However, driving smoothly, anticipating future stops and taking action early is by far and away the single biggest factor you can employ in reducing fuel consumption.

Some of the latest smart vehicles and telematics have built-in anticipation of hills and future road changes so respond appropriately, but a driver in 'anticipation' mode can do just as well as the technology and there are many occasions where the technology would not work but a good driver will.

The other really wonderful thing about these driving techniques is that they will also work equally well with alternative fuels; the laws of physics will still apply and steady speed will result in longer battery or gas life. The only technology that does not work so well with steady speeds is hybrid, where the slowing down of the vehicle is converted back into energy, so they really suit highly variable, stop-start driving conditions.

Tip 3. Gentle use of the right foot

This follows on from Tip 2, above. When either driving downhill or slowing down, coming up to a junction or slower traffic, a modern vehicle will use less fuel if you remain in gear but take your foot off the accelerator. The engine management system recognises that the momentum of the vehicle is driving the engine and shuts off fuel to the engine.

Driving with higher engine RPM obviously consumes more fuel then driving at low RPM for a given road speed, therefore, early gear shifting and low RPM is very beneficial. With automated gearboxes, this is best achieved by a lighter touch on the accelerator, wherever possible, less than 50% on the accelerator position results in the lowest fuel consumption.

If you are serious about changing driver behaviour, which is where most of the savings come from, think about fitting telematics or if you have it, either getting an improved system or using all the features on your current system better; again, there is a chapter on telematics elsewhere in this book (chapter 8).

Cruise control is a useful aid to achieving constant speeds, but it is important to use it on open, smooth roads. It is probably not as good as the driver on hilly or congested roads because of the constant speed variations, however adaptive and intelligent speed control, if fitted, will take care of some, but not all, of those issues.

Tip 4. Avoiding excessive speed

This tip is obviously more important for van drivers than HGVs. The force on a vehicle generated by air resistance increases by the square of a vehicle's speed, or to put it another way, air resistance goes up by a factor of four every time speed is doubled. Therefore, relatively small increases in speed adds significantly to fuel consumption.

DfT figures show that a large van at 70 mph will use 27% more fuel than at 60 mph. Similarly, an HGV at 56 mph will use 22% more fuel than at 50mph. Whatever your vehicles, with or without top speed limiters, it is worth considering dropping their top speed by a few mph for significant reductions in fuel use. The reduction effect on average journey speed will be negligible. In fact, using a smoother driving style not only saves fuel but may actually increase average journey speeds as constant dramatic speed changes do not work well for averages in the long term. Do make sure that with any drop in top speed you consider, the vehicle can still attain top gear and still operates within its "green band", i.e., the vehicle's most efficient engine rev range, else the move will be self-defeating.

Tip 5. Use Air Conditioning sparingly

This one seems to always crop up in most listings of tips. There is no getting away from the fact that air conditioning systems definitively use engine power to achieve their cooling effect. By the laws of physics, this has to burn more fuel. However, I have done countless tests and measurement over the years and although there is a slight drop in performance, I cannot get anywhere close to some of the predicted losses claimed.

The Energy Saving Trust quotes research from ADEME in France (their ecological research organisation) that suggested during the standard European test cycle (NEDC) at 30°C ambient, air conditioning systems working at full capacity consumed around 25% more fuel. This extrapolated to around 5% more fuel than the same models without air conditioning over the period of a year. I suspect this would need a driver to have air conditioning switched on a lot of the time.

However, whatever the actual figure is, there is definitely an increase in consumption, so the advice to drivers should be to only use air conditioning when they need to, instead, perhaps opening the window slightly. Be careful with that advice though, as opening the window more than a small amount at higher speed will incur turbulence and drag, also worsening fuel consumption!

Handy Hint 👍

- It is good practice to have drivers use their air con at least once a month or so, even in winter, in order to keep the air con seals in good condition. Without use, they tend to dry out and may leak.

Tip 6. Vehicle Specification, aerodynamics and reducing drag

If you look at a modern vehicle you can easily see the lengths that all manufacturers have gone to in an attempt to overcome air resistance, with clever designs on steps and door mirrors, some parts looking a little bit like Formula 1 spin-offs. It breaks my heart to then see vehicles with badly mounted roof racks or boxes, sets of ladders, roof bars or horrendous banks of lights, often desired by some owner drivers, which will significantly increase air resistance and hence fuel consumption.

Bear in mind that at low speeds, aerodynamics has little effect. Despite previous comments about air con, there has to be some practicality about it, so for most urban driving, perhaps up to around 40mph, it is usually more efficient to open the windows than use the air con, but at higher speeds the reverse is true.

This also applies to other aerodynamic considerations; if a vehicle is going to be used mainly in urban environments, aerodynamics does not need to be a major issue to give consideration to. However, if a vehicle is likely to spend a good proportion of its time on dual carriageways or motorways, then aerodynamics needs really serious consideration. Be careful if selecting one of the more recent "tear drop" body or trailer designs. Make sure that you still have sufficient height for the load at the lowest corners of the vehicle and that it will accommodate all your products – please don't end up with operational constraints in order to obtain an extra 1 or 2% savings. Remember also, that aerodynamic devices do not all have to look like a spin-off from a formula one car. Even simple items such as putting a slightly larger radius on body corner pillars can make a big improvement on aerodynamics and hence fuel consumption, without noticeably encroaching on load space. Also, lots of small improvements around the vehicle can all add up to make significant savings.

Really the advice for reducing aerodynamic drag can be divided into two:

Firstly, the issue needs to be considered closely at the time of vehicle design. Vehicle designers will try to balance 3 essential factors, namely, weight, drag coefficient and frontal area. For the operator, aerodynamics will usually be a matter of ROI (return on Investment). So, the initial investment of each aerodynamic device has to be matched against the expected potential saving on fuel over time and a judgement made on the cost-benefit of the device. Once again, do not just accept the manufacturer's claims for fuel reduction; find someone with the same device fitted, or using the same body configurations and ask them what savings they are achieving in real life, then apply this to your calculations. As a general rule, don't fit a device unless an ROI of over 25% is anticipated. Also, if other operators can't put a value on their savings, similarly, don't fit it.

The second consideration is that of loading the vehicle, more probably for vans than HGVs, but every opportunity to reduce the frontal drag of the vehicle and help smooth airflow should be taken. The most critical vehicles for fitting aerodynamics to are around 7.5 tonnes, as the weight of chassis and body does not allow for a relatively large payload, so any additional body weight is considered undesirable. Many suppliers therefore offer lightweight equipment in this weight bracket – the trick is to still provide strength and durability at the same time. Also, do not forget any air deflector fitted to an articulated vehicle often needs adjusting to suit the dimensions of the trailer – it is very easy to see many deflectors incorrectly adjusted when travelling the motorways and A roads, therefore causing drag and wasting fuel.

One consideration that often gets overlooked is the final drive axle ratio, which applies equally to all weights of commercial vehicles. In the UK, many vehicles supplied are not built to order. Customers are therefore encouraged, usually by an enthusiastic salesperson, to take the vehicle specification as it came off the production line. A high rear axle ratio will mean lower engine revs at cruising speed, which will give very useful fuel savings over the life of the vehicle.

However, the ratio must not be so high as to affect the driveability of the vehicle as it should still be able to accelerate briskly through lower gears and not struggle on inclines. The ability to use a higher axle ratio is often linked to the vehicle's frontal area – a large frontal area may well require a lower ratio in order to overcome the higher drag. Specification of the correct axle ratio for a vehicle therefore requires someone involved with vehicle knowledge who understands the factors involved. We would be delighted to offer advice on your vehicle build specification – please contact us on 07771 768080 or info@thedwconsultancy.com for a free initial consultation.

Tip 7. Reducing Weight

This tip is often offered to car drivers as many have a habit of filling their boots with items "just in case" that hardly ever get used, if at all. It does, however, have a carry over into some van operations. I do see quite a few vans belonging to fleets of all sizes, which are full of bits and pieces of dubious value, probably put in the van some years ago, perhaps for a specific job and never removed. Specifying a regular clear out session for some vans may well be a very good idea indeed, if for no other reason than safety in the event of an incident.

Handy Hint	👍
• Remember that for any vehicle, whatever the weight or size, any extra body or load weight carried, of any kind = extra fuel being used.	

When replacing vehicles, it will be worthwhile having a review of what equipment is really necessary to be carried and perhaps some items are only necessary for specific jobs. As with aerodynamics above, the reduction of weight is a really serious consideration at vehicle build time as it lasts the lifetime of the vehicle. The world and technology moves on, so each time a new vehicle is specified, take the opportunity to go through the specification and decide what could now be removed, updated or a modern material substituted to bring a weight advantage.

Tip 8 Maintenance

Every fuel-saving list at some point mentions maintenance as being important. I would probably turn that around and say it only becomes important if the reverse is true and you are not having your vehicles properly maintained. If you have read the rest of this book and are still not sticking to proper servicing schedules, then, I'm afraid, there's no hope for you! However, there are some key points to consider here:

In terms of fuel consumption and vehicle maintenance, making sure tyres are correctly inflated are probably number one on the list. As there is a whole chapter elsewhere on tyre management (chapter 12), I won't go any further here. However, on the daily vehicle inspection, for fuel economy, it is also important to check things like tyres, along with making sure steering and brakes are functioning correctly and not binding.

If you read the trade press, from time to time you can read advertisements from wheel alignment specialists, suggesting their service is the complete answer to saving fuel. Certainly, we have all been driving behind a commercial vehicle at some time where one set of wheels appears to point in a very different direction to another and we can only imagine the drag that is causing. From my own experience, regular or routine checks of tracking on vehicles are probably not necessary, however, again in chapter 12, I have suggested a number of key reasons for when you should use wheel and axle alignment services, which should also reduce tyre wear and hence save fuel.

If you have telematics fitted, apart from checking any service issues flagged up and taking action as appropriate, use it as a prompt. If fuel consumption for a specific vehicle starts to rise by any degree and there are no other contributing factors, including a possible driver change, it may be advisable to give it a mechanical check, even if one is not currently scheduled, to attempt to see if there are any maintenance issues as the cause.

If you are not already using fully synthetic oils, they have considerable advantages over semi-synthetic or mineral oils including longer change periods and generally give better fuel economy by 1 to 3% or so and are therefore very worthwhile considering. (see also later in this chapter). Similarly, semi-synthetic will generally give fuel improvements over mineral oils. Also check that your servicing agent is always using OEM specification filters throughout your vehicles, which could have an effect on fuel consumption.

Some people swear by synthetic fuels; the high-priced blended versions offered by fuel suppliers, claiming to improve fuel consumption and clean the engine. Again, I have carried out rough tests over time and been unable to get any measurable differences from them, certainly not enough to justify their higher price. So, I would not advise using them in commercial vehicles, although they are cleaner burning, good to some extent for the vehicle and the environment. I suggest running your own tests of synthetic fuels on each group of vehicles to establish if there are any improvements for your fleet.

However, on the subject of fuel quality for lighter vehicles, I have also carried out tests on supermarket fuels, which are sometimes considerably cheaper than mainstream fuels, but often with a worse mpg return. When you do the sums, the drop in mpg negates any monetary saving from the initial purchase. I am aware of the argument that all fuel in Britain comes from an ever-decreasing number of the refineries in the UK, therefore often the same source, however, mainstream suppliers will add superior additives to the mix which will both cleanse and lubricate the engine, often resulting in better mpg.

Perversely, this lower mpg value from supermarket fuel is not always the case, but it is more often than not, so again I would suggest advising drivers to buy from the cheapest available mainstream fuel provider at a competitive price, rather than just seeking the nearest supermarket in the area. Often mainstream brands around the corner from a supermarket compete on price, so it is not that hard to find a good deal. Some organisations have a fuel policy of always buying from supermarkets and there are cards available specifically for supermarket fuel, simply as they tend to be the cheapest, but as with many things in life, cheapest is not always the best policy.

9) What do I need to know about Oil?

Once again, there could be another book's worth about oil, so let us try and condense the subject into a few paragraphs. When I first started, most workshops would use a single oil tank with one grade of oil, or perhaps two, one for petrol, one for diesel. Now there are so many grades and specifications it is a real minefield to try and pick the right one. Similarly, some vehicles used to use a different grade for running in, another practice consigned to the history books. Now a vehicle comes out of the factory ready to run, although personally, I still give machinery a short running-in period, more of a shake down really, to get any build glitches out of the way. To be honest, I do wonder if the vehicle and lubricant manufacturers need to make this subject quite so complex to select the appropriate grade for your vehicle, however, there is no doubt that oils continue to get increasingly thinner and an awful lot smarter. So, let's try and introduce a little sense into the equation.

Modern Oils can be very High-Tech with an associated Price Tag

It helps if you can understand a little of the technology that goes into lubricating oils. Most people know that the oil grade is made up of two figures, the first, usually suffixed 'W' is a measure of its viscosity when cold, so a low number here will greatly aid cold starting performance and reduce wear when warming up. The second number indicates its viscosity when hot and working hard, again a low number reduces friction and fuel consumption. Oils generally start life in an alkaline condition in an effort to compensate for the acidity produced by combustion products, but they will turn acidic over time, which reduces their ability to protect the engine. Synthetic, and to a lesser extent semi-synthetic, oils are better at resisting oxidation than their mineral counterparts, hence the longer drain times and more stable viscosities over time.

Manufacturers add many other constituents such polymers which tend to reduce the oil's tendency to thin over time, along with additives such as detergents, to help cleanse the oil and reduce corrosion or scoring of engine components. For all modern vehicles, it makes sense to use oils that have a low SAPS (Sulphated Ash, Phosphorus, & Sulphur) content, producing a low volume of ash. For Euro 6 specification vehicles, you will require a maximum ash content of less than 1%, otherwise DPF's (Diesel Particulate Filters) will prematurely clog and may require replacing more often. If you are suffering this problem, it could simply be your operating conditions or it may pay to look at cleaner oils.

Handy Hint   👍

- If you are having problems with clogging DPF's (Diesel Particulate Filters), it may well be due to your particular operation cycles, but it also may pay to see if your current oil specification produces too much ash

---

As oils, especially synthetics, are now so expensive, there is one technique which I have often used over the years, but surprisingly, I rarely see fleet managers use: that of sampling engine oil at intervals. It is quite simple and relatively cheap to do and involves extracting 100 ml or so of oil from the sump and sending to a sampling laboratory. I would suggest using an independent laboratory, rather than your own oil supplier's, simply to give yourself peace of mind. They will be able to tell you if the oil is still within specification as far as viscosity and constituency is concerned, also adding if anything else is found in the sample, such wear particles, or in some cases, fuel dilution. With modern engines and modern oils, it is unusual to detect much beyond a very small trace of wear, however, the constitution of the wear particles will usually identify which components are wearing and can sometimes be a useful diagnostic indicator of potential future problems.

The most important benefit from regular sampling is that it can tell you if you can extend your oil drain intervals. Manufacturers will specify intervals, but these are intended to cover all vehicles in all operating conditions and contain an element of insurance, making sure no vehicle goes past their minimum drain interval. It may well be that your operation and mileage suits whatever oil you are using and could be extended, but you will need some assurance that is truly the case. Through sampling, some operators are finding their synthetic and semi-synthetic oil stays good for some astounding mileages, not even possible to contemplate just a few years ago.

In a few cases, where vehicles are being worked really hard, the intervals may need to be shortened as the oil is falling out of specification before their specified drain period is reached, although this does not often happen unless you are using a really cheap oil, or the wrong specification for your vehicle. Fortunately, you do not need to sample all vehicles all of the time. It makes sense to pick one or two test vehicles initially from each discrete group of vehicles, undertaking roughly the same operation, taking multiple samples to find where the optimum drain period is for each group. Then it is sensible to continue to monitor one or two vehicles in the fleet, at regular intervals, just to give yourself confidence that all is well. You can also use it as a diagnostic tool on individual vehicles exhibiting problems. Sampling is also really useful for operations where engines run without mileage being incurred, such as fire engines and tankers with engine mounted pumps.

With all the marketing hype surrounding oils, it is easy to forget the prime reason for its existence is to protect your engine. The start point for oil specification must therefore be to stick within the grades specified by your vehicle manufacturer and never go outside their specified range for any reason. Manufacturers will normally specify a range of grades that you can select depending on the temperatures you are operating within and the types of operation your vehicles are undertaking.

Then, as downtime, labour and filters all cost money, it makes sense to go for the longest recommended drain interval possible to reduce replacement times, but only if the increased cost of the oil specification more than balances the reduced maintenance cost. Most importantly, drain intervals must also suit your inspection regime; no point in extending the theoretical change period if it still has to be changed earlier.

Lastly, in this day and age, fuel efficiency has to be taken into account. There is a problem with this last factor, namely that the savings in fuel of using a superior oil specification are very likely to be only around 1 to 3 %. That is very worthwhile over the life of a vehicle, however, that means the results of any measurements will mostly be swamped by day-to-day variations in fuel economy, even by such things as the weather. As far as fuel economy of specific oils are concerned, you will either have to hold your own tightly-run discrete tests, perhaps even employing a separate, accurate fuel flow meter, or accept manufacturers claims, providing they are backed up by well documented test results and relate to your vehicles and operation. It is one thing to quote 100,000 km intervals for a vehicle that only runs on motorways between distribution centres, quite another for a stop-start urban delivery operation.

If your maintenance provider is external, don't just accept their standard oil and grades – check they are using the most fuel-efficient oils compatible with your vehicles. The bulk of this section relates to engine oils, as that will be the most often changed and the main lubrication cost for your fleet, but do not forget gearbox and axle oil specifications, which can also save fuel. Hopefully, this will only be for infrequent top-ups or on the rare occasions when a complete change is necessary, but be aware that there are also low-friction lubrication alternatives on the market which also make small, but useful, improvements in fuel consumption.

10) What do I need to know about AdBlue?

AdBlue arrived around the time of Euro IV emissions controls and was initially used only by some manufacturers as an aid to improving emission. Now, however, all Euro VI vehicles at the heavy end of the market use the product in order to meet regulations. Mostly constituted of water, with 32% urea added, thankfully it is non-hazardous, but it is quite corrosive, so you must use dispensing equipment specifically designed for the product to avoid later problems. It is often described as a fuel additive, but it must be kept completely separate from diesel. It is important to keep it clean and completely free from contamination, especially from any oil-based products. AdBlue is used in the vehicle's selective catalytic reduction (SCR) system and gives off ammonia that reacts in the catalyst to convert the increasingly despised NOx (Oxides of Nitrogen) into nitrogen and water.

Vehicles only tend to use small quantities of AdBlue when compared to diesel (somewhere between 2% and 8%, depending on your engine and exhaust configuration), so only need topping up occasionally. However, it is one of those products that is extremely expensive to buy in small quantities, so around 90% of commercial vehicle operators tend to keep their own bulk supplies and utilise their own dispensing equipment. What is really important is to keep track of consumption, exactly as for fuel use, as vehicles can be very variable in the amount they use and if consuming too rapidly, may need attention on service. Although AdBlue costs are small compared with fuel, it is the combined cost that is so important when trying to keep your total running costs under control.

As AdBlue is non-hazardous, providing it is stored correctly, it poses little threat to personnel or the environment. As with fuel and oil, however, the Environment Agency tend to be most concerned about pollution to surface and ground water, so you need to take care to avoid any spills and if they do occur, deal with them rapidly. Again, the Environment Agency can take action if pollution is thought to have taken place.

If you are installing any bulk fuel or AdBlue bulk facilities, you would be advised to follow the latest regulations locally and nationally, also contained on the website for oil and fuel storage at https://www.gov.uk/guidance/storing-oil-at-a-home-or-business. However, previously issued Environmental Agency's pollution guidelines are still a very useful place to start. The key points which the guidance notes highlight are very relevant in the storage of AdBlue, and are:

- It is most important for your storage tank and any associated ancillaries, such as the pump, hose and nozzle, to possess a secondary containment mechanism, such as a suitable bund, capable of holding an additional 10% of liquid stored.

- You must possess both an emergency spill kit and an emergency action plan, plus conduct suitable training on how to deal with spills.

- The dispensing nozzle should be trigger-operated and fitted with an auto shut-off: it must be incapable of being left in the open position.

- The dispensing area's drainage should be isolated from surface water drainage.

- The last point is quite important as it is not always understood - be aware that because AdBlue is heavier than water (unlike diesel), underground interceptors or separators will not prevent AdBlue reaching surface water drains.

How you store and dispense it will depend entirely on the size of your fleet and your consumption. The smallest sensible method of dispensing AdBlue in bulk is probably a 210-litre drum with a simple hand pump fitted. Most average size fleets find an IBC (Intermediate Bulk Container), which holds 1000 litres, is a convenient size, fitted with a dispensing nozzle and flowmeter to register consumption. Such a container can be mounted alongside your fuel island making checking and topping-up a habitual operation.

Larger fleets that use more than 1 IBC container a month may find it more sensible to move to a larger bulk tank, perhaps 10,000 litres or even a 15,000-litre bulk tank installation if demand justifies the investment. Very similar to bulk fuel, these can be fitted with a bund and calibrated dispensing equipment, together with overflow and re-ordering alarms to make stock management much easier. AdBlue is recommended to be stored between - 11 and + 30 degrees Celsius, but is unlikely to be damaged by any freezing that takes place. Most delivery systems take fluid from the bottom of a bulk tank, so supply is unlikely to be interrupted, even in the harshest UK weather.

Top Tips for Fuel & Oil Management ✔

- Bulk fuel installations are usually the cheapest way of providing fuel to the fleet and provide resilience in case of supply interruptions; they do require managing and work best where the fleet returns to base.

- Bulk fuel installations will require regular inspections and a small amount of on-going maintenance to keep in full working order.

- When selecting fuel pumps, go for the most expensive you can afford for reliability, but also have a spare pump, if possible, for back-up; don't over-speed, but ensure they fill quickly.

- When selecting a fuel card, go through the process step by step to get the closest match for your operation – there are so many cards now, one will be bound to match your requirements.

- Since fuel stations have reduced substantially in recent years, mapping a fuel card providers' outlets to your operation has become very important to most operators.

- Getting drivers to employ defensive driving techniques & anticipate traffic better, using momentum to keep their speed stable is the single most effective way of saving fuel, for vans & trucks, whatever the fuel.

- If not already using semi or fully synthetic engine oil, it may be a useful fuel saving technique for your fleet; establish that the increased cost of oil is more than balanced by reduced maintenance costs.

- Random oil sampling is a really useful and underutilised tool to assist you in extending your oil drain intervals & diagnosing potential issues.

- Treat bulk installations for AdBlue in a similar fashion to fuel and monitor usage carefully.

David's Don'ts ✖

- Don't leave any gaps in your fuel management systems – rogue members of staff will always take advantage at some stage.

- Don't let your artic drivers use adjustable air deflectors set in the wrong place – it just wastes fuel and money needlessly.

- Don't let fuel card suppliers hide their suite of fuel reports from you; insist you get your regular information in exactly the format you require, especially any digital information.

The Ultimate Guide to Commercial Vehicle Fleet Management

Chapter 12 – Tyres & Wheels

1) What is the logic behind looking after your tyres?
2) What are the key elements of a Tyre Policy? How do I construct one?
3) How do I select the right tyres for each group of vehicles?
4) How should I monitor our tyre condition and wear?
5) What minimum tread depth should I specify for the fleet?
6) What should drivers do to help manage our tyres?
7) What would constitute good tyre husbandry or management for the fleet?
8) What should I know about wheel fixings?
9) What should I know about wheel alignment?
10) Should I be fitting a TPMS system?
11) Should I be buying tyres on a fixed price or p.p.k. tyre contract?
12) Should I be fitting remoulded tyres?

1) What is the logic behind looking after your tyres?

I have lost count of the number of times a transport professional has said to me "Tyres – they're round and black, aren't they?", usually said with a chuckle, indicating a level of disrespect which is sadly not uncommon within the industry.

And yes, they do only represent around 5% of commercial vehicle operating costs, although tyres can also have a major affect on other running costs, primarily fuel consumption, but also maintenance and insurance costs as well. Tyre spend will range from around £500 per annum for a light van up to £3500 for a six-axle maximum weight arctic. However, this is an average cost for vehicles doing average mileages. In the case of vehicles travelling high mileages or perhaps over rough terrain, the figure for a large vehicle can easily reach £5000 to £6000 per annum. That means for a middle-sized fleet of, say, 100 double shifted Artics, the total tyre bill for the year could easily be more than half a million pounds. Worth paying attention to.

One other factor to bear in mind is that tyres are not big-ticket items, which is why they often get forgotten. However, they represent a lot of relatively small, incremental payments that add up considerably over time to represent collectively, large amounts of money. Due to the volume of tyres that a commercial vehicle will go through, and the way tyres are bought, often from smaller operators providing emergency cover, they are ripe for, let us say, some less than legitimate practices. The difference in cost between a fleet with poorly managed tyres and one with well managed tyres can be at least 50% extra. As with many items in fleet management, in a low margin business, that can make the difference between the organisation making a profit or a loss.

Over the years, tyre manufacturers have made gradual but important improvements in their round, black product, most of which go unnoticed by users. Silica has been increasingly employed in replacing carbon black as a filler in order to give better wet grip and rolling resistance. Tyres carrying lower payloads can also use more synthetic rubber, although truck tyres with heavier payloads still use more natural rubber for strength and durability. Lower rolling resistance tyres, often with a lower starting tread depth used to wear out quicker and have lower wet grip, so these advances have been carefully engineered back into the tyre to get all-round performance acceptable to users. Tyres also contain polymers, oils, waxes and other chemicals in order to get the elasticity and durability we, as users, require.

Commercial vehicle tyre casings need engineering to get acceptable kerb scuffing performance and tear resistance from the tread. Heavier vehicles need differing compounds for steer, drive and trailing axles in order to match the wear characteristics to each. I truly believe every operator should visit, at least once in their career, a tyre factory to help understand just how much technology goes into a tyre. The processes that each car, van or truck tyre goes through has to be seen to be believed and are most definitely not just "round & black". You go in thinking "why are they so expensive?" and cannot help but come out thinking "how do they do all that at the price?" and arrive at a newfound healthy respect for the humble tyre.

2)   What are the key elements of a Tyre Policy? How do I construct one?

The starting point of good tyre management on any fleet must be a well thought through tyre policy. A very useful place to start is to read through "Guide to tyre management and maintenance on heavy vehicles" (readily available on the internet at   https://btmauk.com/advice-about-tyres/professional-road-users/).   Originally produced by the Tyre Industry Federation in 2016, now produced and updated by the BTMA (British Tyre Manufacturer's Association), in association with organisations such as Logistics UK, the RHA and the IRTE. There is a stack of useful information contained within this document, which I will not reproduce here, but I will comment in this chapter on the most important features of the guide to keep in mind. This guide is written for vehicles over 3.5 tonnes, however, there is a very similar guide, available from the same web page, produced specifically for van operators, which contains similar information, but specifically written for lighter weight commercial vehicles.

Once again, there are no right or wrong items to include in a tyre policy, however, as tyres are a 'life & limb' item, there are a number of items that you should really make sure are covered in your organisation's tyre policy.

- Explain in layman's terms how the tyre sizes, types and makes have been decided for each group of vehicles in the fleet.
- Detail the important criteria from your tyre supply contract/s, such as how tyres will be supplied, who will supply them, how they are purchased and any administration procedures including the handling of casings or disposals. Your procedures should include all the contact details that relevant members of staff will require.
- Detail all driver responsibilities including the daily checks on tread, pressure and tyre condition along with the procedures for actioning any repairs or replacements that crop up.
- Explain your policy on minimum tread depths in a way that is unambiguous
- Explain your procedures and responsibilities for checking and maintaining tyre pressures, including operation of TPMS, if fitted (see item 10 below for details).
- Refer to the importance of your wheel changing policy and clarify individual responsibilities to ensure procedures are always carried out on any wheel change.
- Define how spare wheels will be handled for the different categories of vehicles in your fleet, including any storage procedures, ensuring stocks are rotated.
- Explain if there are differing tyre procedures for any leased vehicles on the fleet, including any supplier information.
- Explain clearly and fully your criteria, policy and processes for regrooving and retreading tyres: again, include all the key information from your supply contract/s and who is responsible for the process in your organisation.
- Explain the elements of good tyre husbandry that are in use on your fleet and the responsibilities for ensuring the relative actions are carried out.

For heavier vehicles operating mainly on the highway and not having to travel off-road or on waste or building sites, probably the ideal policy suggested by most premium tyre manufacturers is to aim to have four separate lives for an individual tyre. This means in an ideal world you would buy a premium tyre, recut (or regroove) the tyre at the appropriate point then have that same carcass remoulded with the final life being another recut. Obviously not all tyres will reach this ideal state, due to unrepairable damage and the like, so in-house tyre carcasses will have to be supplemented with quality ones bought in from outside.

The 'four life' principle is brilliant in theory, but harder to achieve in practice and is obviously intended for the heavier end of the market. The key to monitoring the success of any tyre policy is religious documentation of what happens to each tyre, at each point in its life cycle, coupled with calculating the pence per kilometre (or miles in old money) of each tyre fitted. Only then can you really compare the success or otherwise of any particular tyre policy on each type of vehicle within the fleet. At the lighter end of the market, tyres may not be regroovable, which cuts out two of the suggested four lives and it you are not remoulding, you essentially end up by default with one-life tyre policy. All the good tyre husbandry and management principles mentioned elsewhere in this chapter will still apply, however.

There is still a remarkable reluctance amongst some operators to go down the route of re-grooving tyres, although at least half of premium tyre carcasses across Europe are now regrooved regularly. Similarly, turning tyres on the rim, or moving across an axle, can have a marked effect on evening out tyre wear and therefore increasing tyre life, which can also often be usefully carried out on a lighter vehicle. There seems to be a fairly common psychological block amongst many operators against spending slightly more on tyre husbandry, in order to reduce their overall fleet tyre costs, but it makes absolute sense to squeeze the maximum life out of your original investment if for no other reason than to reduce your environmental impact.

Up until fairly recently, operators with at least some element of off-road running would often avoid premium tyres and rely on a cheaper alternative. More recently, premium carcasses have been designed with more chip and cut resistance to suit such rugged operations. Trial and careful monitoring is required here to determine optimum lives and arrive at the minimum p.p.k.

Up until 2018, when anti-trust laws from the EU prevented China from selling cheap tyres at or below cost price on the European market, there was a move away from remould tyres on the basis that a new Chinese tyre could be cheaper than a remould and were treated very much as a throwaway item. During this period, the remould tyre industry's share of the market dropped around 30% due to this so-called "dumping". I was never a fan of most of these cheap imports as their performance was often sub-optimal and moved away from the policy described above, of carefully managing tyres properly throughout the various stages of their life. It gave many operators a false sense of security that they were keeping their tyre costs low, but at a consequential cost to the environment.

Handy Hint   ♨

- Make sure you obtain copies of, and read the guides to tyre management either for heavy vehicles or for vans, produced by the British Tyre Manufacturer's Association – useful for all commercial vehicle operators, light and heavy.

---

3) How do I select the right tyres for each group of vehicles?

Whether starting tyre policy from scratch, or updating an existing one, it is certainly worthwhile having discussions with each of the premium tyre manufacturers' representatives, local or national, to gain all the latest ideas and input from them before deciding on which policy to implement.

When deciding which tyres to buy, the EU tyre labelling guidance at least gives you something to work on regarding the fuel economy, the wet grip and noise produced by an individual tyre. Like most of these test-condition guides they never quite work out the same in practice, however, it's a lot better than no guide at all. It has to be said, that for quite a few commercial vehicle operators, especially those at the heavier end of the market, they ignore these guidance labels and just go on length of life, measured by tread. That is fully understandable, especially if you think tyres are "round and black", but personally, I think it is a little short sighted and hope operators will utilise labels more and more in their buying decisions, as the benefits become clearer.

For fleets with a fair degree of motorway or 'A' road running, the starting point is probably to look for a tyre with a low rolling resistance and hence best fuel economy. As ever there is a trade-off and in this case the best fuel economy may result in lower grip. Remember that with wet grip performance, the difference between an A-grade and an F-grade tyre is up to 30% shorter braking distance, which could be as much as 25 metres shorter stopping distance for a typical truck and semi-trailer operating at 80 km/h.

A small, but important point, is not to let suppliers confuse you when talking about fuel economy, rolling resistance or CO_2 emissions – in effect, it is all one and the same thing. It is a reduced rolling resistance that gives you fuel savings and that saved fuel can be converted directly into CO_2 emission reductions. So, the difficult selection choice is to try to find a tyre that has relatively good fuel economy, but sufficient wet grip performance. And just to complicate matters, you then need to seek a tyre that has both those features and lowest possible noise. Operators undertaking night-time urban deliveries may decide this last factor is for them, the most important, and may come before fuel and wet grip.

That raises some important selection points here. When selecting tyres, the difference between a 70 or 71dB tyre and one with a 74 to 75dB rating may seem very small, but don't forget it is a logarithmic scale, so that few dB increase can make a significant difference externally and perhaps more importantly, within the cab. If you want calm, relaxed and attentive drivers, low noise tyres may well help achieve this objective. Also, a quoted 2 or 3% saving in fuel may not seem very worthwhile. However, remember that fuel can represent 10 to 15 times the running cost of tyres, so to attain a few percentage points reduction in fuel can be well worth paying quite a bit higher on the tyre itself.

The other factor to be borne in mind for a tyre policy is that you are literally as good as your local tyre supplier manager. Even if you have a superb contract with a national organisation this can often be let down in certain geographical areas by a poor local manager. So, at a local level, it is also very worthwhile bringing in your local tyre supplier representative to discuss exactly what they will do for you and how they will do it. If you are having to produce a national tyre policy to cover the country and perhaps a number of depots, it is worth designing in some flexibility in order to cater for the odd poorly managed tyre supply depot.

Up until a few years ago, the idea of having separate tyres for winter use would have been thought of as crazy. Now, of course, you cannot move for winter tyre adverts, appearing in the autumn months. Unless you have particularly arduous operating conditions with a high degree of ice and snow driving, the whole process of removing, replacing tyres and storing summer tyres for the winter months is generally a step too far for many fleet operators. In addition, they suffer higher wear rates on bare tarmac or once the temperatures start to rise again. However, it is true that there are a number of large operators such as the supermarkets, home delivery and utility companies that are now willing to fit winter tyres to a large proportion of their fleet from October to March, so the subject is at least worth looking into.

Thankfully, there are now all-weather design tyres appearing on the market, which have winter operating characteristics that are not far short of full winter tyres, but still operate well in summer months, which would seem to be the ideal compromise. The key to making decisions with such specifications is to test, trial, cost and record all the relevant data for your fleet whilst also encouraging driver feedback, as they are the ones who have to feel happy with the outcomes. Be aware that some countries require winter tyre fitment by law during certain winter months and may also require carriage and use of snow chains, so always check what equipment is required if travelling overseas.

Regular Tyre Inspection is key to keeping costs under control

4) How should I monitor our tyre condition and wear?

The barest minimum is to have tread depths and tyre pressures fully monitored and recorded at least once a month; however, for HGVs and vans running high mileages, I would really recommend at least a brief check at once a week, or once a fortnight if that proves impractical. Depending on their keenness to do business with you, this inspection service can be carried out by your normal supplier and will may cost you a small amount per vehicle per month, well worthwhile to keep overall costs down and give you, and your drivers, peace of mind. Depending on the volume of tyres you purchase, they may absorb the cost into their overall charges, although I am a great fan of knowing exactly what everything is costing you.

The other crucial factor in good tyre management is utilising a good tyre technician. They are some of the hardest working, yet poorest paid, technicians in our industry, but a good one is worth their weight in gold. As well as giving you an accurate and up-to-date picture of the state of your fleet's tyres, they can spot trends in your tyre wear. This can often point towards either poor driver behaviour or may indicate where particular vehicles have difficult terrain to negotiate or may give you early warning of mechanical problems with the vehicle that need attention. Only a tyre technician with considerable experience will possess the knowledge to match uneven wear patterns to particular issues on the vehicle.

When deciding which tyres to use for the groups of vehicles in your fleet, it is really important to run real life trials to establish your cheapest p.p.k. for each area of the fleet. The premium tyre with a re-groove and remix policy at first sight looks expensive, but when trialled over time, may surprise you by being the cheapest p.p.k. Similarly, cheaper tyres feel like you are managing your costs when first bought, but if they are being replaced at a higher rate may well work out more expensive in the long run. The only way to genuinely achieve the lowest cost is to religiously inspect and record tyre condition and wear, including all replacements and repairs in the life of the vehicle. When a vehicle encounters a tyre problem such as a puncture, your instinctive reaction will be to get it repaired and underway as soon as possible. Of course, that is great, providing all the true costs associated with that repair are captured and recorded on your systems so they can be fully analysed at a later date.

5) What minimum tread depth should I specify for the fleet?

This is possibly the single most important factor in your tyre policy as it determines how long you will run your tyre for and therefore what life you can expect each tyre to attain. At the same time, as tyres wear down, your minimum tread depth has a huge effect on the safety of your drivers and vehicles. If you decide on the legal minimum tread depth, your vehicles will probably suffer more accidents, although this will always be difficult to quantify due to the difficulty of separating the true cause of an incident from many other factors. You are also much more likely to be picked up for tyre related infringements when part of the tread goes under the legal minimum and more likely to suffer damage or puncture related incidents.

The legal minimum tread for vehicles under 3.5 tonnes is 1.6 mm over three quarters of the tread width; the corresponding minimum depth for vehicles over 3.5 tonnes is 1 mm over three quarters of the tread width with a visible pattern on the remaining quarter. There is an ever-increasing mass of evidence that for a whole variety of sensible reasons, this legal minimum is insufficient for fleet use. My suggestion would be that whether above or below 3.5 tonnes, your policy minimum tread depth should be between 2 to 3 mm. That is deliberately not a fixed single figure because tyres are hardly ever obliging enough to wear evenly.

So to clarify, tyres showing tread depth below 3 mm over part of their tread should be earmarked for replacement or re-grooved either immediately or very soon, (at the next service, or the next tyre inspection, or before that, if waiting represents too long an interval). The idea of this policy is that no part of the tread ever reaches below 2 mm. However, I would not suggest replacing before 3 mm as you are then throwing away a good proportion of the useable tread on a tyre. You can see there is a fine balance between the two, which makes regular inspections, particularly on high mileage vehicles, so crucial, so as never to let any portion of your fleet's tyres fall below 2 mm.

There is a wealth of evidence to show that retaining at least 3 mm of tread is necessary both for water dispersal and to reduce braking distances. The aforementioned 'Guide to Tyre Management' from the BTMA gives facts and figures about the increase in braking distance at minimum legal tyre tread depths, in some cases, increasing stopping distances by 30% compared with a tyre with 3mm of tread. Even with today's wider tread patterns, it is still a very small patch of rubber in contact with the road and that patch needs to be of good quality.

All you have to remember is that by replacing at slightly more than the legal minimum, you are giving your drivers the best chance to avoid having an accident and therefore once more, reducing your overall costs. In addition, if you aim for legal minimum tread as your fleet policy, which I am afraid some operators do, it is certain that at some stage, some tyres will go past that minimum, resulting in illegal tyres and by the law of averages, they will be picked up by the enforcement authorities, or be involved in an incident.

None of this precludes the most important factor in tyre management of all, which is once again, the daily inspection by drivers. All operators need to be conducting regular training or coaching sessions, including regular reminder toolbox talks, which, amongst other issues, should describe exactly how drivers should look after their tyres during the daily inspection.

6) What should drivers do to help manage our tyres?

Sadly, despite operators trying very hard to educate staff, the daily vehicle walkaround check is still seen as a mundane task by many drivers, however, its importance especially relating to tyres should not be underestimated. By carrying out just a few simple checks, especially a simple assessment of tyre condition, commercial vehicle drivers can greatly reduce the risk of breakdowns and improve safety on the roads. Drivers need to remember that this check is not designed as an in-depth inspection; their role is to pick up all clear, easy to spot defects which are then reported so action can be taken; that's all. The daily check should provide information on the state of the wheel rims, wheel retaining indicators, tyre inflation, tyre wear, and should spot any visible tyre damage including anything embedded in the tread or tyre.

The drivers should look out for the following:

- Cuts or damage to the tyre, ignoring any superficial damage which should not affect the tyre durability; however, any deep cuts to either the tread or sidewall that show ply exposure must be reported immediately. Also check the tyre tread and sidewall for damage such as punctures, cracks, bulges, cuts, chipping, tread or sidewall separation, torn out tread lugs or visible reinforcing cords, which again must be reported immediately.

- Punctures or embedded objects including nails or foreign objects that have penetrated the tyre, or stones trapped between twinned wheels should be reported immediately and should not be removed by the driver, due to possible sudden pressure loss. However, stones trapped in the tread grooves should be removed by the driver to prevent them working through the tread into the belt structure and tyre damage.

- A simple visual check of the inflation pressure by checking sidewall deflection. A distorted sidewall shape would indicate significant under-inflation and needs attention. Continuing in service would probably cause flexing and heat build-up, compromising the tyre's structural integrity and potentially leading to premature tyre failure. If a TPMS is fitted (see item 10 below), drivers should use the manual check feature.

- Wheel rims – look for buckling, scraping or other obvious signs of damage, ensure there are no visible cracks, especially around the fixing holes. Check also there are no missing wheel nuts, missing (or moved) wheel nut indicators and no visible signs of looseness.

- Check tyre tread depth, using the wear indicators positioned in the tread grooves, which will show the tread is above the legal limit. However, to comply with the organisation's suggested 3 mm limit, the driver should be issued with a simple tread depth gauge and shown how to use it. Drivers should also check for uneven wear across the tread, flat spots and sidewall scuffing; sidewall markings (now including date of manufacture) must be legible on at least one side of the tyre.

- After reporting, if management have any doubts about a tyre's condition, they should seek appropriate technical assistance.

7) What would constitute good tyre husbandry or management for the fleet?

A piece of research conducted jointly by Highways England and Bridgestone Tyres in the 18 months up to August 2016, recorded 58,612 tyre-related breakdown incidents on the strategic road network.

https://www.gov.uk/government/news/tyre-related-deaths-and-injuries-preventable-say-highways-england-and-bridgestone

Of these, 20,007 (34 per cent) involved commercial vehicles, yet they represent only 15% of the total vehicle parc. Yes, of course these vehicles cover higher mileages than the average motorist, but it does indicate the real need to manage your fleet's tyres to avoid these costly incidents. Sadly, that same exercise also checked around 30,000 commercial vehicle tyres and discovered 1 in 12 tyres were underinflated by more than 20 per cent from their nominal pressure, likely to cause premature wear and possible failure and more likely to be the prime reason for increased tyre breakdowns on commercial vehicles.

So, what can you do to avoid having tyre related incidents? The prime way to avoid problems is by using good tyre husbandry. In no particular order, this should include the following items:

- Daily inspections of tyres by drivers are paramount to capture issues early (I know I have said this before, but it cannot be repeated enough!).

- Note: if you are operating off road, especially if you have twin wheeled vehicles or trailers, it is particularly important for drivers to check for cuts, bulges and exposed cords, not just on the daily check, but each time they stop on off-road sites, to have a quick walk-around the vehicle; also check no foreign objects are trapped between the wheels.

- Install a good tyre maintenance regime utilising your local tyre agent, especially pressure and tread-depth management regimes to help avoid tyre breakdowns.

- Your tyre agent inspection regime (minimum once a month) should include checking for wheel and tyre damage, individual tyre pressures, individual tread depths, the potential to regroove, adherence to the fitment policy, missing valve caps, broken or missing wheel nut indicator caps and any other minor items that need reporting.

- If your tyre agent identifies any vehicles that have come back from service (internal or external) with incorrect pressures, ensure your workshop or service agent is clearly instructed on correct procedures for the future.

Make sure your tyre markings show the same size and load ratings across the same axle; the ratings should be the same or higher than the vehicle plating certificate (and check they are under 10 years old on steering axles).

- Have your tyre agent (and drivers with some training) look for abnormal patterns of tread wear in order to try to spot mechanical issues early, e.g., over or under inflation, wheel alignment or suspension damage. Diagnosis requires some expert knowledge, so a good tyre technician is essential.

- Good husbandry includes training your drivers and staff on the more detailed points of tyre management over time and something that many operators forget, is to regularly sweep the yard to keep it free of potential puncture risks. I see so many hazards in client's yards and it is a bit of an own goal to pick up a puncture in your own yard!

- Really important - always focus on pence per kilometre, or cost per mm of tread, not just the purchase cost of tyres.

- Think of good tyre husbandry as simply preventative maintenance for tyres, just like vehicle inspections are for vehicles.

- If you are managing your tyres yourself, you can copy a tyre company's p.p.k. contract management methods to best advantage. They know the best ways to keep costs down – simply imitate them.

- Insist on regular and full fleet checks as often as possible; ensure the tyre management reports are fully actioned as soon as possible after receiving the report, else your supplier may lose enthusiasm and confidence in your management.

- Tyres marked "regroovable" are made to be regrooved, so use every opportunity to reduce your cost per mm of tread – have tyres ready to be regrooved highlighted in your regular inspection reports.

- For maximum savings, manage your tyres in-house unless you have a more productive role for your staff or require reduced risk fixed outgoings.

- Never lose an opportunity to have a pressure check undertaken, or consider fitting TPMS; ensure pressures are correctly measured and recorded on vehicle service.

- When vehicles are going off-fleet, check that no nearly new tyres or remoulds disappear with them; swop tyres with good tread for tyres with reduced (but of course, fully legal) tread before disposal, unless that infringes any leasing or other agreements.

- True cost savings will arise from good tyre management, aim for a win-win contract with your tyre management company & service providers, not the cheapest price. At the outset, agree a set of KPI's for the contract and monitor them closely.

- You need consistent management and staff from your supplier so that they come to know your operation and vehicles - so please do not change your provider too frequently.

- If you are moving to a tyre p.p.k or fixed price contract, be aware that your supplier will want considerable amounts of data from you before you start and will probably ask for at least a two- or three-year minimum contract period in order to justify their investment in time and tyres for your fleet. The more data you can provide, the cheaper the contract offering is likely to be.

- Tyre technology, especially tyre sizes and prices, are in a continuous state of flux, so revisit and challenge your established tyre policies, with advice from manufacturers and suppliers, at least once a year.

- Ensure any gauges or other tools used in-house are calibrated regularly and check your tyre supplier does the same. If you run an in-house workshop, consider sending technicians on a tyre-fitting course – establish the true costs (take the full labour cost into account) of doing tyre work yourself measured against your tyre supplier.

A quick note here on tyres over 10 years old. There has been significant discussion recently about new legislation banning the use of 10+ year old tyres, which since February 2021 should not be fitted on any steer axle wheel of a heavy vehicle. The sheer fact is rubber degrades over time due to flexing, abrasion, temperature changes, ultraviolet light, chemical and liquid attack, physical ageing and many other factors. To be honest, personally, I do not think you should be using 10-year-old tyres at all, except in exceptional circumstances such as a museum item or ultra-low mileage, low-speed vehicles. As well as making sure all required markings are still showing (and visible) on the tyre sidewall, it also prompts the advice to check the date stamp on the sidewall of the tyre or remould (a legal necessity) upon purchase as your supplier could have been sitting on old stock. Make sure you always have a sensible life-usage still to go on any tyre supplied to you.

Good Tyre Husbandry avoids many unnecessary minor breakdowns

8)   What should I know about wheel fixings?

Wheels have been detaching themselves from commercial vehicles for far too long. 35 years ago, we hired a test track primarily for testing aerodynamic fuel saving devices but also for testing other equipment. At the same time, we decided to see if we could deliberately get a wheel to come loose from an articulated vehicle. Even hitting the tank test track far too fast with nearly all the wheel nuts removed, which shook the fillings out of my teeth, did not result in a wheel coming loose, so why they were coming adrift on the road was not immediately obvious to me. What I did discover at that time, however, was that the design safety factor for a commercial vehicle wheel was only 1.4:1, meaning it only took a bit of dirt, paint or rust to shift and the wheel could start to come loose. Compare that to the wheel on a commercial airliner, where the design safety factor is around four or five times that figure. To date, I have never yet seen a tyre fitting van chasing down the runway after a 777 airliner!

In the intervening 35 years, I had hoped that a better design of wheel and fixing may be devised by the manufacturers, but sadly, no. For the foreseeable future, therefore, the solution to the, so called, wheel loss "mystery", is to follow a strict maintenance regime, which is pretty ridiculous in this day and age, but unfortunately completely necessary. Devise your wheel fixing and retorquing policy to suit your operation and make absolutely certain everyone involved, especially drivers and your service agents, know the policy in full and stick to it religiously. The problem with having such a low design safety factor for commercial vehicle wheels is that one slip in the process and you could lose a wheel with potentially disastrous consequences to your organisation and perhaps a member of the public.

Any wheel change policy for your organisation must therefore include the following important features:

- How to correctly identify wheel nuts and studs for both steel and alloy wheels.

- The consensus now is that a little light lubrication (on the stud threads only), is necessary to get the right clamping force at the wheel, but no lubrication whatsoever should be allowed on the wheel face.

- You can use an air gun very carefully (do not cross threads else you should throw the nut and stud away) to run the nuts up at a setting of less than 100 Nm, but **only** use a manual calibrated torque wrench to tighten the nuts in the correct sequence to the correct torque.

- Make sure you have the correct torque figures identified for each vehicle and wheel type; stickers for torque and tyre pressure applied above the wheel arch are really beneficial and save time.

- The more difficult part of the process; whatever the vehicle is doing, you must arrange to have the wheels re-torqued after 40 to 80 km travelled.

- All of this operation needs to be fully recorded and auditable.

- All this process and a lot more is available in the IRTE/RHA/Logistics UK best practice guide for wheel security. Available from the SOE (Society of Operational Engineers) at:
  https://www.soe.org.uk/resources/wheel-security-guide-2020-pdf.html

In theory that is all you have to do until the next time a wheel is removed. However, most operators use some form of additional safety device, of which there are many. There are simple push-on indicators, which are intended to show if a wheel nut has moved since tightening. This can be usefully examined at least at every daily walk-round check. Alternatively, there are devices which attempt to hold nuts from turning or there are locking wheel nuts as an alternative to the ordinary wheel nut. Every operator seems to have their own favourite and their own set of reasons for their choice of device.

New initiatives are constantly appearing; the latest is a cover and two-colour indicator; the colour is changed when the wheel has been re-torqued which looks to be quite a useful reminder. You will have to conduct your own market survey and discuss the issue with colleagues to form your decision on what device to use, then ensure they are fitted across the fleet. By-the-way, if you are a van fleet operator and feeling a little smug, do not be, as you too should be following the same re-torque procedure. I have to say, sadly, many operators do not. Neither do most van operators use the additional indicators or locking mechanisms which although available for lighter weights, tend to be aimed for the above 3.5 T market.

9)   What should I know about wheel alignment?

Most wheel alignment companies who cater for commercial vehicles will encourage you, quite naturally, to have very regular wheel alignment checks. Personally, I do not think they are entirely necessary as a routine matter of course. The rationale behind the practice dates back at least 10 years to a study undertaken by the government's Freight Best Practice initiative which demonstrated both fuel savings and tyre savings were available from having regular alignment checks. Instead, I believe there are certain instances when a check should most definitely be undertaken and should then include the full gamut of measurements such as wheel camber and caster, kingpin inclination and so on. Measurement these days will invariably use laser technology for accuracy. Accurate measurement is one thing, the most difficult part of the operation is the adjustment, as varying one particular aspect of the suspension geometry will almost certainly change the setting of another. It is possibly one of the most frustrating operations you can undertake on any vehicle.

So, when should vehicle wheel geometry and alignment be checked? For heavier multi-axled vehicles, I would recommend an annual check as a starting point, which is therefore probably best carried out at the time of MoT. Somewhat perversely, depending on the vehicle specification and the body fitted, I would also probably recommend an additional check when the vehicle receives its first service. This is because the vehicle should be spot on when coming out of the factory but may then be fitted with a body, which in turn should be carrying a load, possibly up to maximum capacity. This will result in suspension components settling, which may well affect alignment. Some sensibility has to be applied to both the annual and in-service check. If you find either of these are just not requiring any adjustment, then extend the alignment check intervals or delete the check altogether.

For any vehicle, there are then specific times when further wheel alignment checks should always take place. These are:

- When uneven or abnormal tyre wear has been identified on particular wheels. You cannot undo the damage done, but an alignment should prevent further wear, especially when the tyres are replaced.

- Where tyre wear on one particular vehicle is consistently greater than its sister vehicles.

- Where axles look visibly out of alignment.

- When replacing steering components such as track links, track bars and ball joints – the age-old practice of counting the number of threads when replacing suspension items will be roughly correct, but not accurate enough to prevent wear.

- Any major maintenance work to axles or suspension.

- When the driver complains that the vehicle is pulling to one side or other, or the steering wheel is not centring itself when in the straight-ahead position (before having alignment checked make sure that tyre pressures are correct and that your tyres have even tread across the axles).

- If the vehicle has suffered a major accident which has resulted in some structural deformation and repair.

- Where wheels and tyres show significant 'kerbing' has taken place.

- If a vehicle is continuously operating in an arduous environment, such as off-road driving, building site or a landfill tip, consider additional checks and intervals to suit the adjustments found.

10) Should I be fitting a TPMS system?

TPMS (Tyre Pressure Monitoring Systems) have been a mandatory required on passenger cars since 2014 and faults on their systems has been an MoT failure issue since 2015. TPMS was extended to commercial vehicles in 2019 and will be required across Europe (and hence the UK) by 2022. As with many issues, even being out of the EU, the UK will almost certainly follow these regulations, not least because they represent a step forward in safety and tyre management. Most tyre manufacturers offer their own version of the system as do most vehicle manufacturers, both parties have been working for some time on developing and improving their systems.

There are many surveys in existence in the UK, and indeed in the EU, on the state of their commercial vehicle tyres, as mentioned earlier in this chapter. Invariably these indicate that a large proportion, estimated at as high as 30 to 40% of commercial vehicle tyres in some surveys, are run, on a consistent basis, with tyre pressures greater than 10% adrift from their optimum settings. This results in much higher tyre wear for underinflated tyres, also resulting in excess fuel use and increased premature tyre failure. Tyres are also one of the largest sources of unscheduled breakdowns on commercial vehicles. With that background, it is fast becoming an issue of "when and what do I fit?" rather than "should I?".

Elsewhere in this chapter, I suggest that the best method for managing the two key tyre variables, namely, pressure and tread depth, is to regularly inspect your fleets tyres, or have them inspected for you. Monthly is good, weekly is even better. This method of tyre husbandry has been in existence for a very long time, only really improved more recently by better recording techniques. The obvious problem with this tried and tested system is the amount of time and money it consumes. Also, a tyre survey, at best, can only ever be a snapshot of the state of your tyres at one specific point in time.

 Although TPMS will slightly increase costs at the outset, and has a few disadvantages when replacing or moving tyres, there is no doubt that moving to this technology is yet another significant step forward for the transport industry and enables management of the fleet's tyres in real time. A number of fleet managers using the system have pointed out to me that the increased cost of providing and managing the system is more than compensated for by the reduction in unplanned tyre punctures and breakdowns, especially if the lost opportunity cost to the operation is taken into account.

There are effectively two types of TPMS in operation currently, first kind is called 'indirect TPMS' and works on changes in the rotational speed of the wheel and tyre, usually calculated through the ABS signals from the wheel. The second kind of system is called 'direct TPMS' and uses a sensor mounted within or on the wheel, sending a signal to an ECU (Electronic Control Unit) mounted on the vehicle which translates the data, when required, into alarms and messages for the driver. TPMS for commercial vehicles are now largely all direct and of two types. Firstly, those where the transponder (which comprises of a sensor, data processor and communication device) is fitted to the interior of the wheel rim or to the interior of the tyre, these obviously require the wheel and tyre be removed to fit or replace. Secondly, the transponder is fitted within the tyre valve. The latter has the disadvantage that pressure adjustments potentially disturb the arrangement, however, their internal parts are easily replaceable as a kit.

Battery life for these sensors is somewhere between five and seven years; that is naturally reduced if many warnings are issued during its lifetime. Failure of the sensors can be through moisture ingress or damage on fitting, but 75% fail due to expired batteries and the whole unit has to be replaced. Both systems can suffer from false alarms; indirect due to a wheel or tyre change or significant pressure adjustment, direct systems that are sensitive enough can be set off by a large pothole in the road. Sadly, there are enough of those around at present. Both systems can be relatively easily reset to stop erroneous warnings.

By and large, the indirect systems are much cheaper and simpler to operate, however, as ever, there is a drawback. They are not so responsive and rely on a drop of pressure of up to 20+ % in order to trigger a signal, so considerable damage to a tyre could have already happened by the time the alarm sounds. If all wheels slowly drop in pressure at the same rate, some systems do not alarm at all. In contrast, direct systems are far more responsive, however, the drawback is they are more expensive, a little bit more difficult to set up as they have several component parts and require some maintenance over time.

When fitted, each wheel and tyre has a unique ID which has to be logged either to the system app or to the vehicle system in order for warnings to be issued. Depending on the system, pressure settings can be displayed in-cab, on a technician's hand-held terminal, on a depot-based screen and via telematics to any appropriate device. Most recent systems include an app which can be used on a driver's mobile device, showing relevant pressures and warnings.

Increasingly, tyre pressure monitors will also monitor tyre temperatures, which give a further indication of tyre condition, and if mounted on the wheel rim, can also give an indication of potential brake issues through heat transference. This is a useful secondary benefit – if the tyre is not overheating and the pressure is within tolerance, a high temperature alert on its own could well be an early indication of dragging brakes or a similar mechanical problem. If there are no brake issues, a high tyre temperature can prompt a thorough examination of the carcass to ensure no degradation has taken place as tyres do not tend to respond well to excess heat. The way the tyre pressures and temperatures are behaving can give a technician or manager significant diagnostic information about potential faults, whether it is a tyre, wheel or brake issue and therefore what action to take in order to rectify the situation.

As to whether to fit or not, I suggest a trial is required to test their effectiveness on your fleet. Certainly, I know of quite a number of fleet managers who now swear by TPMS, saying that it moves whole tyre game from one of being reactive, to being truly proactive. Instead of responding after the event to defect notices or call outs to change or repair a tyre; now low pressures can be investigated quickly and with sufficient advanced warning, so tyres are checked or changed before an incident or degradation happens. This considerably reduces breakdown charges and associated missed delivery slots, resulting in beneficial operational savings. A number of operators claim the ROI on TPMS systems is less than a year, but this obviously depends on fleet mileage and usage.

Commercial fleet managers therefore have to decide if and when this technology becomes a 'must fit' for them. The starting point must be to look at operational records to see how many tyre breakdowns occur and on what vehicles. It would make sense to trial a number of vehicles, preferably a whole depot if appropriate, to establish what savings may be available for your operation. It then becomes a simple ROI calculation to see if retrofitting part of, or the whole fleet, makes economic sense, but do not forget to add in the time and cost involved of replacing broken-down vehicles, along with an estimate of how much underinflated tyres are costing your operation. You may also be able to mitigate the cost of implementation by negotiating with your current tyre supplier and including installing TPMS as part of your contract.

Handy Hint 👍

- If you are using a Tyre Pressure Monitoring System (TPMS) make sure you have a system in place to act on the information it gives you and have tyres checked and problems indicated by the system adjusted or repaired before the end of a shift to maximise the benefits of the system.

Having said how good TPMS is, as ever, there is a caveat. The European Federation for Transport and Environment commissioned a report on TPMS in 2018 (https://www.transportenvironment.org/publications/eu-drivers-risk-under-inflated-tyres) which clarified that vehicles fitted with TPMS were safer than those without and that the direct measuring systems were more effective and efficient than the indirect; no surprises there. However, it also concluded that similarly to exhaust emission measurements, both systems were not operating as well in the real world as they did under test conditions. This was evidenced in their research findings that 8% of the vehicles fitted with TPMS had at least one tyre in a dangerous condition of underinflation. The report suggested there was room for the manufacturers improve their products and the commission to improve their required standards.

Almost as fast as I write this section of the chapter, the manufacturers are extending their offerings in automated tyre management. At least one manufacturer is offering a "back to base" drive-over reader that records the vehicle registration number, along with individual tyre pressures and tread depth, thus automating the weekly or monthly manual check, potentially every time the vehicle enters the depot. Vehicles that do not often return to base will still require in-wheel or in-valve sensors, which will record pressure and can record temperature, however, tread depth will still be required to be taken manually. It is also worth knowing that 2nd generation tyres will have RFID (Radio Frequency Identification) tags bonded into their sidewalls, meaning they can be tracked for their entire life, even when regrooved or remoulded. This will greatly aid those fleets who like to retain their tyre carcasses for later life.

Suppliers have seen the trailer market as an obvious target as tyres tend to get overlooked on trailers that do not stay paired with a unit. At least one supplier combines tyre data with other vehicle and trailer data including EBS (Electronic Braking System) data on the braking system performance. There is at least one supplier that goes one step further and provides for automated tyre inflation through the axles, should pressures ever drop too low, useful on trailers that do not often return to base. One of the major tyre companies recently bought a leading telematic supplier as part of this development and has also announced a joint venture with a major vehicle manufacturer in order to provide joint truck and trailer TPMS. Other suppliers are also looking at similar cooperative ventures in order to reach a larger section of the market.

11) Should I be buying tyres on a fixed price or p.p.k. tyre contract?

The standard approach to looking after tyres means operators generally agree various levels of tyre management with their supplier or suppliers, which includes a fitment and service policy, a menu of service items with a negotiated price for each (often referred to as "pay-as-you-go"), generally a collation of invoices into a single weekly, or more usually, a monthly bill, with further options on management information and reporting. Providing it is well managed, which means sufficient and accurate management information, this is normally the best option for operators who want to minimise tyre costs. As well as more regular inspections, there should be a comprehensive monthly fleet audit to measure a range of criteria such as damage, tyre pressures, tread depths, the potential to regroove, adherence to the fitment policy, missing valve caps and any other minor items that need reporting.

If all these items are being monitored and managed correctly, along with drivers doing their bit by reporting tyre issues promptly, this is probably the cheapest method of tyre management. However, there are definite advantages to some operators of a fixed p.p.k. contract, varying only with the distance run, especially if the vehicles are working on a specific customer contract. It means a known tyre cost with no surprises for however long the contract runs, so suits risk-averse operators.

If you know your tyre costs and your provider can beat that cost because they think they can run it more efficiently, then you effectively put the onus on them to reduce your operating costs. It can also insulate an operator from tyre price increases.

Additionally, the tyre provider can offer a fixed-price non-variable solution, however, for obvious reasons, the operator is usually paying something for this benefit. Nearly 20% of operators in the UK utilise this option, so it is worth looking at if you like more predictable costs.

There is also a psychological benefit to the operator; previously, if the tyre supplier declared there was some tyre "husbandry" work to be carried out, such as turning, re-grooving or twinning, the operator may well hesitate as it will cost money, albeit knowing it will be cost effective. Under a p.p.k. contract, the supplier will have no such qualms as they know it will reduce their operating costs, probably thinking in terms of a unit cost per mm of tread. Bear in mind a p.p.k. or fixed-price tyre contract is likely to have a built-in inflation clause with a number of indices included such as the price of rubber and RPI in order to be fair to both parties and minimising exposure risks. There may also be an element of "open-book" accounting so that both sides can see the real cost of operating the contract.

In essence then, tyre contracts are worth looking at if you want to hand over control in order to have fairly fixed charges for the duration, very useful for vehicles on a contract. If you have good data on your current tyre use and spend, it will be worth seeing what quotations you can obtain. The whole concept of a tyre supply contract is that good management by your supplier will allow them to achieve better p.p.k.'s. However, unless you are not very good at management and control right now, do not expect any massive improvement as the supplier has to better your tyre spend and make a profit otherwise it is not really worth it for them.

12) Should I be fitting remoulded tyres?

Due to an ever-increasing drive by most fleet managers to improve their organisation's corporate social responsibility and reduce the environmental impact of their fleet, the use of retreaded or remoulded tyres is obviously a more sustainable and readily accessible solution to help reduce an organisation's carbon footprint. As mentioned earlier, since the reduction in cheap tyre imports, remould tyres have become more popular again. Remould tyres are manufactured from similar compounds to new tyres, but utilise most of the old tyre carcass and hence use far less raw materials. They are required by law to be manufactured to the same performance criteria and undergo stringent performance checks on the quality of the carcass, prior to remoulding.

This testing involves a number of processes, including a non-destructive shearography test (as used on aircraft tyres). As the full history of these tyres can never be known, these tests are intended to detect if there are any inherent defects or separations within the casing, some of which are impossible to detect with the naked eye, to give a high level of confidence in the finished product. Remould tyres can therefore be considered to offer comparable levels of performance, durability and safety to their new tyre equivalents. The whole process is very transparent and as previously mentioned for new tyres, I would strongly recommend any potential fleet manager or fleet engineer to visit a remould plant at least once; I can almost guarantee you will be pleasantly surprised by the quality of production.

Due to the stresses placed on a steer axle tyre, for safety, most operators and manufacturers do not recommend fitting a remould on the steer axle/s. Remould tyres will probably, but not necessarily, have different ratings to the rolling resistance, noise and grip that apply to the original tyre. They will also probably give different mileage ranges to a new tyre. Although manufacturer's talk about the four potential lives of a tyre, providing they pass subsequent quality checks, in fact they can actually be remoulded more than once, thus extending their environmental credentials even further. It is worth saying that remoulds used to be viewed as the poor-man's alternative to premium tyres. This is no longer the case; they are a premium product that have a place within any quality fleet tyre policy. Most supermarket fleets are well known to utilise a high proportion of retreaded tyres.

Cold retreading means that a patterned and prevulcanised tread is applied to the buffed casing. The tread is placed under tension, together with an unvulcanised bonding ply, onto the buffed casing, which ensures that the tread adapts to the tyre contour to effectively bond the parts together. The tyre is then simply packed into a tube for the curing process. It is probably fair to say that the qualities of the tyre, such as fuel economy and grip, are more likely to vary from the original tyre on a cold retread than a hot retread, which generally use compounds very close to, or matching, the original tyre.

For a hot retread, the tyres undergo a virtually identical process to those found in the production of completely new tyres. It is this quality which makes hot retreads the favoured option for UK fleets. The balance between hot and cold retreads in Europe is about even at 50/50, whereas hot retreads in the UK consistently tend have a higher percentage of the market. Hot retreading generally uses the same profiles and rubber mixtures that are used in new tyre production, with the tyres reworked from bead to bead. The main advantage of hot retreading is that the side walls are effectively renewed and the tyre remains regroovable. At the end of the day, tyre selection and the use of retreads is all about the careful monitoring of new tyres, retreads, casings and the fitting process, then through measuring and monitoring, tailor your purchasing policy in order to give the lowest p.p.k.

Top Tips for Tyres & Wheels ✔

- Use the EU tyre labelling guidance as a start point guide to selecting tyres – balance the 3 criteria of fuel economy, wet grip and noise to suit your operation and drivers.

- Have regular inspections carried out on all your tyres, noting pressure, tread depth and condition as often as you can – always act immediately on the information provided.

- Use good tyre husbandry by re-grooving (where possible), turning tyres on the rim or the axle and re-positioning to maximise tyre life and reduce overall costs (watch out for uni-directional tyres).

- Make sure tyres are regularly included in any driver training sessions, especially what to look out for in their daily checks. The driver is always the most important point of contact for vehicle and tyres.

- For drivers of off-road vehicles, try to get them into the habit of checking their wheels and tyres at every stop (or at least before coming back on-road) and not just at the beginning of the shift.

- Make sure you have an anti-wheel loss policy in place, including a re-torquing procedure and ensure staff and suppliers stick to it rigidly; this applies equally to lighter van operators as well.

- It is good practice to check wheel alignment annually, then whenever tyre wear appears on a wheel or axle, or steering components are replaced, or the vehicle pulls to one side, or tyres have been 'kerbed' often, or has been in an accident, or operates off-road.

- Tyre Pressure Monitoring Systems (TPMS) already have a good track record in fleets; conduct trials to investigate the potential savings for your organisation, including savings to the operation through reduced breakdowns.

David's Don'ts ✖

- Don't overlook tyres in your management KPI's; measure performance by pence per kilometre or mile – managing your tyres efficiently can have a major impact on the bottom line.

- Never wait to replace tyres at their legal minimum tread depth; for vans or trucks, stipulate 3 mm as the nominal point of change so no part of the tread ever reaches 2 mm depth.

- Don't dismiss remould tyres as the poor relation to newly manufactured tyres; they are now a high-quality product with a place in most operators' tyre policy.

The Ultimate Guide to Commercial Vehicle Fleet Management

Summary

Right at the start of this book I promised there would be a summary at the end of the best advice contained in these pages for all those who like the shortened version. Well, here it is.

If any subject is of particular interest to you, I would urge you to go back and read the relevant section where everything is explained in more detail.

Of course, if you would like further help and advice on any topic or anything is not clear, we would love to hear from you. You can contact us through the website www.thedwconsultancy.com or email directly to dwilson@thedwconsultancy.com or telephone 07771 768080

Whichever way you choose, we would love to hear from you.

Chapter 2 Summary - The Commercial Vehicle industry background and future

- In the drive to decarbonise transport, Battery Electric Vehicles are likely to be the vehicle of choice for most van users in the near to middle future, as through continued research and development, weights gradually reduce, vehicle ranges increase, charging times reduce and there is a much-increased investment into the nation's charging infrastructure.

- Due to the energy density of diesel, it will remain the number one choice for HGVs for the foreseeable future, however, technical advances will continue to reduce emissions and increase efficiency. Euro 7 legislation, with even tougher targets, is due to be introduced around 2025; industry pundits disagree amongst themselves, but oil prices are most likely to rise over the period, however, not enough to drive alternative fuel advances on their own.

- The drive to decarbonise HGVs will continue apace, the most likely alternative will be a move to hydrogen fuel in the medium to longer term, providing so called "green" hydrogen becomes more widely available and affordable. This will be supported by cleaner gas and biofuel in the shorter term and alternatives such as battery electric (including hybrid), or direct electric in the medium to longer term.

- Brexit and to some extent, Covid, has left the automotive industry with some considerable challenges to be overcome, including vehicle battery provision.

- The cost of electricity for vehicles is unlikely to stay low for long; as EV adoption increases and hydrocarbon fuel duty revenue to the exchequer drops, it is likely to be either taxed directly, providing vehicle use can be separately measured, or some other form of road user charge will be introduced.

Chapter 3 Summary – Fleet Strategy & Planning

- Your fleet management strategy should link up directly and clearly with your organisation's other strategic aims and priorities and support their objectives, especially your financial and environmental objectives.

- A brief Service Level Agreement (SLA) between fleet and operations is beneficial to both users and providers alike.

- The core to a fleet strategy will be to publish the intended average age of each section of the fleet, along with the maximum ages for vehicles and maximum mileage for each vehicle group, so colleagues can clearly understand when vehicles will get replaced.

- At least once yearly, probably most usefully at budget time, conduct a brief but detailed calculation on the optimum economic point to replace your vehicles, for each discrete group of vehicles, to ensure you are still replacing vehicles at the optimum point for minimum overall cost.

- It is really important to declare what Key Performance Indicators (KPI's) you will be using to manage your fleet and why you selected them. You should be clear how often you will report the KPI's, to whom and what happens if they are not met, so there are no surprises for anyone involved in fleet.

- Your Fleet Strategy should explain how it will intersect with other departments such as finance, operations and HR. Make sure it spells out in clear terms how the communication between departments will work, to avoid any clash of responsibilities or misunderstandings in taking business decisions.

- Include environmental targets within your strategy to demonstrate how you will be reducing your organisation's fuel use & emissions. Include any mitigating activities and a future strategy on alternative fuels, however, try not to be too specific with targets for alternatively fuelled vehicles, allow flexibility for price, technology and infrastructure changes.

Chapter 4 Summary – Vehicle Procurement

- The point of when to replace a vehicle does not always match the theoretical one; the real cost vs time graph is probably flatter and stepped, not smooth like the theory.

- You will almost certainly have to use 'soft' replacement factors such as emissions, image and condition, along with 'hard' cost facts to help decide when to replace vehicles.

- Using true whole life costs is the best way to determine when to replace, but for practicality, you will probably still declare a mileage or age limit on each discrete group of vehicles.

- Standardising specifications helps greatly at replacement time and is one of the most important ways of reducing fleet costs.

- Good purchasing negotiation skill is both an art and a science, which you can learn and improve with experience. Make sure you brief senior decision makers on the progress of negotiations before presenting final figures for approval.

- Good project management during the build stage is hugely important, as is keeping in regular contact with all your suppliers and keeping other departments informed throughout the project.

- Allow time for new vehicle inspection throughout the process and only ever publish a realistic lead-time to your organisation.

- Involve drivers and operations early in the vehicle replacement process to get 'buy-in' from them throughout the project, however, never let them dictate makes and models, ensure you get a full operational specification to convert into the correct vehicle specification.

Chapter 5 Summary – Commercial Vehicle Finance & Funding

- Generally, if cash flow and reserves allow, buying outright is the cheapest and safest way to acquire vehicles for your organisation, however, there may be better uses for that cash, giving a better return elsewhere in the organisation.

- If going for a leasing or finance option, always shop around and evaluate the market fully, rates can vary enormously between similar suppliers.

- Get independent financial advice on your funding choice as the supplier may be selective in their offerings, and always get Tax and VAT advice before making a final decision.

- Whenever entering a finance agreement always spend time checking the small print fully, make sure that all vehicle activities and responsibilities are clearly laid out before signing – if an item is not in the contract, don't assume, get clarification.

- If an evaluation into self-insurance shows a benefit to your organisation, make sure you have the administrative capability and expertise in place before starting.

- Evaluate your main insurance risks and put an action plan in place as soon as possible to reduce them, reviewing at quarterly intervals.

- Telematics coupled with cameras are currently probably the most effective interventions to reduce your vehicle insurance premiums.

Chapter 6 Summary – New Technology and Alternative Fuels for Commercial Vehicles

- Always research the basic facts and figures for any new fuel or technology, do not rely on any grand performance predictions from the supplier.

- Check all available background data and experience of existing operators before making any decisions.

- It is best not to count on predicted infrastructure improvements from a provider, instead check how rapidly it has grown up to present, also where both existing and new finance is coming from, to enable you to make your own estimations.

- The buying decision for many new technologies appearing on vehicles remains one of balancing the potential benefits against costs.

- Accept that existing or promised incentives such as grants or reductions in tax to assist in acquiring alternatively fuelled vehicle can be withdrawn at relatively short notice.

- Do not rely on grid electricity prices remaining relatively low for too much longer.

Chapter 7 Summary – Bolt-on Commercial Vehicle Technology

- The drive behind the increase in fitting additional equipment to new and existing vehicles in the last 5 years has clearly been the expansion of local regulations and standards for commercial vehicles.

- Minimise the number of alarms or screens in the vehicle cab to avoid overloading driver senses.

- Regularly check the calibration of nearside sensors and alarms to avoid excessive false alarms.

- If you do not fit reversing alarms as a matter of course, conduct a specific risk assessment into reversing and consider fitting aids such as ultrasonic or radar sensors or cameras.

- If considering fitting forward and rearward facing cameras in the cab, involve staff and unions in trials and discussions early on.

- Avoid fitting cameras anywhere on the vehicle where road dirt already accumulates; try to stick with just one camera supplier and layout so drivers get acclimatised to the product.

Chapter 8 Summary – Telematics

- Prior to installing telematics, accept it will take up considerable amounts of management time, however, the benefits will far outweigh the time spent – as well as saving significant amounts of fuel, most organisations installing telematics find they uncover numbers of vehicles they can dispose of due to major under-utilisation.

- Telematics can massively improve the retention of driver training, helping to retain good habits.

- Alternatively fuelled vehicles benefit equally, if not more, from improved driver behaviour as conventional engines.

- Remember how intrusive telematics is for drivers, they will need the benefits of the system sold to them early.

- Ensure you establish ownership, or at least rights, to all your data before implementing any system; apply all your usual GDPR protocols to any personal data held on the system.

- Decide early on what the KPI's are that you wish to measure, telematics provides so much data that it is best to focus on just a few key parameters that are useful to your operation.

- Customer service from telematics suppliers is far more important than features; suppliers offer fairly similar packages – establish a rapport with your contract manager and support team before purchase.

Chapter 9 Summary – Fleet Management Systems

- Maximise buy-in from the main users of the system by involving them in deciding what core outputs you require - start with a blank sheet of paper; the first item should be to provide you with your most important Fleet KPI's, in a simple, accurate and timely fashion.

- To encourage all the main users to get the most out of a fleet management system, spend time setting up dashboards for them to highlight the KPI's they need to be watching on a regular basis.

- Attempt to consolidate or integrate any and all systems involved in fleet for simplicity and always aim for data entry just once.

- Very important is to check out your potential supplier's customer support – speak to the actual people you will be contacting to establish they are helpful and understandable.

- Organise system training at the time of purchase and make sure it happens at the appointed times.

- Involve your IT support early when selecting a new system to gain their agreement and ensure future internal support.

- Stick just to the core requirements from the system and do not be tempted to purchase unnecessary add-ons.

- Most importantly, establish ownership of your data – you will need access later if you want to move supplier.

- Allow enough time to cleanse old data before transferring to a new system – don't carry over unnecessary items of data.

Chapter 10 Summary – Vehicle Repair & Maintenance

- Corporate responsibility and operator recognition schemes mean van operators now need to utilise similar maintenance regimes to HGVs. A full daily walk-round check (before each shift) for both vans and HGVs is the cornerstone to a good maintenance regime.

- Defects found on service or inspection are good indicators; if too many, ensure daily checks and previous maintenance were carried out properly. Very few defects are usually good news, as long as inspection items are not missed, but may possibly mean service intervals can be extended.

- Having your own workshop eliminates travel time and costs, which can be considerable if your agent is not local. An MoT or ATF facility (when allowed) can be a useful revenue stream for your own workshops & can generate 3rd party work; but ensure future throughput figures are sensible before investing.

- The two most important KPI's by far for managing your own workshop are Efficiency and Utilisation. A well-run parts operation is also crucial to improve workshop efficiency.

- For contract maintenance, inspect your supplier's premises and specify the contract details carefully for a smooth-running operation. Where available, utilising a suppliers' extended opening times, (some even 24 hours a day), can remove downtime and a considerable number of 'spare' vehicles from the fleet.

- It is important to record every single call or instruction to your maintenance contractor and log all actions and events. Hold regular meetings to discuss and improve performance and iron out issues quickly.

- Contracting out your maintenance does not absolve you from your maintenance responsibilities and records; this equally applies to non-HGV operators.

- Take care with the quality of parts from independent workshops and especially for insurance repairs – specify up front if you require OEM parts and constantly monitor repair quality.

- If not already doing so, van operators should be measuring both their planned and unplanned maintenance time by vehicle.

- If still using a paper driver defect reporting system, review the many digital systems available and their advantages for compliance recording.

Chapter 11 Summary – Fuel & Oil Management

- Bulk fuel installations are usually the cheapest way to fuel the fleet and provide resilience in case of supply interruptions, but will require managing, regular inspection and a small amount of maintenance. They obviously work best where the fleet returns to base.

- Select the highest quality fuel pump you can afford for reliability, with a back-up if possible; do not over-speed, but ensure they fill quickly.

- There are now a huge variety of fuel cards available, match your requirements precisely against their offerings; mapping a card providers' outlets to your operation is a good start point.

- Ensure card suppliers demonstrate their full suite of fuel reports and can provide regular information in exactly the format you require.

- Drivers employing defensive techniques & anticipating traffic, using vehicle momentum to keep speed stable, is the single most effective way of saving any type of fuel, for both vans & trucks.

- If not already using semi or fully synthetic engine oil, it may be a useful additional fuel saving technique for your fleet; providing the increased cost is balanced by reduced maintenance time and cost.

- Problems with clogging DPF's (Diesel Particulate Filters) may be due to your particular operation cycles, but you may also be using an oil specification that produces too much ash.

- Random Oil sampling is a really useful and underutilised tool to assist you in extending your oil drain intervals & diagnosing potential issues.

- Treat bulk installations for AdBlue in a similar fashion to fuel and monitor usage carefully.

- Do not leave any gaps in your fuel management systems – rogue members of staff will take advantage at some stage.

Chapter 12 – Tyres & Wheels

- Use the guides to tyre management produced by the British Tyre Manufacturer's Association as your guide to managing tyres, useful for all commercial vehicle operators, light as well as heavy.

- Use EU tyre labelling guidance as a good start point guide when selecting tyres – choose the right balance of the 3 criteria to suit your fleet operation.

- Have regular inspections conducted, as often as possible, on all your tyres; record pressure, tread depth and condition - use good tyre husbandry by re-grooving (where marked), turning tyres on the rim or axle and re-positioning on the vehicle.

- Include tyres in your driver training sessions and explain what to look out for in daily checks.

- Check HGV multi-axled wheel alignment annually, then for any vehicle whenever necessary through signs of wear or maintenance that might affect alignment .

- Put an anti-wheel loss policy in place, including a re-torquing procedure and ensure staff and suppliers stick to it rigidly; this applies equally to lighter van operators.

- Consider trialling and introducing TPMS for your fleet, include operational savings in your ROI calculations.

- Do not overlook tyres in your management KPI's, measure overall performance by pence per kilometre or mile.

- Do not replace tyres at their legal minimum tread depth; for vans or trucks, make 3 mm the nominal minimal depth so no part of the tyre tread ever gets below 2 mm.

- For appropriate weight vehicles, consider remould tyres as an active part of your quality tyre policy.

Summary

The Ultimate Guide to Commercial Vehicle Fleet Management

Acknowledgements

As ever, there are a whole bunch of people I have to thank in helping me write this book – they need a mention here.

First off, I have to thank Sandra and the rest of the family for all their considerable support and patience during the long hours of writing. Whilst talking of patience, I think I should also mention my business coach, Angel Angelidis for his extreme forbearance during the (longer than it should have been) gestation period.

Then there are some really great people who kindly took the time to review the first drafts of this volume and provide me with the considerable benefit of their advice. All were involved in fleet management, but many were experts in their own fields, so their contributions were absolutely invaluable. In alphabetical order these generous people were:

Adrian McMullan	Lightbulb Analytics Ltd.
Prof. Colin Tourick	Colin Tourick & Associates Ltd.
David Payne	Pegasus Logistics Engineering Ltd
Eddie Cross	ProSolution Management Services Ltd.
Glen Davies	AtoH
James Tillyer	Transformotion Ltd
John Gorton	Head of Transport Kent and Essex Police
Lawrie Alford	LATC Apprenticeships UK
Norman Harding	London Borough of Hackney
Phil Lloyd	Logistics UK
Sara Lovell	Canal & River Trust
Shane Webb	Copart UK Ltd
Susan Carte	A La Carte Advice & Consultancy

More thanks must go to Adele Abbott of Teletrac Navman, Daniel Moir of the SOE, Junior Cunningham of Getty Images and Albert Golukhov of Excess Logic for the use of images and references used in the text.

I'd also like to sincerely thank Chis Sturman, for kindly taking the time to write a forward to the book and Mark Gedye, of InterPro Solutions, for the very comprehensive proof reading and formatting of the final volume. Thanks also to Yasir Nadeem for his care and diligence in creating the cover.

David Wilson August 2021

Acknowledgements

The Ultimate Guide to Commercial Vehicle Fleet Management

Explanation of Acronyms used throughout the book

Acronym	Meaning	Additional Comments
ABS	Anti-lock Braking System	
AC	Alternating Current	
ADAS	Advanced Driver Assistance Systems	
AdBlue	Trade name for Diesel Exhaust Additive	
ADEME	The French Agency for Ecological Transition	
AEBS	Advanced Emergency Braking Systems	
AI	Artificial Intelligence	
AIF	Alcohol Interlock Facilitation	
AMT	Automated Manual Transmission	
APT	Air Pressure Transducer	
ATF	Authorised Test Facility	
Brexit	Britain Leaving the European Union	*Event took place in December 2020*
BTMA	British Tyre Manufacturer's Association	
BVRLA	British Vehicle Rental & Leasing Association	
CAP	Car Auction Prices	*Originally for cars, now resale values for most vehicles*
CAZ	Clean Air Zones	
CCS	Carbon Capture & Storage	
CEO	Chief Executive Officer	
CNG	Compressed Natural Gas	
CO2	Carbon Dioxide	
Covid-19	International Viral Pandemic	
CPC	Certificate of Professional Competence	*(Mainly for managers, also available for drivers)*
CPD	Continuous Professional Development	
DAF	Vehicle Manufacturer	
DC	Direct Current	

Acronym	Meaning	Additional Comments
DDAW	Driver Drowsiness Awareness Warning	
DEFRA	Department for Environment, Food & Rural Affairs	
DfT	Department for Transport (UK)	
DNO	Distribution Network Operator	*Electrical Power Distributors*
DOC	Diesel Oxidation Catalyst	
DPF	Diesel Particulate Filter	
DVLA	Driver and Vehicle Licensing Agency	
DVS	Direct Vision Standard	
DVSA	Driver & Vehicle Standards Agency	
EA	Environment Agency	
EBS	Electronic Braking System	
ECU	Electronic Control Unit	
EGR	Exhaust Gas Recirculation	
ESC	Electronic Vehicle Stability Controls	
EST	Energy Saving Trust	
EU	European Union	
Euro X	European Emission Standards for Vehicles	*(X Ranges from 1- 6 to date)*
EV	Electric Vehicles	*Generally, Battery Electric*
EWTVA	European Whole Type Vehicle Approval	
FM	Fleet Management	
FOI	Freedom of Information	
FTA	Freight Transport Association	*(Now Logistics UK)*
GANTT	Type of bar chart, illustrating a project schedule	*Named after the originator, c. 1910*
GCSE	General Certificate of Secondary Education	
GDPR	General Data Protection Regulation	*Colloquially, Data Protection*
GPRS	General Packet Radio Service	*Colloquially, Mobile or Cellular Communications*
GPS	Global Positioning System	*Used to describe most satellites, actually a US system*
GTL	Gas to Liquid (Fuels)	
GVW	Gross Vehicle Weight	
H2	Chemical Symbol for Hydrogen	
HGV	Heavy Goods Vehicle	

Acronym	Meaning	Additional Comments
HM	Her Majesty's (Treasury)	
HMRC	Her Majesty's Revenue and Customs	
HR	Human Resources	
HSE	Health and Safety Executive	*UK Organisation*
IBC	Intermediate Bulk Container	
ICE	Internal Combustion Engine	
ID	Identity Document	*Used colloquially for most forms of identifier*
IFRS	International Financial Reporting Standard	
IMI	Institute of the Motor Industry	
IoT	Internet of Things	*Concept of interconnected systems & devices*
IP	Ingress Protection (Water) Standard	*International EN 60529, British BS EN 60529, European IEC 60509.*
IRTE	Institute of Road Transport Engineers	
irtec	Independent accreditation of the competence of technicians	
ISA	Intelligent Speed Assist	
IT	Information Technology	
JIT	Just in Time	
km	Kilometre (length)	
KPI	Key Performance Indicator	
KTN	Knowledge Transfer Network	
kW		
LED	Light-Emitting Diode	
LEVC	London Electric Vehicle Company	*Vehicle Manufacturer*
LNG	Liquified Natural Gas	
LOLER	Lifting Operations and Lifting Equipment Regulations	
LPG	Liquified Petroleum Gas	
m	Metre (length)	
MAN	Vehicle Manufacturer	
MD	Managing Director	
ML	Machine Learning	
MoT	Light Vehicle Safety Check (Ministry of Transport)	
MPG	Miles per Gallon	
NEDC	New European Driving Cycle	

Acronym	Meaning	*Additional Comments*
NOx	Nitrogen Oxide	
NVQ	National Vocational Qualifications	
O Licence	Operator's Licence for Heavy Goods Vehicles	
OCRS	Operator Compliance Risk Score	
OEM	Original Equipment Manufacturer	
p.p.k.	Pence per Kilometre	
p.p.m.	Pence per Mile	
PDI	Pre-Delivery Inspection	
PIN	Personal Identification Number	*Numeric or alpha-numeric security code*
PLC	Public Limited Company	
PSV	Public Service Vehicle	
PUWER	Provision and Use of Work Equipment Regulations	
QR	Quick Reference	
R&D	Research & Development	
R&M	Repair and Maintenance	
RDE	Real Driving Emissions	
RHA	Road Haulage Association	
ROI	Return on Investment	*Payback Calculation as % or time*
RPI	Retail Price Index	*Specific Measurement of Information*
RPM	Revolutions per Minute	
RTC	Road Traffic Collision	*Formerly Road Traffic Accident (RTA)*
SAE	Society of Automotive Engineers	
SAPS	Sulphated Ash, Phosphorus, & Sulphur	
Sat-Nav	Satellite Navigation	
SCR	Selective Catalytic Reduction	
SLA	Service Level Agreement	
SME	Small & Medium Size Enterprises	
SMMT	Society of Motor Manufacturers and Traders	
SOE	Society of Operational Engineers	
T	Tonnes - Metric unit of weight	
TC	Traffic Commissioner	

Acronym	Meaning	*Additional Comments*
TCA	Trade & Cooperation Agreement	
TEDx	Talks of less than 18 minutes	*Usually on topics of global importance*
TfL	Transport for London	
TPMS	Tyre Pressure Monitoring System	
TUPE	Transfer of Undertakings [Protection of Employment] Regulations	
TV	Television	
UK	United Kingdom	
ULEZ	Ultralow Emission Zones	
VAT	Value Added Tax	
VECTO	Vehicle Energy Consumption Calculation Tool	
VED	Vehicle Excise Duty	
VOL	Vehicle Operator Licensing system	
VTOL	Vertical Take-Off and Landing	
VW	Volkswagen (Vehicle Manufacturer)	
WLC	Whole Life Costs	
WLTP	Worldwide harmonised Light vehicle Test Procedure	
6 x 2	3 Axled Vehicle, 6 sets of wheels, 2 Powered	*Common shorthand for total axles and numbers powered*

INDEX